Search Engine

Finding Meaning in Jewish Texts
Volume 1: Jewish Life

Rabbi Gil Student

KODESH PRESS

Search Engine

The Publisher extends its gratitude
to Rabbi Yeshayahu Ginsburg
for his assistance with this project.

Letter from Rav Menachem Genack, CEO of OU Kosher

Orthodox Union

Union of Orthodox Jewish Congregations of America • איחוד קהילות האורתודוקסים באמריקה

Eleven Broadway • New York, NY 10004-1303 • Tel: 212-563-4000 • Fax: 212-564-9058 • www.ou.org

KASHRUTH DIVISION

MOISHE BANE
President

Gary Torgow
Chairman

Rabbi Yitzchak Fund
Vice Chairman

HABBI MENACHEM GENACK
Rabbinic Administrator; CEO

RABBI ALEXANDER S. ROSENBERG
Rabbinic Administrator (1950-1972)

בס"ד

ידידי הרב החשוב ונכבד [handwritten text, illegible]

Letter from Rav Shlomo Aviner,
Rosh Yeshiva of Yeshivat Ateret Kohanim

SEARCH ENGINE

Letter from Rav Yitzchak Breitowitz,
Rav of Kehillat Ohr Somayach

ק״ק אהבת תורה
Woodside Synagogue Ahavas Torah
9001 Georgia Avenue
Silver Spring, MD 20910

4 Kislev 5778
21 November 2017

Rabbi Emeritus
Yitzchak Breitowitz

Rabbi
Moshe Walter

President
Richard Sassoon

*Vice President for
Administration*
Chanoch Kanovsky

*Vice President for
Programming*
Adina Gewirtz

*Vice President for
Membership and
Community Relations*
Alida Friedrich

Treasurer
Jerry Saunders

Secretary
Daniel Friedman

For almost 15 years, first in Hirhurim and now in Torah Musings, Rabbi Gil Student has educated, inspired and entertained thousands of people with his perceptive and comprehensive essays on halacha, Jewish thought and Jewish history. He is one of the true pioneers in harnessing the power of the internet to convey the timeless and eternal truths of the Torah and it is no accident that his blogs have been consistently recognized for their excellence.

For the second time, he has collected many of these pieces in book form. In almost 300 pages, R. Gil covers a wide variety of topics—marriage, Shabbat and holidays, prayer, food, recreation, death. All of the essays, as brief as many are (a concession to the diminished attention span of the online generation!), are well-thought out, organized and cogent. He addresses his topics with clarity and roots his conclusions in authoritative Torah sources. Moreover, his tone towards rabbonim and poskim, even those that he may disagree with, is consistently respectful. He debates ideas, not personalities. As such, both in style and substance, his work is a pleasure to read and is of real benefit not only to beginners but even to accomplished Torah scholars.

May R. Gil continue to spread the Dvar Hashem in his "Yeshiva without walls."

Yitzchak A. Breitowitz
Rav, Kehillat Ohr Somayach
Jerusalem, Israel

Letter from Rav Aharon Rakeffet,
Rosh Yeshiva at RIETS

ישיבה יוניברסיטי בישראל ע״ר
Yeshiva University in Israel
RIETS Kollel - Aaron Rakeffet
Caroline and Joseph S. Gruss Institute
40 Rechov Duvdevani,
Bayit Vegan, Jerusalem ISRAEL 9641423
Tel: 972-2-531-3000 Fax: 531-3021

בס״ד

The bon mot that contemporary rabbis often cited was about the question that the Orthodox rabbi received. It concerned the appropriate bracha when one obtains a new Lamborghini. The rabbi responds "What is a Lamborghini?" The same question was then asked of a Reform clergyman. He answered, "What is a *bracha*?" When I went over Rabbi Gil Student's new volume I felt like the Orthodox rabbi in this lark.

What are Combat Exoskeletons, Instagram, Kosher switches, Powerball, Soundcloud and many other phrases in this publication? Rabbi Student has admirably brought Jewish Law into the twenty-first century in this volume. He exhibits a wide range of knowledge and cites many sources of both contemporary and classic rabbinical literature. While many issues that are discussed have still not reached a rabbinical consensus, this work will provide much data for future dialogue.

I have known Rabbi Gil Student for many years now. He is a true example of the best in the Torah world who attempt to strive in contemporary civilization.

May I express my blessings to the author

שיזכה להוציא את חידושיו הנכונים על פני תבל מתוך בריות גופא
ונהורא מעליא, ורוב נחת מבנים ובני בנים העוסקים בתורה ובמצוות.

Aaron Rakeffet

אהרן רb
פרופ׳ ואb/ רקפת
אל רב שb

Letter from Rav Arie Folger, Chief Rabbi of Vienna

ISRAELITISCHE KULTUSGEMEINDE WIEN

ARIE FOLGER, MBA
OBERRABBINER - CHIEF RABBI

אריה פאלגער
הרב הראשי דק"ק וויען יצ"ו

RABBINAT רבנות

Approbation for the sefer "Search Engine" by Rabbi Gil Student

Vienna,   the 15th of Kislev 5778

To readers of the Sefer "Search Engine,"

For many years, Rabbi Gil Student has been concerned with matters pertaining to the klal and has applied his ability to handle the written word in order to educate and elucidate. He has done so with essays he published into book form some fifteen years ago, has done so through a publishing label he had launched, with which he published a variety of thought provoking books, and most importantly, was ahead of the curve in understanding the internet's potential to spread Torah, particularly addressing timely topics. Through his Hirhurim - Torah Musings web site, initially a blog, which later became a full fledged internet periodical in which numerous authors teach Torah, Rabbi Gil Student has consistently aimed to present Torah responses to contemporary issues, as well as to sift the wheat from the shaft regarding what one might, using the Rashbam's idiom, term *hapeshatim hamitchadshot bekhol yom.*

As Rabbi Student notes in his introduction, we do not suffer from too few books. Books are readily available. If anything, we suffer from information overload. Through well researched halakhic essays and well founded book reviews, Rabbi Student helps us sift through this humongous pile of information, finding the gems while disregarding - at times subjecting to critical inquiry - some of the less solid material out there. But his isn't just a scholarly undertaking. Reacting to a phenomenon Rabbi Alfred Cohen once labeled presenting "The Torah in a Brown Paper Bag," Rabbi Student goes out of his way to do the opposite and show the reader how compelling Torah is.

Rabbi Student's commitment to halakha is profound. Following in the footsteps of the Rov, Rabbi J. B. Solovitchik, he stresses that halakha is not distinct from Jewish theology, but is rather applied Jewish theology. It is surely in this spirit that we find him addressing both philosophical and halakhic issues, at times blending both in a

A-1010 WIEN · SEITENSTETTENGASSE 4 · TEL. +43/1/531 04-111 · FAX +43/1/531 04-155
rabbinat@ikg-wien.at · www.ikg-wien.at

DVR 0112305

manner that injures neither one nor the other, but rather allows our understanding of each to enrich the other. One example is found in the book review he includes in the present volume of Rabbi Eliezer Melammed's sefer on marriage and marital intimacy. Seeing the unity of halakha and hashkafa is what sets that sefer and its approach apart, and allows it to stay clear of some pitfalls of other approaches.

Though I must admit to only having read some of the essays in the present volume, I can confidently say, based on the essays I have seen, as well as numerous other writings of Rabbi Student, that they are well researched, compellingly written, and infused with yirat shamayim, coming from a solid commitment and also of a realistic understanding of society, in the spirit of educating a student ba'asher hu sham. I therefore much appreciate the appearance of the present volume and am eager to see the appearance of the other two forthcoming volumes he announced in the introduction of the present volume.

May he succeed in drawing more people to more intense Torah learning, and even draw readers to delve into the sources included in his footnotes. May be we'll even develop a somewhat longer attention span. I wish this volume much success.

Arie Folger

Table of Contents

Preface

I thank God for allowing me to complete this book and pray that He allows me to continue learning and teaching.

In 2004, I started the *Hirhurim* blog for publishing my Torah thoughts. To my surprise, the blog grew in popularity, starting an exhausting marathon of daily writing and publishing about Torah texts, laws, and thought. Along the way, co-bloggers added important content to the blog. Among them were Steve Brizel, Joel Rich, and R. Ari Enkin. I thank them for their years of contributions to the blog.

The blog opened many opportunities for me, including speaking and writing for newspapers and magazines. In 2013, I dropped the blog format and transformed *Hirhurim* into an online periodical, titled *Torah Musings*, with an editorial board and more formal literary style. The editorial board includes R. Basil Herring and R. Moshe Schapiro. Efraim Vaynman does a lot of work on the website behind the scenes, often going above and beyond the call of duty. Regular contributors to the magazine include R. Gidon Rothstein, R. Daniel Mann, and Joel Rich. R. Micha Berger served as an invaluable early source of advice and editorial assistance during the transition to *Torah Musings*. I thank them all for their continued efforts to spread Torah. This book emerges from my contributions to *Torah Musings* over the past four years.

Alec Goldstein of Kodesh Press served as the impetus for this volume. In addition to being a good friend, he is an excellent editor. His tireless work and precision has made this process a pleasure. I also thank Yesh Ginsburg for his editorial work on the book.

It would be difficult for me to name every teacher who has influenced me or taught me, and I certainly do not want to imply that they agree with everything that I say or write. However, I would be negligent if I did not acknowledge their contributions to my education. What follows is a list of synagogue and school rabbis from whom I have learned: R. David M. Feldman, R. Ephraim Kanarfogel, R. Feivel Cohen, R. Mordechai Marcus, R. Yisroel Hirsch, R. Baruch Pesach Mendelson, R. Shalom Z. Berger, R. Yitzchak Goodman, R. Shlomo Stochel, R. Menachem Meier, R. Benzion Scheinfeld, R. Mordechai Willig, R. Hershel Schachter, and in particular R. Mayer Twersky. I also highlight the influence of R. Aharon Rakeffet and R. Menachem Genack. I thank them all for inspiring and educating me in the path of Torah. My lifelong friends, R. Daniel Z. Feldman and R. Benjamin G. Kelsen, have been constant sources of support and advice. I thank them for always being there for me.

I would not be where I am, for better or for worse, without the dedication of two people who have set me on my current path: my mother and father. Their devotion to our family and Jewish education, and their encouragement for each of their children to grow in their own ways, serves as an inspiration to me and my children.

And, of course, nothing in my life would have been possible without the loving patience and support of my wife, Miriam. She is a true partner in everything that I do. I thank her every day for bringing joy to my life. Our four children—Deena, Shea, Shmuly, and Tzaly—have always been blessings and sources of pride. Our family was recently joined by our son-in-law Dovid, and even more recently by our granddaughter, Ayala. We have so many blessings for which to be thankful. We pray for all their continued success in a Torah-infused life.

Gil Student
gil.student@gmail.com
12 Kislev 5778 / November 30, 2017

Introduction

I. Why *Halakhah*?

Imagine if someone asked you to name the most important elements of Judaism or the most relevant parts, the things that really speak to you. I doubt this book's table of contents will help you answer that question. As mentioned in the Preface, this book contains essays published on the Torah Musings website. This volume contains primarily halakhic essays that cover daily life and the annual cycle of holidays. This is not a book of fundamentals nor of inspiration.

Readers can legitimately ask why we are so focused on the minutiae of law. Is our vision so limited that we get caught in the weeds of rabbinic debate, focusing on texts rather than people, details rather than the breadth of human experience? If Jewish life is only about how to cut and pass *challah* around the table, where does God play a role?

This question has many answers. The first is that while this volume focuses on law, the next two projected volumes, already in draft form, address other issues. Tentatively, the next volume will be about Jewish leadership and the subsequent volume about Jewish thought, topics that, arguably, are considered by many to be more relevant. So, yes, there is more to Jewish life than details of Jewish law.

II. *Halakhah* and *Hashkafah*

However, the very question belies a mistaken attitude. The divide between the spirit and the letter of the law derives from gentile sources. In Judaism, law is applied theology. Human beings cannot be divided between our thoughts and our actions. These aspects of human existence interact with and influence each other. Our actions impact our beliefs, and vice versa. The *Sefer Ha-Chinukh* repeatedly explains various commandments as intended to influence our beliefs—"our hearts follow our actions" or, more poignantly, "a person is acted on by his own actions."[1] And similarly, our emphases and focuses reflect our beliefs of what should be a priority and what meanings lie in specific actions.

Jewish law, *halakhah*, represents God's will in this world. Rabbinic enactments, as well as rabbinic disagreements, reflect human attempts to discern the divine message and intent. When we study *halakhah*, we are studying practical theology. And when we debate *halakhah*, we are engaging in a millennia-long attempt to explore the revealed wisdom contained in Jewish sacred literature.

I am not trying to conflate genres. *Moreh Nevukhim*, Rambam's *Guide for the Perplexed*, is not the same as his *Mishneh Torah*, his halakhic code. In a sense, both are different sides of the same coin, utilizing different tools and languages. Rambam agrees that truth comes from many sources, both logic and science on the one hand and revelation on the other. *Moreh Nevukhim* uses philosophical tools, guided and limited by revelation, to arrive at religious truth.[2] *Mishneh Torah* uses revealed texts and ideas, as discussed by the Sages over the centuries, to arrive at practices that reflect a life striving for religious truth.

---

1. *Sefer Ha-Chinukh*, no. 16.
2. See Marvin Fox, *Interpreting Maimonides: Studies in Methodology, Metaphysics, and Moral Philosophy* (University of Chicago Press, 1990), ch. 2.

III. What is in This Book?

This book is not comprehensive. *Mishneh Torah* contains 1,000 chapters, and was subject to extensive criticism for failing to reveal and discuss its sources. It would take thousands of pages to fully address all of *halakhah*.

This book contains essays on timely halakhic issues. Some essays deal with current questions (e.g., Skype), some with future questions (e.g., combat exoskeletons), some with theoretical questions (e.g., superheroes), and some with questions from the past that reflect the long journey from the Talmud to today. *Halakhah* has evolved in one sense, although not as religious radicals may wish. Questions that were once debated have been authoritatively concluded, creating new precedents with which future questions can be addressed. I find this fascinating, and include a few essays on how *halakhah* has evolved (e.g., pocketwatches, home fires).

IV. Why a *Sefer*?

A colleague asked me why I, a relative pioneer of online Jewish scholarship, am publishing this as a *sefer*, a Jewish book. Don't I know that the printed word is hopelessly out of date? My answer takes us to the core relationship between Jews and the *sefer*. Jews have been traditionally called the "People of the Book." We maintained a culture of literacy even before public education became a societal goal. My gentile business colleagues are often surprised when I tell them that my children learn to read Hebrew before English. Reading, particularly religious texts, is in our blood and our culture. In contrast to the Catholic Church's pursuit of heresy among early translators of the Bible into English, Jews have generally treasured translations into the common language. We are commanded to read the weekly Torah portion with a translation, and we have an ancient tradition, albeit largely abandoned today, of reading the Bible in synagogue each week accompanied by a translation of each verse.[3] Everyone, not just rabbis, must be well versed in the Torah.

The Talmud (*Gittin* 60b) says that, originally, only the Bible was allowed to be written. We had to retain the oral nature of our other traditions. However, due to the danger of forgetting these sacred ideas, the Sages eventually permitted us to write them down. This led to the publication of the Mishnah and Gemara, Midrashim, and all subsequent Torah books. While there is a dispute today whether someone who publishes an unnecessary book violates this prohibition, everyone agrees with the vital importance, the national necessity, of publishing original Torah insights.[4] So important is the publication of Torah books that we are told to set aside this prohibition rather than risk losing these ideas.

But Jewish book sales are down. On its own, this is unsurprising during difficult financial times. However, I think that something larger than penny-pinching is occurring. Even as the economy improves, there is a larger trend that remains and jeopardizes the future of the *sefer*.

V. A Tale of Revolutions

A brief history of publishing revolutions can help us see what lies in the future. For centuries, publishing was largely a matter of hand-copying manuscripts. During the Second Temple era, scribes gathered in the Temple in Jerusalem and copied books from a primary manuscript. These copies were then distributed and sold.[5] This tedious process continued in varying forms,

---

3. On Christian translations, see encyclopedia entries for John Wycliffe and William Tyndale. On Jewish use of translations, see *Shulchan Arukh, Orach Chaim* 145 and 208.
4. See *Responsa Chasam Sofer, Orach Chaim* 208; *Responsa Be-Tzel Ha-Chokhmah* 4:84.
5. Rav Saul Lieberman, *Hellenism in Jewish Palestine* (New York, 1994), p. 85.

among Greeks, Christians, Muslims, and Jews, until the fifteenth century when Johannes Gutenberg's invention of the printing press changed the world. Books could be produced *en masse* and sold at more reasonable prices. Those who could read had access to a much larger library of knowledge.

This technological revolution was the third in a series that changed humanity. Rav Lord Jonathan Sacks, in an impassioned argument for educating the third world, describes the dramatic effects of these three innovations.[6] Writing, initially with pictograms, created civilization. It enabled the permanent transfer of information from one person to another. However, reading and writing were limited to the few who mastered the complex written language, who studied as many as twenty years to acquire these skills. The development of alphabets, which encapsulate entire languages in only twenty to thirty characters, opened information to wider classes of people. The alphabet broke down barriers of society. It created the possibility that anyone could acquire the knowledge that allowed for exercising societal power.

The printing press brought literacy to the masses. Within fifty years of its invention, readers had access to more than fifteen million copies of over 35,000 titles across Europe. This spreading of knowledge eventually led to political and religious revolutions. The newfound wisdom empowered the public and gave people the ability to disagree with and overturn the ruling classes. Five centuries later, publishing has experienced another revolution.

VI. The Internet As a Game-Changer

Writing created information. The alphabet spread it. Printing democratized it. The Internet is drowning it. With the Internet, people now have access in their palms to more information than ancient Egyptians could find in the entire Library of Alexandria.

---

6. Rav Jonathan Sacks, *The Dignity of Difference* (London, 2003), 125.

Vast stores of knowledge are available online. Google Books is a massive project to digitize libraries. If I come across a phrase that sounds like it was stated by Rav Joseph B. Soloveitchik, I search for the phrase on Google Books and, faster than I could flip through a card catalogue, I find through this website the exact book and page in which the phrase appears.

HebrewBooks.org started as a website to perpetuate the many obscure *sefarim* published in America. After philanthropic grants allowed substantial expansion, the site now provides an extensive library of downloadable books in searchable PDF format, free of charge. Responsa and codes, Talmud and commentaries, encyclopedias and journals are all available immediately on one's laptop. Daat.co.il is another incredible online library, full of complete books of Jewish thought, law, and biblical commentary. And there is much more available all over the web, and even on new devices.

Yet, as we gain access to so much information through such powerful tools, we face a new danger. We are bombarded with too much information. News comes to us all day from multiple sources. Opinions, both essays and comments, abound. *Parashah* insights flood our inboxes. Daily digests, hourly updates, constant data flows, libraries at our fingertips—the human mind is not equipped to handle this much information at once. We lack, if not the capacity, then the training to adequately process it all.

And it isn't just a matter of digesting everything; we need to decide how much credibility to assign the information. Readers of all ages encounter massive amounts of information, with no guide to determine its accuracy or relevance. Just because something is on the Internet does not mean it is true. We live in a library whose bookshelves have collapsed on us, and we are struggling to make our way through the rubble of constant information. But volume is not the real issue.

VII. Give It to Me Quickly

The problem facing the *sefer* is not why to pay for enlightenment when you can get it for free. It is that we have so much information online, we lack the time for books. Once we finish catching up on our e-mails, blogs, tweets, and Facebook updates, we have no time for books. The saving grace for Orthodox Jews is Shabbos, when we shut off all our communication devices. Finally, in between prayer, family, friends, and food, we have time for books. But can we totally turn off the effect those devices have on us?

The bombardment of information is not only time-consuming, it has also changed the way we process knowledge. We have stopped reading carefully and only pay attention to the newest and most exciting pieces. We often fail to read to the end of e-mails and articles. We skim, so we can cover more ground. The information triage our brains perform six days a week cannot be easily turned off on the seventh. The world has collectively lost its attention span, and Orthodox Jews suffer from the same symptoms. Any given person can, and in my opinion should, avoid this pitfall or retrain himself to frequently read long books and articles. But we would be naïve to believe that any such movement will take place on a wide scale. Instead, we find the *sefer* endangered by a decreasing ability to focus. Unless the *sefer* can adjust.

VIII. A New Kind of *Sefer*

The solution to the Internet is to embrace it on our terms. If people process information differently, then books need to be written in a different way. We must produce books that accommodate the new way of reading. The "*vort*" genre, in which books consist of short Torah insights, is perfect for our unfocused generation. Articles can be shortened and footnotes can serve as hyperlinks, offering more information and suggestions for further reading to readers interested in a specific point. Concluding summaries can highlight the main points for impatient readers. Long books can be broken down into bite-size sections that people can read in spurts.

Generally speaking, the essays in this book are brief, with detailed citations so motivated readers can pursue further research on their own terms. Throughout this book, section headers turn short essays into even shorter segments, each readable on its own. Journalists have long known how to gain readers' attention by using provocative headlines and placing the most important information at an article's beginning because most readers will not reach the end. Today, we must all be journalists. The essential Torah content cannot be changed, but the form in which it is presented must.

The *sefer* isn't dead. It merely needs to adjust to changing realities. This book is my attempt to create a reader-friendly exploration of serious Torah subjects that consists of brief, varied, and self-contained topics. It is an experiment, one which certainly does not fully represent the ideal to which it strives. It is not authoritative, it is not always interesting, and sometimes it goes on for too long. Please accept my apologies. Most importantly, because of the need to be brief and varied, and because of my other personal limitations as a scholar, this book should be treated only as reading material, not as a religious guide. Engage with the different views; look up sources in their original; but always consult with your rabbi before putting anything into practice. You are not a halakhic authority and neither am I. More on that in the next volume, God-willing, on Jewish leadership.[7]

---

7. Large portions of this introduction originally appeared as "The Future of the Sefer" in *Jewish Action*, Spring 2011.

PART 1: MARRIAGE & FAMILY

The Super-Mitzvah to Have Children

The Logical Imperative to Procreate

The "Shidduch Crisis," the growing number of older singles in the Orthodox community, is not a uniquely Jewish phenomenon, nor should it be. Contemporary society is also undergoing a "Singles Crisis." This should give us pause when proposed solutions to the Shidduch Crisis, no matter how clever (and especially when too clever), only address concerns specific to our community. Can it really be a coincidence that we are suffering from the same problem as the culture around us? If not, we need to recognize this within our proposed course of action.

Additionally, acknowledging this link to general society gives us opportunity to consider why this phenomenon is so troublesome as to be called a "crisis." Yes, we see the very real human suffering, but we have to look more deeply and ask: *Why* are these humans suffering?

I. The Half-Servant

The first commandment in the Torah is to be fruitful and to multiply (*peru u-revu*), i.e., to have children. This was said first to Adam and Chavah as a blessing, like that said to the other animals, and again to Noach as a blessing and command (Gen 1:28, 9:1, 9:7). Since it was not repeated after the Torah was given, this mitzvah only applies to Jews. Gentiles are not obligated to be fruitful and multiply. However, we see a curious development twice in the Talmud.

When slavery was allowed, centuries before the Emancipation Proclamation, the Talmud (*Gittin* 41a) discussed the case of a half-servant. A servant is bought by two owners in a partnership and one owner sets him free. The half-servant is in a state of limbo—he cannot marry a free woman because of his servant half and he cannot marry a maidservant because of his free half. Therefore, the Sages decreed, the other owner must set the man completely free. The prophet declares: "*Lo sohu vera'ah, la-sheves yetzarah,* [God] did not create [the world] to be barren, He created it to be settled" (Isa. 45:18). This teaches an overriding obligation to have children (a mitzvah of *sheves*) that even applies to a servant.

Why did the Talmud quote a verse in Isaiah and not one of the three verses from Genesis about being fruitful and multiplying? Is not an explicit commandment in the Torah more compelling than a prophetic passage? Two students of the great Tosafist, Rabbenu Tam, disagree how to interpret this passage.[8] Rav Yitzchak of Dampierre (Ri) explains that the prophet emphasizes the importance of this mitzvah (*peru u-revu*) to the divine plan. Even though a half-servant is not really obligated in this commandment, his master should still free him to allow him to fulfill this great mitzvah.

Rav Yitzchak ben Mordekhai of Regensburg (Rivam) sees in *sheves* a different mitzvah. Why should an owner free his stake in a servant, suffering a financial loss, to allow a half-servant to fulfill *peru u-revu*, a commandment in which he is not technically obligated? It is true that a half-servant is not obligated to be fruitful and multiply. However, he is still obligated to settle the world by having children. Everyone, freeman and servant, man and woman, is obligated in *sheves*.

---

8. Tosafos, *Gittin* 41b sv. *lo*; *Chagigah* 2b sv. *lo*; *Bava Basra* 13a sv. *she-ne'emar*.

II. Women and Procreation

The other talmudic reference to *sheves* limits the sale of a Torah scroll. Normally, you may never sell a Torah scroll, perhaps the most sacred possession an individual or community can acquire. The Talmud (*Megillah* 27a) allows for the sale of a Torah scroll in only two circumstances: in order to study Torah or to pay for an orphan's wedding expenses. The latter exemption is supported with the above verse from Isaiah. Since *sheves* is so important, or so all-encompassing, it overrides the sanctity of the Torah scroll in this respect. Commentaries to the *Shulchan Arukh* note that the Talmud uses the masculine form of the word for "orphan." What about a female orphan?

It is quite surprising that the Torah only obligates men to have children (*Yevamos* 65b). *Peru u-revu*, childbirth and childraising, is a mitzvah placed only on males. Certainly, most people find this contrary to their biological, psychological, and sociological instincts. The most popular explanation for this curious halakhic position was offered by Rav Meir Simcha Ha-Kohen of Dvinsk in his *Meshekh Chokhmah* (Gen. 9:7). Rav Meir Simcha argues that the Torah is merciful and does not obligate people in tasks that are necessarily painful (see *Yevamos* 87b). The Torah exempts women from the obligation because childbirth is extremely painful for them.

That exemption takes a surprising turn. We may sell a Torah scroll to enable an orphan to fulfill the mitzvah of marrying. However, women are not obligated in the mitzvah. Therefore, perhaps we may not sell a Torah scroll to fund the wedding of a female orphan. Commentaries struggle with this surprising and counterintuitive conclusion. *Chelkas Mechokek* (*Even Ha-Ezer* 1:1) adopts it while *Beis Shmuel* (*Even Ha-Ezer* 1:2) and *Magen Avraham* (153:9) dispute it (see also *Ba'er Heitev, Even Ha-Ezer* 1:2; *Otzar Ha-Poskim* 1:11). Who needs communal assistance more than a female orphan? One answer lies in the debate between Ri and Rivam.

According to Ri, there is only one mitzvah to have children; *sheves* is the same as *peru u-revu*, from which women are exempt. However, Rivam sees these as two separate *mitzvos*. All people, men and women, are obligated in *sheves*. Therefore, since the permission to sell a Torah scroll is based on the verse in Isaiah about *sheves*, this permission must include orphan women. Note that according to the Ri, the discussion is not over. There might be other reasons to extend the permission to orphan women, as discussed in *Otzar Ha-Poskim* 1:11.

III. The Source for *Sheves*

The idea that *sheves* obligates everyone to procreate requires explanation. Where do we see women receiving such a commandment? And why would the Torah mercifully exempt women from *peru u-revu* and then turn around and re-obligate them in the very same thing via *sheves*?

I suggest that *sheves* is not a direct command. The prophet is not telling us what to do but explaining to us God's will, posing a simple syllogism:

1. God put people on this big planet
2. God does not do things without a reason
3. Therefore, God wants the world populated.

This is not an unassailable argument. Maybe God wants people to occupy only one place, even though the planet is large. Maybe He only wanted us on this world for a short time. How are we expected to fully grasp the divine will?[9] In this case, prophecy

---

9. And does this make space travel, settling the vast universe, a religious obligation?

does not command us but educates us, informing us of God's will. *Sheves* does not command us but tell us what God wants.

Yet, we did not need this revelation. Merely observing the world teaches us that people were created with innate biological and psychological desires to have children. God must have implanted within creation the drive for procreation for a reason. The suffering of singles in this "crisis" is a symptom of spiritual unfulfillment, a sign of the divine plan of marriage and procreation. Genesis 1-2 is part of our inherent psychological makeup.

Once we know that God desires procreation, we are bidden, as His created beings, to fulfill His will. He wants people in the world, a full world. Therefore, we cannot allow humanity to dwindle. We must continue the human chain, implementing God's will. Having children is one way in which we can fulfill God's desires.[10]

This is not a meta-mitzvah, an overarching command like "And you shall do the right and the good" (Deut. 6:18). Rather, it is a logical mandate supported by prophecy. It is founded in the fundamental duty of every created being to fulfill his master's will. As such, it presumably obligates all people, gentiles and Jews, every created being seeking to fulfill the will of its Creator.[11]

If this is correct, then God, through His merciful Torah, does not command women to have children. However, the continuation and growth of the human species is God's will, which all people— men, women, Jew and gentile—must fulfill and through which they achieve their highest purpose. Their suffering, the communal and societal crises, demonstrates this need.

---

10. One can argue that we need not fulfill God's will, only His commandments.

11. After writing this, I was gratified to see that Rav Aharon Lichtenstein takes a similar approach, albeit not within Rivam's view. See his article "'Peru U-revu' and 'Shevet'" on VBM-Torah.org.

All-In-One Weddings

I got engaged during my last semester of college, in which I was taking a Hebrew Literature course. After missing two classes in a row, I explained to the professor, "*Hishtaddakhti* (I got engaged)." He looked at me funny and asked, "*Hitarasta*?," ostensibly correcting my Hebrew, at which point I switched to English to clarify my intent. The confusion is a combination of historical development and my occasional pedantry. In Modern Hebrew, engagement is called *eirusin*. However, in halakhic terminology, *eirusin* means "betrothal," the first stage of marriage, and *shiddukhin* means "engagement." I refused to call my engagement an *eirusin* because that would be halakhically imprecise. However, this confusion of terminology is not a modern phenomenon but the product of a long historical progression.

I. Two Parts to a Wedding

The familiar Jewish wedding ceremony we see today is very different than it was in talmudic times. Certainly the music, dancing, and food are very different. But even the core religious acts have changed. The Mishnah (*Kesubos* 48b) explains that first *eirusin* was performed, in which the groom and bride are betrothed, officially married but unable to live together. Up to a year later, the *nissu'in* was held, which is the final stage of marriage. The delay allowed the families time to prepare food, clothing, and housing for the celebration and afterward. At some point, we know

30

that *shiddukhin*, "engagement," preceded any part of the wedding. Without *shiddukhin* two people could quickly marry when feeling attracted to each other, without proper forethought. One talmudic sage, Rav, went so far as to excommunicate people who married without *shiddukhin* (*Kiddushin* 12b).

Today, Jews almost universally conduct *eirusin* and *nissu'in* one immediately after the other, under the *chuppah* at the wedding ceremony. The groom gives the bride a wedding ring, reciting the proper formulation, and the presiding rabbi recites the blessings over the *eirusin*. Another rabbi then reads the *kesubah* (marriage contract), and perhaps someone speaks about the couple. Then the *nissu'in* begins with the seven blessings and the couple going to a *yichud* room.[12]

The *eirusin* and *nissu'in* used to be separated by months. Now they are separated by minutes. When and why did this change? I set out to investigate this and found some very interesting answers. After a good deal of my research, I was fortunate to be directed by a friend to an extensive study, *Seder Kiddushin Ve-Nissu'in Acharei Chasimas Ha-Talmud* by A.H. Freiman.[13] Many of the sources I quote below are from his book.

One thing to keep in mind as we go through the sources is that an alternate custom developed called second *kiddushin* (or second *eirusin*). When *eirusin* and *nissu'in* were separated by long periods of time, a second, symbolic *eirusin* was performed at the *nissu'in*. In some places, only the blessings on the *eirusin* were recited but not a second betrothal. It is not always clear whether sources are referring to the complete joining of the *eirusin* and *nissu'in* ceremonies or merely a repetition of the *eirusin*. We will see what we can determine and what remains ambiguous.[14]

12. Exactly what constitutes *nissu'in* is slightly different for Sephardim. See Rav Ovadiah Yosef, *Yabi'a Omer*, vol. 5 *Even Ha-Ezer* no. 8.
13. Mosad Ha-Rav Kook, 1945
14. I don't think Freiman succeeded in separating these two developments.

Another issue is that there were always exceptional circumstances, such as betrothal of a minor or someone who lived far away. I can envision a historical custom that the entire wedding take place on one day except in those unusual cases. If so, responsa about those cases are not entirely relevant to our question.

II. Ge'onim

A problem arises when the blessings on *eirusin* and *nissu'in* are recited in quick succession. Before both, we recite the *borei peri ha-gafen* blessing on wine. But if we recite it once, why do we need to repeat it just a few minutes later? And if we repeat it, do we need a new cup or can we perform two *mitzvos* on one cup?

Rav Natronai Gaon (*Otzar Ha-Ge'onim, Kesubos* 82) rules that you should preferably recite a blessing on two separate cups of wine. If there is not enough wine, then you may recite a single *borei peri ha-gafen* for both ceremonies.

Clearly, already in Rav Natronai Gaon's time—the ninth century—the blessings on both *eirusin* and *nissu'in* were at least sometimes recited at the same time. However, it remains uncertain whether this was a repetition of *eirusin*, a delay of the blessings on *eirusin*, or the unification of *eirusin* and *nissui'in* into a single unit of ceremonies.

III. France and Ashkenaz

People who attend contemporary Jewish weddings are familiar with the reading of the Aramaic text of the *kesubah*, the wedding contract, in the middle of the ceremony. Rashi instituted this practice. The Mordekhai (*Kesubos*, first page) quotes a responsum of Rashi in which he states that we read the *kesubah* in between *eirusin* and *nissu'in* to serve as a break between the two. For both, we recite a blessing on a cup of wine. The break of the reading of the *kesubah* resolves the problem of repeating the same blessing in quick succession.[15] Rashi's grandson, Rabbenu Tam, and a correspondent, Rav Meshullam, state explicitly that Rashi instituted this reading (*Sefer Ha-Yashar*, nos. 660-661). However, it is unclear whether Rashi meant that the two units of the wedding ceremony both took place on one day or that this was a delay of the *eirusin* blessings or repetition of the ceremony.

Three other responsa of Rashi are relevant and offer a different picture of weddings in his time. In *Teshuvos Rashi* (no. 192), he discusses whether the blessings on *eirusin* should be recited at all at the time of *nissu'in*. This implies that the two ceremonies were performed separately. Rashi's institution of the reading of the *kesubah* could have been only for occasions in which the *eirusin* and *nissu'in* were performed together.

Teshuvos Rashi (no. 193) addresses a case in which both *eirusin* and *nissu'in* were performed on the same day but the witnesses signed the *kesubah* improperly. The mention at the beginning of the question that both ceremonies were performed on the same day suggests that this was not always the case. If it was standard practice, the questioner would not need to mention it.

The third responsum (*Teshuvos Rashi*, no. 194) is the most interesting and important for our purposes. Rashi officiated at, or at least attended, a wedding in which both *eirusin* and *nissu'in* were performed in succession but only one *borei peri ha-gafen* was (accidentally) recited. Rashi insisted they go back and recite the second *borei peri ha-gafen*. People asked him why he insisted on this, which prompted his responsum.

In his answer, Rashi explicitly addresses the joining of the two ceremonies with an explanation that resonates well today. If *eirusin* and *nissu'in* were celebrated separately, then each celebration would require its own feast. If the feast for the *eirusin* is too small,

---

15. The responsum is also quoted *Hagahos Maimoniyos, Hilkhos Ishus* 10:3. And see Tosafos, *Pesachim* 102b sv. *she-ein*.

the groom and his family will be offended. Therefore, presumably because of the expense (Rashi only implies this aspect), the two ceremonies were effectively combined so the families need only pay for one feast.

However, the question still implies that this was not a universal practice. If it was, there would have been no need to mention that the *eirusin* and *nissu'in* were done together. But it also implies that otherwise the blessings on the *eirusin* would not have been recited at the time of the *nissu'in*. It seems that in Rashi's time, people were starting to combine the two ceremonies for economic reasons.

Let us continue our discussion of wedding practices in what we call Ashkenazic communities (France, Germany, and Poland). By the time of the Maharam of Rothenburg, it was standard practice to recite the blessings of *eirusin*, read the *kesubah*, and then recite the blessings on the *nissu'in*. The book of customs from his school records this as the universal practice (*Sefer Minhagim De-Vei Maharam b'r Barukh Mi-Rothenburg*, p. 82). Similarly, Maharam Mintz (Responsa, no. 109) describes the wedding ceremony with the *eirusin* followed by the *nissu'in* on the same day. However, neither specify whether *eirusin* was only performed at that time or possibly earlier, as well.

The *Terumas Ha-Deshen* (1:207) is clear, though. He writes that, in the overwhelming number of cases (he approximates 99%), *eirusin* and *nissu'in* were performed together. He says that separating the ceremonies is considered an improper practice, only done by those attempting to somehow trick a woman into marrying him.

IV. Provence (Southern France)

Southern France was a separate community from France and Germany, with significantly different customs. The *Sefer Ha-Ittur* (*Hilkhos Birkas Chasanim*) writes that the custom in his place was to perform *eirusin* a year or two before *nissu'in* but in other places the ceremonies were performed at the same time. It appears that in his time, practices differed throughout Provence. The *Sefer Ha-Manhig* (*Hilkhos Eirusin*, no. 107) testifies that, during his travels, he saw differing practices in France and Provence.

However, the Meiri (*Magen Avos*, no. 5) states that in his day in Provence, *eirusin* and *nissu'in* were always performed together. He offers a surprising explanation for this practice. He suggests that it harks back to a time, mentioned in the Talmud Yerushalmi (*Kesubos* 1:5), when the gentile lord would demand to spend the wedding night with every new bride. If the lord insisted on that right the night of *eirusin* while the husband would only live with his wife a year later after *nissu'in*, there would be a long gap during which the bride had been only with the lord. Therefore, the Meiri claims, *eirusin* and *nissu'in* are performed on the same night, so the bride and groom can be together before the lord intervenes.

This seems like a historically dubious and generally implausible explanation, since joining the ceremonies had only recently become standard at the time of his writing. However, it does testify to the practice in Provence. Additionally, the Meiri's goal in *Magen Avos* was to defend the customs of Provence against those of Spain. From his words, it seems that the only objection from Spain was that in Provence they only recited one *borei peri ha-gafen* for both *eirusin* and *nissu'in*. The Spanish scholars did not object to the combining of the two into a single unit of ceremonies.

V. Spain

The Ramban (*Kesubos* 7a s.v. *ve-tzivvanu*) explains that we recite separate blessings on the *mitzvos* of *eirusin* and *nissu'in* because we perform them at separate times. However, *Talmidei Rabbenu Yonah* (*Shitah Mekubbetzes, Kesubos* 7b s.v. *tanya idakh*) implies that there were places where the two were performed together.

Similarly, Ritva (Responsa, no. 19) wrote to a community where *eirusin* and *nissu'in* were joined into one unit of ceremonies.

The Rivash (Responsa, 82) states that the reason for second *eirusin* in the unusual case in which *eirusin* was performed in advance through a messenger is that the standard practice is to join the two ceremonies into a single unit. If the groom failed to perform *eirusin* at the wedding, guests might think that he had skipped it entirely. Apparently, by the late fourteenth century, the universal practice in Spain was to perform both *eirusin* and *nissu'in* at the same time, so guests would be surprised if it was omitted.

VI. Other Communities

The *Tur* (*Even Ha-Ezer* 62), writing as a German immigrant in Spain, states that the standard practice was to join *eirusin* and *nissu'in* into one unit. Rav Yosef Karo (*Beis Yosef*, ad loc.), writing in Israel, disagrees. He states that this was only true in the *Tur*'s place, but customs differ by community. Rav Moshe Isserles (*Darkhei Moshe* 34:5), writing in Poland, states that the practice in his time was to perform *eirusin* and *nissu'in* together, as the *Tur* stated.

In Jerusalem, there was an enactment to always perform *eirusin* and *nissu'in* together. apparently in the seventeenth century. In the mid-eighteenth century, Rav Raphael Meyuchas, the chief rabbi of Jerusalem, wrote that those who wished to perform *eirusin* earlier did so outside the city limits (*Pri Ha-Adamah*, vol. 4 p. 22 col. 3, quoted in Freiman, p. 280). This is also mentioned in *Minhagei Yerushalayim* (*Dinei Kiddushin*, no. 2; Freiman, p. 281).

The practice in Yemen followed the Rambam throughout the ages. Rav Ya'akov Sapir (*Even Sapir*, vol. 1 p. 60b; Freiman, pp. 305-306), following a visit to Yemen in 1858, reported that they performed *eirusin* at the time of engagement (*shiddukhin*) and the *nissu'in* only after all the preparations were made, i.e., at the wedding.

This led to a small crisis in Jerusalem in 1885. A Yemenite immigrant performed *eirusin* according to the Yemenite tradition and contrary to the enactment in Jerusalem. The Jerusalem rabbis sent a delegation to the leaders of the Yemenite community, asking them whether they are Ashkenazim, Sephardim, or their own separate community. The working assumption was that Ashkenazim were not bound by the enactment of Sephardic rabbis in Jerusalem. After a good deal of debate, the Yemenites agreed to follow the customs of the Sephardim in Israel (Freiman, p. 282).

In Iraq, they performed *eirusin* at, or not long after, the engagement well into the twentieth century (*Responsa Rav Pe'alim*, vol. 4, *Even Ha-Ezer*, no. 3). An 1892 booklet of Iraqi wedding customs, *Tzorkhei Chuppah*, does not even list the blessing on *eirusin* (Freiman, p. 294).

VII. Language Confusion

With all this development of customs over the centuries, with the shift of *eirusin* from a betrothal that served as an engagement to a part of the final wedding ceremony, it should not be surprising that people confused the terminology. Rav Ya'akov Bassan (Responsa, no. 36) writes that people frequently called an engaged woman an "*arusah*," a betrothed woman. Freiman (p. 218) cites three responsa that he claims involve uncertainties about whether a term means "betrothal" or "engagement," although I did not see it in my review of the first responsum he mentions (*Responsa Mahari Mintz*, no. 12).

Be that as it may, it seems that usage of the term "*eirusin*" in Modern Hebrew for "engagement" reflects this historical shift in practice. What was once a pre-wedding betrothal is now part of the wedding ceremony. Yet the pre-wedding engagement is still called, at least in Modern Hebrew, "*eirusin*." However, I still maintain my stubborn refusal to use the halakhically imprecise term.

Do Husbands Own Their Wives?

A common misconception about Judaism is that in the wedding, a husband acquires his wife and subsequently owns her. This is generally an idea accepted by people with significant Jewish education, and for a good reason. The first Mishnah in *Kiddushin* states that a woman is acquired by her husband in any of three ways. Clearly, it would seem, a woman is her husband's property. However, this is incorrect, and a number of prominent authorities—in contexts far from polemics and apologetics—disprove this theory.

The Netziv, Rav Naftali Tzvi Yehudah Berlin (d. 1893), wrote a responsum on this subject to a rabbi who had concluded that husbands do, in fact, own their wives (*Meishiv Davar* 4:35). The Netziv emphatically denies this conclusion. He points to two sources that might imply an ownership relationship and explains them differently.

I. Ownership

The Torah (Deut. 22:13) describes marriage as a man taking a woman (*ki yikkach ish ishah*). The language of taking seems to imply acquisition and ownership.

Only a *kohen* may eat from from the *terumah* portion of food, which other Jews give to *kohanim*. The Torah (Lev. 22:11) states that anyone owned by or born to a *kohen* may also eat from that food. The Sages (*Yevamos* 66b) infer that a *kohen*'s wife may eat *terumah* from the ownership clause (*kinyan kaspo*), implying that a *kohen* owns his wife.

II. Independence

However, with a somewhat complex deduction, the Netziv proves that a man does not own his wife like he owns slaves. The Sages decreed that a woman's wages belong to her husband unless they reach a contrary arrangement, and in exchange a husband is obligated to support his wife (*Kesubos* 58b). They enacted this to simplify household finances and protect marital harmony. However, because family situations vary, the Sages provided women an opt-out ability. Women can declare themselves financially independent, thereby keeping their own wages and freeing their husbands from the obligation to support them.

The Netziv argues that this rabbinic enactment would be unnecessary and the opt-out ability impossible if a husband owns his wife. A slave's earnings also belong to his master, but that is a function of ownership, not a rabbinic enactment. The fact that a wife's earnings do not automatically flow to her husband prove that she is independent, not owned by her husband. A woman's status is in direct contrast to a slave, who is truly owned by his master.

III. Exclusivity

However, the Netziv believes that a husband owns a specific right to his wife. To explains this, let me take a brief detour that the Netziv does not explain. As we recently discussed, there are two stages to a Jewish wedding—betrothal (*eirusin* or *kiddushin*) and marriage (*nissu'in*). The first stage is establishing a unique relationship between the man and woman, so that no other man may marry her. A betrothed woman is not yet allowed to live with her husband but must receive a *get* to remarry. The second stage is when husband and wife live together as a married couple, after *nissu'in*.

The Netziv explains that the wedding includes a husband acquiring the exclusive rights to sleep with his wife. Before then, no man is allowed to sleep with her. After that point, she is allowed to sleep with him but no other man (absent a divorce). This is an acquisition, not of the woman in totality, who remains independent, but in the rights to marital relations. In theory, a woman should also acquire such rights in her husband but, by strict Torah law, she cannot because a man is allowed to have multiple wives (later forbidden by rabbinic fiat). Instead, the Netziv points out, a man is biblically obligated to sleep with his wife (Ex. 21:10), in fulfillment of the mitzvah of *onah*.

This is a highly unromantic view of a marriage. It describes the underlying mechanics, the theory of a wedding and not the emotions. A marriage is a joining of two individuals into a union. Exactly how that union is accomplished legally, the technical workings of the marriage, is beside the point.

IV. Acquiring

A debate ensues among later authorities which part of the wedding consists of a husband acquiring this right. Rav Yitzchak Rabinowitz (d. 1919), also known as Rav Itzeleh Ponovizher, argues that the *eirusin* is the mechanical part of the wedding (*Me-Chiddushei Ha-Gaon Rav Yitzchak Rabinowitz, Kiddushin*, no. 1). At that point, a wife is forbidden to all other men even though the couple is only betrothed and not fully married. This would also explain the Mishnah's language of three methods of acquisition in describing *eirusin*—at that point, the husband acquires the sole right to be with the wife.

However, Rav Yoav Weingarten (d. 1922) argues that *nissu'in*, which historically was performed up to a year after the husband gave the wedding ring to his wife, is the point at which the husband acquires these rights (*Chelkas Yoav, Even Ha-Ezer* 6). He points out that the Torah states it almost explicitly. In the context of exempting a recently married man from military service, the Torah (Deut. 20:7) says, "Who is the man who betrothed a woman but did not take her?" Apparently, taking her, the acquisition, is only a function of the second stage of a wedding.

Regardless of which of these two is correct, all three of the above scholars argue that a woman is not the property of her husband. She is a free and independent individual. However, by marrying, she gives up her right to potentially sleep with other men. In practice, a man also gives up that right, but only according to rabbinic law, and therefore through a different mechanism.

Equalizing and Nullifying Weddings

At a 2017 conference of Jewish feminists who identify as Orthodox, a session was given on inequality in the wedding process. One speaker pointed out that the wedding ceremony is inherently unequal—the man takes the woman as a wife. Another speaker suggested that the ceremony should be changed so that, in addition to the man acquiring the wife, the woman should also acquire the husband. Indeed, she did just that at her wedding. That made me wonder whether anyone who does this is halakhically married.

I. Under the *Chuppah*

At a Jewish wedding, a man gives a woman an item of value (for centuries, a ring). With her acceptance, the man acquires exclusive marital rights and obligations. As we have explained, the man does not acquire the woman herself because she remains a free, albeit married, woman. If a woman attempts to acquire a man in this same way, it raises questions whether either of the agreements worked.

Traditionally, a Jewish wedding involves the man giving the woman a ring. This contrasts with Christian weddings, in which the couple exchanges rings. Rav Moshe Feinstein (*Iggeros Moshe*, *Even Ha-Ezer* 3:18, 4:13) was asked about the propriety of a Jewish double-ring ceremony, in which the man gives the woman a ring and then the woman gives the man a ring under the *chuppah*. Rav Feinstein forbade a double-ring ceremony for two reasons. First, it is a Christian practice, and we may not model our religious ceremonies on those from other religions. Additionally, it might lead to confusion about the nature of the Jewish marriage ceremony, in which the man takes the woman. If the wife wants to give her husband a ring, she should do so later and not at the *chuppah*. If she insists on giving it at the *chuppah*, the rabbi should announce that this ring is merely a gift and not part of the actual wedding process.

II. Invalid *Chuppah*

In recent responsa, Rav Osher Weiss (*Minchas Asher*, vol. 1 no. 71, vol. 3 no. 98) goes even further. Rav Weiss was dealing with women who married under the auspices of a Conservative rabbi. One woman obtained a Conservative divorce, remarried, and had children from the second marriage who are now Orthodox. Are these children considered illegitimate? If the original wedding was halakhically valid but the divorce invalid, they are considered illegitimate and may not marry into the general Jewish community. The second woman is trying to obtain a divorce from her husband. However, because Jewish divorce must be mutual, he has the right—which he is invoking—to prevent the divorce. Rav Weiss explored reasons to invalidate the original weddings, rendering the children of the first woman legitimate and the second woman unmarried. As with all responsible attempts to annul a marriage, the deliberations are complex and specific to individual circumstances.

One argument Rav Weiss advances is that a double-ring ceremony is invalid. He writes (vol. 3, p. 333):

The entire concept of *"kiddushin"* according to Torah law is that the man consecrates and acquires the woman. Even though the earlier commentators already wrote that this is not a financial acquisition and a wife is not the property of her husband, the Torah still says, "When a man takes a woman" (Deut. 24:5). He acquires her regarding marital matters. Therefore, when she gives him [a ring] and she says ["I am consecrated to you with this ring"], there is no *kiddushin* at all (*Kiddushin* 5b). This understanding completely contradicts the concept of marriage in the modern world, according to which there is only mutual and equal connection and obligations.

Indeed, people testified that the man and woman in this case exchanged rings under the *chuppah*—he gave to her and she gave to him. It seems to me that if the man and woman had that intention, there is no *kiddushin* at all.

According to Rav Weiss, the wedding ceremony and marriage process is inherently non-egalitarian. The man has one role and the woman has a different role. Any attempt to equate those roles risks voiding the marriage.

In the cases Rav Weiss discusses, he includes other considerations to annul the marriages. And despite the multiple considerations, he still insists on a divorce with a *get* whenever possible. I am not suggesting that a woman who marries with a double-ring ceremony does not need a *get*. Additionally, the precise details of what takes place under the *chuppah*, the words said and actions done, affect the outcome.

However, despite all this, Rav Weiss makes a point that is important to consider: The wedding is supposed to include different roles for the man and woman. In this respect, the Torah is in fundamental opposition to the egalitarian concept of a wedding. When we face that contradiction, we are supposed to side with the Torah. Failure to do so, attempting to make the male and female roles the same, undermines the wedding process. This technical claim of the invalidation of the wedding is bold, which Rav Feinstein seems to reject since he does not raise it. However, when attempting to change customs—particularly regarding weddings and divorces—we would do well to take into account the view of an important contemporary halakhic authority.

Orphans and Affirmative Action

The Torah commands us to treat orphans with special care, leading to an important halakhic question: Who is an orphan? The answer has, I believe, an important ethical message that still resonates today.

I. In Search of a Definition

We are prohibited from causing harm to a widow or orphan even more than others: "You shall not afflict any widow or orphan. If you afflict them in any way—for if they cry at all to Me, I will surely hear their cry..." (Ex. 22:22-23). Effectively, the Torah mandates affirmative action for orphans.

But who falls into this category? While we should treat every individual with care, widows and orphans receive preferential treatment. If two cases come before a court at the same time, the orphan's case goes first (*Shulchan Arukh, Choshen Mishpat* 15:2). Additionally, an orphan, or his trustee, may charge rabbinically prohibited interest (*Shulchan Arukh, Yoreh De'ah* 160:18). In order to properly apply these rules, we must define the category of an orphan.

Perhaps anyone who loses a parent is considered an orphan. The pain of losing a parent is a permanent scar, even for an adult whose parent passes away. But if this is the case, nearly everyone becomes an orphan eventually (except those who sadly predecease both parents). This would create a system of preferential treatment for the older generation and effectively undermine rabbinic prohibitions of charging interest. That may be the intention of the laws but it seems farfetched. It seems more likely that only a small minority of people ever fall into the category of orphans that receives preferential treatment.

II. The First Definition

The Rambam (*Mishneh Torah, Hilkhos Dei̇os* 6:10) sets down the first definition of an orphan. He writes that a child who loses a mother or father is classified as an orphan until he no longer needs an adult to take care of him but can take care of himself like other adults. With this, Rambam limits orphanhood to children. Similarly, Rambam writes elsewhere (ibid., *Hilkhos Nachalos* 7:5) that a court only appoints a trustee (*apotropus*) for a child orphan, not an adult. Note that Rambam includes the phrase "like other adults." No one is completely self-sufficient; everyone needs help from friends and family. An orphan is mainstreamed when he becomes as self-sufficient as his peers.

Characteristically, Rambam provides no sources for his rulings. The second ruling about appointing a trustee is explicit in the Gemara (*Bava Metzi̇a* 39a). However, the earlier and more detailed definition confounded commentators for centuries until its source was conclusively identified in the early twentieth century.

Despite the unknown source, other authorities adopted Rambam's definition. *Sefer Ha-Chinukh* (65) paraphrases the Rambam's definition: "Until they do not need an adult in their matters but take care of all their own needs like other adults." Similarly, among Ashkenazim, Rav Moshe of Coucy (*Semag*, prohibition 8) paraphrases Rambam's definition, as does Rabbenu Peretz in his glosses to *Semak* (87). These post-Maimonidean scholars could have known Rambam's source or they may have accepted his definition on his substantive authority. Or perhaps they found the definition intuitively compelling.

Rav Yisrael Isserlein (*Terumas Ha-Deshen* 1:300) addresses a case of the converse. Is someone who cannot manage his own affairs and whose parents will not help him considered an orphan even if his parents are still alive? A young married couple received dowries and was then cut off by his parents. However, the groom was incapable of managing his own affairs. The bride's father asked whether he could establish a fund for them that lends money with rabbinically prohibited interest, since the groom was effectively an orphan. Rav Isserlein replied that since the groom's father is alive, the groom cannot be considered an orphan. Youth, lack of parental support, and inability to manage one's affairs, define the limits of orphanhood but do not constitute an independent definition.

III. Modern Definitions

Rambam's definition was effectively codified in *Magen Avraham* (156:2), subsequently quoted by *Mishnah Berurah* (ibid., 4). Similarly, Rav Meir Eisenstadt (Maharam Esh, in *Panim Me'iros* 1:37 s.v. *ve-tzarikh*) writes that a self-sufficient adult, or a married woman whose husband provides for her, is no longer considered an orphan.

However, a slight modification was offered by an important Turkish authority. Rav Binyamin Pontrimoli (*Responsa Shevet Binyamin*, no. 229, last par.) points out that an orphan is allowed to independently sell the land he inherits when he reaches the age of twenty. He suggests that this is a general definition of an orphan: The status ends at the age of twenty. Rav Pontrimoli's grandson and namesake rules likewise in his *Pesach Ha-Devir* commentary on *Shulchan Arukh* (156:5). Rav Yaakov Chaim Sofer of Baghdad (*Kaf Ha-Chaim* 156:14) quotes the *Pesach Ha-Devir* approvingly.

I have found that these definitions are quoted by contemporary authorities in conjunction. To qualify halakhically as an orphan, an individual must have lost one parent, must be incapable of managing his own affairs like other adults, and must be younger than twenty.[16]

IV. The Source

In 1905, Rav David Tzvi Hoffmann published an annotated edition of the long-lost *Mekhilta De-Rashbi*. Rav Hoffmann points out in a footnote that a comment of this ancient midrash seems to be Rambam's elusive source for his definition of an orphan (Ex. 22:21, p. 150 n. 70). The *Mekhilta De-Rashbi* asks: "Until when are they called orphans? Until they can stand on their own." This implies financial self-sufficiency, as Rambam and subsequent authorities ruled.

In his *Avodas Ha-Melekh* commentary (*Dei'os* 6:10), Rav Menachem Krakowski agrees with Rav Hoffmann and adds that a similar statement appears in *Tanna De-Vei Eliyahu Rabba* (ch. 27, p. 143 in the Ish-Shalom edition). The midrash refers to orphans in their times (*yesomim bi-zmanan*), implying that the status is limited by age or phase of life. Subsequent commentaries accept these sources, including Rav Yosef Kafach's edition (ad loc., n. 59) and Rav Nachum Rabinovich's *Yad Peshutah* (ad loc.). Rav Menachem Kasher (*Ha-Rambam Ve-Ha-Mekhilta De-Rashbi*, pp. 160-161) also agrees that the *Mekhilta De-Rashbi* is Rambam's source.

V. Implications

This limited definition of an orphan has profound implications. Life is full of challenges. If we offer preferential treatment to everyone who has suffered setbacks or encountered difficult or even traumatic circumstances, then the preference would be nullified by abundance. As many have pointed out, if everyone is special, no one is special. A child separated from his parent or

---

16. See, for example, Rav Simcha Rabinowitz, *Piskei Teshuvos* 156:11 and Rav Yitzchak Ya'akov Fuchs, *Halikhos Bein Adam Le-Chaveiro*, 18:11.

whose parent is unable to raise or assist him is not an orphan but still must overcome difficult challenges. Why doesn't he receive preferential treatment? The Torah reserves this treatment for the unique, tragic case of an orphan. Everyone else receives our sympathy and encouragement, as well as our charity and support, but not preferential treatment.

Additionally, and perhaps important for contemporary discussion of affirmative action, adults must take responsibility for their situations. The disadvantages and setbacks of our upbringing do not entitle us to perpetual special treatment. Even those who seem to come from charmed backgrounds carry emotional baggage. Children need guidance and support, and therefore orphan children receive preferential treatment. Adults, though, need to take control of their lives. While we must deal with every individual sensitively, we have no Torah-based affirmative action for adults.[17]

---

17. At least for adult men. Widows are in a different category because they lost their caregiver.

Jewish Sexual Ethics

I. Two Responses to Society

We live in a hyper-sexualized environment in which the media and society bombard us with messages and images that are not just immodest but outright explicit. A community that attempts to remain traditional when confronted with this relentless assault has two options. It can go farther in the contrary direction or walk in step with society as much as possible. A relatively recent Hebrew book, currently being translated into English, takes a middle approach.

One response to a sexually permissive society is to emphasize asceticism as the ideal, to step away from sexuality as much as possible. Given the vast ascetic literature in Judaism, and the Mussar and Kabbalistic hesitations about sexual pleasure in particular, this direction flows naturally for a Jewish community.

Another approach moves toward leniency. According to this view, it is better to permit as much as possible. Considering all the temptations facing people, offer them as many permissible avenues as possible to keep them within the fold. Due to the wide spectrum of views within Judaism, this path can be plausibly taken without damaging the halakhic method.

Both approaches face risks. A counter-cultural approach is all-or-nothing. Widening the gap between Jewish and general society forces people to choose—and many will opt out of traditional Judaism. On the other hand, going along with society sets the stage for breaking boundaries. It adopts secular values and only partially fulfills them. Deviance is all but inevitable.

Complicating this issue is the talmudic requirement to teach these matters only privately. The Mishnah (*Chagigah* 11b) says that you may not teach about marital relations to a group of three or more people. The Gemara (ibid.) explains that the concern over teaching to a group is that people might pay insufficient attention and mistakenly believe that the forbidden is actually permitted. Today, any public discussion of these matters raises so many jokes, digressions, and pop culture references that people can easily reach an incorrect conclusion. These are not issues for a podcast or blog post.

II. A Third Approach

Rav Eliezer Melamed, author of the extremely popular code of contemporary Jewish law, *Peninei Halakhah*, published a Hebrew volume on marital relations titled "Family Joy and Its Blessing." This book is written in the same style as *Peninei Halakhah* but kept apart from the set because of its intended mature audience. For those who understand the talmudic euphemisms he uses, the author gets as explicit as possible without turning the book into a how-to manual. In general, his attitude is fairly lenient. However, he avoids the pitfalls of the first approach mentioned above by building a bigger picture.

Rav Melamed incorporates into his work a theology of marriage. A person is only complete when living happily with his spouse. While childbearing is an important mitzvah, marital relations is not just about having children. It is also about pleasing your spouse, which is an explicit mitzvah in the Torah, particularly on the husband. Therefore, even the otherwise permissible marital activities are only allowed if they are mutually pleasing. Instead of thinking about marital relations as receiving pleasure, one has to view it as giving pleasure.

Rav Melamed's vision of marriage is purely heterosexual, as is any legitimate reading of the vast Torah literature. His sections on homosexuality reflect on recent societal changes. In the past, it was common for many people with homosexual feelings to marry and have children. Rav Melamed encourages everyone who can marry and procreate to do so, as long as they can please their spouse and remain faithful (he also discusses when one should reveal in advance same-gender attractions to a potential spouse). In his final section on this topic, Rav Melamed tells active homosexuals that even if they violate this prohibition, they are still obligated in every mitzvah. And even regarding this prohibition, every time they overcome their desire and refrain, they receive reward.

III. Law and Theology

Rav Melamed embeds his leniencies in a framework that focuses not just on what is permitted but also what is forbidden. He discusses self-stimulation, birth control, and abortion. While even there his views tend toward leniency, he operates within a structure of obligations and prohibitions. He emphasizes this by including a companion volume with in-depth analysis of rabbinic sources (*Harchavos*), as he does with some volumes of his *Peninei Halakhah*, this time written by his study partner, Rav Maor Kayam. Rav Melamed's approach is not an anything-goes attitude but a textually sound, lenient guide towards marital holiness through *halakhah*.

Rav Melamed's final chapter adds a Religious Zionist twist to a messianic vision of gender. Rav Melamed adopts the increasingly popular approach that male and female will become equal in messianic times. Initially, in a courtship and marriage, the man and woman have different roles. The man is the initiator and the influencer; the woman is the supporter. After many years they develop equal footing with each other. Just like this relationship evolves within a marriage, it also evolves within humanity. Living as we do in pre-messianic times, as many Religious Zionist thinkers contend, we are in a transitional period regarding gender equality. The confusion we see in the world, the preliminary and somewhat chaotic shifts regarding gender, is due to the proximity to the messianic era.

Rav Melamed devotes a lengthy discussion to personal sanctity. He explores the proper intentions to have during relations and the proper role of asceticism in religious life. Perhaps most importantly, he elevates the role of marital relations even when intended selfishly, for one's own pleasure. Even if not ideal, this, too, is holy. When a married couple remains faithful, even without the loftiest spiritual intentions, they avoid the forbidden sexual prohibitions. As Rashi (Lev. 19:2) teaches, avoiding those prohibitions brings holiness. This is a simple but often overlooked statement about the silent nobility of a simple religious life.

When Did Jewish Childhood Begin?

We tend to project our views on others, especially the attitudes we take for granted. In 1960, historian Phillipe Aries published a book challenging our assumptions about childhood in pre-sixteenth century Europe.[18] According to Aries, Medieval Europeans did not recognize a unique period of childhood. Until the age of seven, children were cared for but were not educated, trained, coddled, or enjoyed, perhaps due to the high mortality rate. After passing that stage, children were treated like little adults. There were no games or special clothes for children, nor educational stages.

After great debate, historians have largely dismissed this theory. A recent study of British childhood from the Middle Ages through today directly addresses this question without quoting Aries. Hugh Cunningham (*The Invention of Childhood*, London, 2006) asks: "Was this really how it was? Was there no recognition that children needed special care in their upbringing?" (p. 28) and proceeds to argue at great length that this was not true in many ways.

What do Jewish sources say about it? Rav Ephraim Kanarfogel (*Jewish Education and Society in the High Middle Ages*, ch. 2)[19] explores Medieval Jewish texts for indications about childhood. *Pirkei Avos* (3:10) warns people to stay away from the "conversation of children." The commentary attributed to Rav Yedayah Ha-Penini,

---

18. *L'enfant et la Vie Familiale Sous L'ancien Regime*, translated into English as *Centuries of Childhood: A Social History of Family Life* (Vintage, 1965).
19. Wayne State University Press, 2007.

but really written by Rav Yitzchak Ben Yedayah of thirteenth-century Provence, explains that people naturally enjoy younger children more than older children. However, young children will waste time talking about nonsense and cause others to speak about nonsense, as well. A father's time is spent better on other things than playing with a young child. However, the comment implies that young children have a uniquely enjoyable quality to them.

Sefer Chasidim (770) says that a person who is feeling troubled on Shabbos should speak with a child, which will cheer him up. However, a man should not hold his son on his lap right before *Mincha* because the child will cry and the man will be thinking about the crying child during prayers (no. 432). Again we see that children are enjoyable and worthy of care and notice.

When Rav Elazar Rokeach mourned the murder of his six-year old daughter by Christians, he included in his eulogy that she played with him and sang (*Sefer Gezeiros Ashkenaz*, pp. 166-167). This touching mention reveals that the parental instinct and love for young children that we take for granted today also existed in Medieval times.

Talmudic texts disagree about when a child's Torah education should begin. Tosafos (*Kesubos* 50a s.v. *ve-safei*) state that a child should begin studying at age five, although others suggest age six. Other texts also express the obligation on parents to inculcate proper character traits in child from a very early age (see the glosses of Rabbenu Peretz to *Semak*, no. 4).

Rav Kanarfogel concludes that, unlike the portrait Aries presents of relative neglect in early childhood, "in Jewish society of northern France and Germany parents did enjoy their children and that some were clearly cognizant of the distinct nature of childhood" (p. 39).

The Late *Mohel*

There is a fascinating exchange of letters from the summer of 1865 between two grandsons of Rav Akiva Eiger.[20]

I. Delaying A Circumcision

Rav Leibele Eiger was a *chasid* who served as a *mohel* in Lublin. His practice was to engage in intense meditative practices for many hours before a circumcision, effectively delaying the ceremony until the afternoon. Some residents of his city complained about this, and Rav Leibele felt it necessary to receive approval from local rabbinic authorities (which he did) and from a prominent rabbinc authority from elsewhere. Therefore, he wrote a letter to his cousin, Rav Shimon Sofer (son of the Chasam Sofer and grandson of Rav Akiva Eiger), asking for his approval.

After explaining the circumstances, Rav Leibele pointed out that the rabbinic saying is "*zerizin makdimin LE-mitzvos* – the zealous begin early FOR *mitzvos.*" He argues that this does not mean that we have to perform the actual mitzvah early because then it would say "*zerizin makdimin HA-mitvos* – the zealous begin THE *mitzvos* early.*" Rather, the formulation we have means that we begin preparing early for a mitzvah. He adds that he has other proofs but chooses not to elaborate so as not to belabor the point.

---

20. The letters are published in *Iggeros Soferim* (Vienna-Budapest, 1928), section 4 pp. 43-51.

II. Spiritual Preparation

Rav Leibele notes that the *"chasidim ha-rishonim* – the early pious ones" of the Talmud would prepare for an hour before praying. Nowadays, when we are on such a low spiritual level, we have to prepare that long for every mitzvah.

These long spiritual preparations before a circumcision are, he claims, an established custom in his region. Therefore, even though Rav Shimon Sofer's custom is to the contrary, Rav Leibele asks his cousin to recognize the differing practices and to validate his.

III. Do Not Delay a Circumsion

Rav Shimon Sofer replied within days. He writes that the concept is correct—it is appropriate to delay a mitzvah in order to perform it better, as the *Terumas Ha-Deshen* (Responsa, no. 35) and *Chakham Tzvi* (no. 45) ruled. However, how is the *mitzvah* enhanced by having a more holy *mohel* perform it? The parents should just use a different *mohel* who takes less time to prepare.

Furthermore, Rav Sofer argues that there is a good reason for rushing to perform a circumcision. The foreskin is considered offensive and must be removed as soon as possible. Rav Leibele needs to bring a source that spiritual preparation is sufficient to delay removing the offensive foreskin for hours.

In fact, the universal custom, Rav Sofer states, is to perform the circumcision as early as possible. Rav Sofer ignored Rav Leibele's claim that his region had a different custom, perhaps because he assumed that it was a relatively recent (Chassidic?) innovation.

IV. The Holier *Mohel*

Rav Sofer then quotes a midrash that Moshe and Aharon performed circumcisions in the Sinai Desert, which presumably delayed some of the circumcisions by hours. There must have been someone else who could have done it but people still waited for

Moshe and Aharon. Evidently, this is a proof that one may delay a circumcision for hours in order to utilize an important and holy person as a *mohel*.

Rav Sofer cautions that not everyone can claim to be sufficiently holy to be compared to Moshe and Aharon, but his cousin is surely one who can. Therefore, his practice is acceptable.

V. Keep Your Holiness to Yourself

Rav Sofer later added an addendum. In the age in which they lived, when so many people were improperly claiming to be great Jews and accepting upon themselves inappropriately pious practices, we need to be extra-cautious and not appear to be sanctioning such a misguided approach by acting similarly. While the early pious ones of the Talmud prepared for an hour before prayer, it seems clear that the later pious ones did not.

The reason for this later practice is that the generations have declined, yet false pious ones pretend to be greater than they really are. To stop them, the true pious ones abandoned all extra-pious practices in public, keeping them only for privacy when no one would see. Rav Sofer wrote that this was what his father, the Chasam Sofer, would do—when in public he followed the same practices as everyone else but in private he would follow certain kabbalistic practices.

PART 2: JEWISH EDUCATION

It's All About Education

I. Education is the Key

The past half century of Jewish experience has taught that education is the key to ideological success. Whichever group controls the schools wins the hearts of succeeding generations. But what seems clear in retrospect was not obvious at the time. In Rav Ya'akov Ariel's telling, Religious Zionism failed to recognize this and suffered great losses due to this blindness and accompanying institutional rigidity.

Rav Ariel's recent book of religious ideology, *Halakhah Be-Yameinu*,[21] includes two essays on the history of Religious Zionist education in Israel, the first on educational differences and the second on the broader history as it intersected with his personal experiences. I find this fascinating because it explains so much. However, I recognize that this is one man's anecdotal, ideological narrative rather than a comprehensive history. Be that as it may, it still bears consideration. To avoid undue focus on issues such as gender and ethnicity, which excite so many of us, I will only address native Israeli male education.

II. Lack of Success

The founding rabbis of Religious Zionism emerged from what we would now call Charedi yeshivas. When they established educational institutions for the Religious Zionist community, these

---

21. Machon Ha-Torah Ve-Ha-Aretz, 2010.

leaders assumed that the same types of yeshivas would continue to produce great students who would fill roles in the Religious Zionist community. To some degree, they were correct. Leading rabbis, such as Rav Shlomo Goren, studied in yeshivas like Chevron and Ponevezhe. However, overall, the opposition to Religious Zionism grew so strong in these institutions that these rabbis were the rare exception and were insufficient to fill the many rabbinical roles required in the growing state. Mercaz HaRav, the central Religious Zionist yeshiva, all but collapsed after the death of its dean, Rav Ya'akov Moshe Charlap, in 1951. There was another reason for the failure to establish Religious Zionist post-high school yeshivas— lack of students.

The initial Religious Zionist elementary and high schools, with a few noteworthy exceptions, were patterned after Western European gymnasia. They were essentially secular schools with some classes on religious subjects. The religious studies teachers did not set the school's tone and did not have any more influence than any other teacher. While the goal was to attract the less committed students and fight against an oppressively secular culture, the result was a generation full of religiously uninspired and uneducated students. Graduates of these schools were interested in high achievements in career and army rather than in Torah.

III. Torah Revolution

In Rav Ariel's narrative, the savior was the Bnei Akiva youth movement. Its inspired youth demanded change, often meeting institutional opposition but slowly overcoming and eventually dominating. After they pushed for the establishment of Religious Zionist yeshivas, Kerem B'Yavneh and HaDarom were established and Merkaz Harav was revitalized at approximately the same time. These institutions of higher Torah learning not only taught Israel-centric values but encouraged army service among its students and graduates, often within the groundbreaking Hesder program.

Additionally, these activist youths successfully started elementary and high schools with more of an Eastern European flavor—with a rabbi as the primary instructor for each class whose job was to guide his students toward a life of religious devotion. These schools were yeshiva high schools. Rather than the secular studies setting the tone for the religious studies, the influence flowed in the reverse direction. The yeshiva high school, as opposed to the religious high school, succeeded in feeding the post-high school yeshivas. In turn, the yeshiva elementary schools grew with a similar model and fed the yeshiva high school. The reverse trajectory of this loose and disorganized movement as well as its grassroots nature led to slow growth.

IV. Growth

The Six-Day War was not a turning point but an inflection point. The religious fervor of the moment boosted the expansion of this educational movement just as it was reaching maturity. The expansion not only grew the existing framework into the normative model but added another level—kollel. The Religious Zionist educational system was now ready to produce its own exceptional Torah scholars. And it did. These yeshivas and kollels have graduated hundreds of exceptionally capable rabbis, leaders, judges, and decisors, not to mention laymen accomplished in Torah and secular pursuits. They have allowed outstanding students to devote many years to growth in Torah knowledge and wisdom.

However, the focus on Torah achievement creates social boundaries which have already generated responses. Not every yeshiva high school graduate is prepared to devote many further years to yeshiva study and army service. The growth of the Hesder yeshiva led to a perception of Torah elitism and a split in the community between those with advanced Torah education and those without. This was answered in two ways.

V. Specialization

Specialized yeshivas emerged, focusing on different aspects of the religious personality. Yeshiva frameworks within academic institutions, most notably Bar Ilan, offered additional alternatives. Students with many different needs can find their place within the Religious Zionist system of Torah study, although Rav Ariel cautions about the need for proper proportions in areas of focus.

Additionally, to the surprise of many, the army preparation schools wildly succeeded in attracting students. These schools generally teach intense one year courses in Jewish law and thought for those intending to enlist in regular army service (as opposed to Hesder). The schools' success has been bittersweet because they attract students from across the spectrum, including many who would otherwise have enrolled in multi-year yeshiva programs. However, Rav Ariel praises these programs for successfully instilling faith and devotion in its graduates, some of whom eventually end up in a yeshiva.

Rav Ariel addresses some criticisms of the Religious Zionist educational system. He accepts its many flaws but argues that it has sufficiently succeeded to merit continuation, even if with nuanced changes. Rav Ariel's favored educational framework is one of personal choice grounded in Torah basics and a religiously nourishing environment. He savors the uniquely Israeli (i.e., Religious Zionist) aspects of study—Bible, history, geography, theology—that have flourished over the past few decades. In retrospect, the Religious Zionist community could not grow during the early life of the country until its religious educational system was put into place.

Religious Zionism and Kollel

The issue of kollel study serves as the basis of many heated debates in the Orthodox community. The right-wing advance full-time Torah study as the standard while the Modern Orthodox promote work, studying Torah while in college and while working. However, a number of Modern Orthodox communities house local kollels, sponsored by Yeshiva University, indicating a middle ground that requires elaboration. What is perhaps the founding text of Religious Zionism discusses this issue and demonstrates a nuanced middle position that I think represents the dominant Modern Orthodox view.

In 1862, Rav Tzvi Hirsch Kalischer published his magnum opus, *Derishas Tziyyon*, calling for Jewish settlement in Israel and the reinstitution of animal sacrifices in Jerusalem. The book made waves, generating discussion among leading rabbis for decades. In particular, Rav Kalischer raised funds for the organization Chevras Yishuv Eretz Yisrael, which sponsored the existing settlement in Israel and its proposed expansion.

I. Work is a Mitzvah

In the book's Preface, Rav Kalischer discusses possible objections to his fundraising request. Among them is that the expansion of agricultural work opportunities in Israel would draw its impoverished inhabitants away from studying Torah. Rav Kalischer responds on two levels. First, not everyone in the Israeli settlements are learning Torah. If they work, they will be able to support their local Torah scholars. However, he adds that he is only referring to the elderly and weak. Young, strong men should work the land and study Torah in their free time. The Talmud (*Berakhos* 35b) quotes Rava as telling people that he did not want to see them in the study hall during the harvest and pressing times of Nisan and Tishrei so they would earn money.

Rav Kalischer adds two more points. First, working in Israel—developing the land—is an additional mitzvah. Second, people who work for a living, who are not compensated for their Torah study, learn with entirely pure intentions. He quotes *Tanna De-Vei Eliyahu Zuta* (18) and *Berakhos* (7a) that someone who works for a living and learns Torah, i.e. who is financially self-sufficient, will be rewarded in this world and the next.

All this seems to argue for kollel for retirees only. Those who are able to work should do so and learn Torah in their free time. In 1866, Rav Kalischer republished *Derishas Tziyon* with additional comments called *Rishon Le-Tziyon*. In his additions to the Preface, Rav Kalischer adds more nuance to his position on kollel.

II. Learning Torah

Berakhos (35b) records a debate between R. Yishmael and R. Shimon Bar Yochai. The former believed you should learn Torah when you are not working. The latter believed you should always learn Torah. The Gemara concludes that many tried R. Shimon Bar Yochai's approach and failed, implying that the proper approach is to work, as stated by the *Tanna De-Vei Eliyahu* mentioned above.

Rav Kalischer adds three more points. We have to be realistic: Not everyone who works will rise to the challenge and learn Torah in all his free time. Rav Kalisher quotes the Maharsha's commentary to *Berakhos* (17a) that people will inevitably learn different amounts outside of work. As long as their intentions are pure, they will be rewarded equally in heaven.

Additionally, Rav Kalischer expresses concern that a young man will spend all his time working without learning Torah at all. An ambitious worker will set his sights high and spend all his time progressing in his career. When will he learn? Therefore, it is important for a young man to spend time in yeshiva without any worries beyond learning Torah. Kollel has its place for the young, to develop their skills and command of Torah.

III. Kollel Compromise

However, some people will show such dedication to Torah that they should dedicate their lives to learning it full time. Rav Kalischer states that none of his comments refer to those who rise on the ladder of spirituality and permanently find their place in the study hall. Such people should learn Torah without restriction.

In the end, Rav Kalischer's view seems to be that full-time yeshiva and/or kollel is appropriate for the young, the old, and those few unique individuals who exhibit exceptional devotion and promise. The majority of people should spend the majority of their lives working, contributing materially to society, and learning Torah as much as possible in their free time. In practice, much of the Chareidi world—particularly outside of Israel—functions this way, as well. However, they see kollel study as the ideal while Rav Kalischer, and the Modern Orthodox community, sees working as the ideal.

Who Really Started Jewish Education?

I. Three Educational Developments

Common wisdom has it that Yehoshua ben Gamla, in either the first century CE or the first century BCE, instituted universal Jewish education. This is probably wrong.

The Gemara (*Bava Basra* 21a) says:

> Rav Yehudah said in the name of Rav: However, remember that man for good and Yehoshua ben Gamla is his name. If not for him, Torah would have been forgotten from Israel. At first, a child who had a father, his father taught him [Torah]. Someone without a father would not learn. From where do we derive this? "And you shall teach them" (Deut. 11:19) — and *you* shall teach. They enacted that children's teachers should be appointed in Jerusalem. From where do we derive this? "Because from Zion the Torah will go forth" (Isa. 2:3). Even so, if a child had a father, the father would bring him to Jerusalem. Someone without a father would not go and learn. They enacted that teachers should be appointed in every city and enter them at the age of sixteen or seventeen. Someone whose teacher got angry with him would reject him and leave. Until Ben Gamla enacted that children's teachers should be appointed in every district and town, and that children should enter school at the age of six or seven.

We see four stages in this history of Jewish education:

1. Homeschooling
2. Centralized in Jerusalem
3. Local high schools
4. Local elementary schools

Only this last stage is attributed to Yehoshua ben Gamla, not the two earlier enactments. However, that would be enough to earn Yehoshua ben Gamla the title of the father of Jewish education, if not for a competing text.

II. The Pharisee

The Talmud Yerushalmi (*Kesubos* 8:11) lists three enactments of Shimon ben Shetach:

1. A man should use his wife's *kesubah* in commerce (so he takes its financial obligation seriously)
2. Children must go to school
3. Glass utensils can become impure

According to this text, Shimon ben Shetach enacted universal Jewish education, not Yehoshua ben Gamla. Interestingly, Tosafos (*Bava Basra* ad loc., s.v. *zakhor*) say that the Yehoshua ben Gamla who enacted the educational decree is the same man named in *Yevamos* (61a) as Shimon ben Shetach's brother-in-law, whose wealthy wife bought him the high priesthood. Presumably based on this, Rav David Frankel (*Sheyarei Korban*, *Yerushalmi Kesubos*, ad loc.) suggests—not unreasonably—that they issued the decree together.

However, Rav Yitzchak Isaac Halevy (*Doros Ha-Rishonim* part 1, vol. 2, p. 465ff., in vol. 3 of the current edition) offers a more complex back story. Shimon ben Shetach was involved in a prolonged battle to wrest the Sanhedrin back to the Pharisees from the Sadducees. He slowly expelled Sadducee members and replaced them with his colleagues and students. If he had issued an educational enactment, the Sadducees would have reacted with suspicion and undermined the non-partisan decree. For the sake of the children, Shimon ben Shetach gave credit to the otherwise unremarkable and innocuous Yehoshua ben Gamla. The Babylonian Talmud, which was discussing the history of Jewish education, reported the official name associated with the decree. The Yerushalmi, which was not discussing the education but Shimon ben Shetach's personal accomplishments, gave him credit as the brains behind the enactment. Rav Aharon Hyman (*Toledos Tannaim Ve-Amoraim*, vol. 2, pp. 622-623) accepts this historical recreation.

III. Splitting the Honor

In an interesting responsum, Rav Yehudah Leib Graubart (*Chavalim Ba-Ne'imim*, vol. 3, no. 94) rejects this explanation. In a responsum sent to Rav Avraham Bornstein of Sochatchov on the subject of rabbis who purchase their positions, Rav Graubart addresses a responsum of the *Bach*, which cites Yehoshua ben Gamla's purchase of the high priesthood, which the Talmud criticizes. Rav Graubart distinguishes between that case and the early twentieth century rabbi in a number of ways. He also quotes the historical recreation of Rav Halevy and rejects it as baseless and failing to explain why the Babylonian Talmud praises Yehoshua ben Gamla so strongly.[22]

---

22. Rav Graubart's responsum is dated 13 Kislev 5668, Saturday [night], Dec. 12, 1908. Rav Bornstein passed away in 1910. However, Rav Aharon Hyman only published *Toledos Tannaim Ve-Amoraim* in 1910. If so, how could Rav Graubart quote it in a 1908 letter? One colleague suggests that Rav Graubart added the reference to the responsum when he published it in a book, years later.

If so, who enacted the educational decree—Yehoshua ben Gamla or Shimon ben Shetach? Rav Graubart explains that they both issued educational decrees. As we see in the Gemara above, there were multiple enactments throughout history. Shimon ben Shetach enacted the first decree, establishing schools in Jerusalem. Yehoshua ben Gamla issued the final and most effective decree, establishing local elementary schools. While Rav Graubart does not discuss this, there is reason to think that there was another Yehoshua Ben Gamla who lived slightly before the destruction of the Second Temple, and therefore could have issued a decree well after Shimon ben Shetach.

Na'amah Sett, in "Education As A Communal Obligation in *Mishpat Ivri*" (Hebrew), quotes Prof. Eliav Shochetman (undergraduate thesis, p. 19) and Rav Yisrael Stepanski (*Ha-Takkanos Be-Yisrael*, vol. 4 p. 286) as similarly suggesting that Shimon ben Shetach enacted the second decree and Yehoshua ben Gamla the third decree. According to this understanding, Yehoshua ben Gamla was one of the fathers of Jewish education, as was Shimon ben Shetach. This contrasts to the view of Rav Halevy and Rav Hyman who deny Yehoshua ben Gamla any significant role in the development of Jewish education.

Are Kabbalah Classes Kosher?

The fundamental principle of public Kabbalah and Chassidus classes is inherently self-contradictory. Esoteric teachings are intended for the intellectual elite, not the masses; otherwise they would not be esoteric. Comprehension of complex material requires a solid foundation of requisite knowledge. There is so much Torah to learn before Kabbalah, so many intriguing and important ideas, that few achieve sufficient mastery to reach the next level.

Yet there is a powerful argument to the contrary. On reviewing an important responsum on this subject, I noticed a gaping hole that is all the more remarkable because of the author. In turn, this raises an important question that deserves attention.

I. Secrets of the Torah

I am not sure precisely when but, at some point, an Israeli organization began advertising classes in Kabbalah. Rav Ovadiah Yosef was asked on his weekly radio show about its propriety. His response appears in *Yechavveh Da'as* (4:47), a volume originally published in 1981. A similar responsum appears in Rav Yosef's *Yabbi'a Omer* (10:YD 23) dated 1964.

The sources are clear about this. The Gemara (*Chagigah* 13a, 14a) states that one may only share the "secrets" of the Torah with a great Torah scholar. Kabbalists, like Rav Chaim Vital (introduction to *Eitz Chaim* 1d) and the *Shelah* (vol. 1 29b), explicitly say that only great scholars should learn Kabbalah. Halakhists, like Rav Moshe Isserles (*Shulchan Arukh, Yoreh De'ah* 246:4 and *Toras Ha-Olah* 3:4) and the Vilna Ga'on (*Yoreh De'ah*, ad loc. and Prov. 21:17) agree. Rav Yosef, with his famous encyclopedic knowledge, quotes other sources that reach the same conclusion.

Before reaching his prohibitive conclusion, Rav Yosef adds another consideration. Any Torah teacher must be pious but a Kabbalah teacher even more so. The chain of transmission must be personal, through a teacher-student relationship, rather than through books. Therefore, an organization whose Kabbalah teachers have questionable piety must be avoided.

II. The Missing Piece

Yet Rav Yosef omits important information in these responsa. Chassidic leaders teach that in the years preceding Mashiach's arrival, these esoteric teachings must be shared with the masses. For example, Rav Chaim Elazar Shapira, a previous Munkaczer Rebbe, writes this explicitly in a responsum (*Minchas Elazar* 1:50). It is inconceivable that Rav Yosef was unaware of this responsum. Not only was he famous for the breadth of his knowledge but he quotes from *Minchas Elazar* on other subjects. Indeed, that set of responsa contains important halakhic precedents and sits on most rabbinic bookshelves (including my own). After seeing one of Rav Yosef's responsa on this subject, it took me less than five minutes to find a contradictory source. This is so uncharacteristic of Rav Yosef that it cannot have occurred accidentally. The omission calls out "*darsheini* — explain me."

What follows is my suggestion. However, I have to add the caveat that I have not read the recent biographies of Rav Ovadiah Yosef. I am aware of his battle to return Sephardic *halakhah* to the *Shulchan Arukh*, after its kabbalistic detour exemplified in the rulings of Rav Yosef Chaim of Baghdad (author of *Ben Ish Chai*).

Rav Yosef was not opposed to customs based on Kabbalah. A good deal of contemporary practice includes kabbalistic customs. However, Rav Yosef insists that halakhic sources take precedence over kabbalistic sources, which caused great controversy within the circles of Sephardic halakhists. I suspect that has something to do with our subject. However, I think there is a simpler answer.

III. Mashiach and Kabbalah

The very notion that Kabbalah must be restricted generally but may be revealed prior to Mashiach's arrival seems impossible to apply. Jews believe that Mashiach will arrive imminently. Imagine what Jews thought one thousand years ago. They believed that Mashiach would arrive soon. While history proved that belief premature, why would they refrain from teaching Kabbalah to the public?

Put differently, what makes our era different from any previous era? While I personally believe that evidence abounds for Mashiach's imminent arrival, so did people in previous generations. If so, why didn't the greatest kabbalists of the eleventh century, for example, open a Kabbalah Center in France?

In truth, something like that did happen, although perhaps not in France. We see from the responsa literature that some people taught Kabbalah to the masses in the Middle Ages. For example, Rivash (Responsa, no. 157) complains about improper kabbalistic beliefs, albeit confessing to lacking expertise in the subject. Rashbash (Rav Shlomo Ben Shimon Duran; Responsa, no. 189) explicitly complains about ignorant masses claiming expertise in Kabbalah. He writes: "If they are secrets of the Torah, they should not be revealed." Rashbash certainly believed in the imminent arrival of Mashiach. Why didn't he permit the public study of Kabbalah on that basis? These two important halakhic authorities lived in Spain and Algeria in the late fourteenth and early fifteenth centuries but are far from unique.

Rav Yair Chaim Bachrach, of seventeenth century Germany, objects to widespread study of Kabbalah (*Chavvos Yair*, no. 210). These esoteric ideas must be taught directly by experts to uniquely qualified Torah scholars. Anyone else lacks the prerequisite knowledge to properly understand the secrets of the Torah. This author certainly believed in Mashiach's imminent arrival but still forbade teaching Kabbalah to anyone other than elite scholars.

IV. Conclusion

If so, the cumulative weight of all these opposing views defeat the Chassidic (and otherwise) argument that today we can teach Kabbalah to the masses. From the perspective of the teacher, there should be no difference between today and fourteenth-century Spain or seventeenth-century Germany. If it was forbidden then, it should be forbidden now.

I am suggesting a big leap, putting words into Rav Yosef's mouth. However, my question began with his omission so it must be answered by what he did not say. Maybe I am wrong. But that still leaves the question, why was Rav Ovadiah Yosef so quick to forbid teaching esoteric Torah to the masses?

PART 3: SHABBOS

Shabbos Guides

I. Shabbos Isn't Simple

I have a working theory that the complexity of a halakhic topic is inversely proportional to the length of its treatment in the Written Torah. When more will not be enough, less is better. The laws of Shabbos, whose thirty-nine categories of labor only begin to describe the Torah's requirements, are only mentioned in general in the Bible, with but a handful of exceptions. Instead, the Oral Torah leads the way.

The *Kitzur Shulchan Arukh*, the concise nineteenth-century code of Jewish law, seems to take a similar approach and only offers highlights of *Hilkhos Shabbos* rather than a comprehensive treatment. However, writers of popular compendia of religious practice have stepped up to fill in the gap. The 2013 passing of Rav Yehoshua Neuwirth, the author of arguably the greatest such book in the twentieth century, offered us the opportunity to think about the genre and discuss a number of examples published over the past few decades.

To be sure, popular compendia on *Hilkhos Shabbos* are nothing new. A recurring observance of this nature demands intricate familiarity of its guidelines. Rav Avraham Danziger, author of the *Chayyei Adam*, wrote *Zikhru Toras Moshe* in the late eighteenth century to help older boys learn the laws of Shabbos. This book is an excellent resource for adults, as well. More recently, Rav Gedaliah Felder's *Yesodei Yeshurun* (vols. 3-5), published from

1958 to 1965, covers the laws of Shabbos in a popular format, adding important rulings of his own on contemporary issues. I would like to limit our discussion here to Rav Neuwirth's *Shemiras Shabbos Ke-Hilkhasah* and a few—certainly not all—similar Hebrew and English books published since.

II. Strict or Lenient?

Three decisions stand out to me as crucial in writing a popular work on the laws of Shabbos. The first is the level of stringency. Do you want to rule strictly, to prevent the unsophisticated public from making mistakes? Or do you want to rule leniently, because the broader public should not be subject to anything not absolutely required. My own preference is that an author call it like he sees it, but that only pushes the question to the personality of the author: Does his training and temperament tilt him toward leniency or stringency?

In evaluating a book, I often find it difficult to decide whether the author is strict, lenient, or neither for a few reasons. First, what is mainstream? Sometimes it is cultural, the norm in a particular community, which is difficult to determine from a distance. At best, you can compare similar books and determine relative approaches—this book is stricter than the other.

Second, an author can be lenient in one place and strict elsewhere. You have to do a broad comparison of many different rulings to establish a pattern, or lack thereof. Additionally, you have to compare the text to the footnotes. Are the conclusions different, as often happens? Does the author explain why he is ruling strictly or leniently, based on a local reason or a broad approach? Because of the complexity of this evaluation, I leave it for others with more interest in this particular issue, without discounting its importance.

III. Order and Depth

A second consideration is the structure of presentation. The *Tur*, followed by *Shulchan Arukh* and commentaries, teaches the laws of Shabbos in rough order of the day. It starts with the laws of Shabbos preparations, proceeds through the order of the evening, onto the morning and afternoon, filling in laws where appropriate and then adding more at the end that had no obvious place. The result is quite confusing. I often tell people that they cannot learn the laws of Shabbos from the *Mishnah Berurah* because, for a novice, the presentation is so confusing. Any commentary to *Shulchan Arukh* must follow this order, although the *Mishnah Berurah* and *Arukh Ha-Shulchan* mitigate the confusion by adding periodic overviews.

Another approach is to teach each of the thirty-nine Shabbos labors separately, with proper introductions, overviews, and miscellaneous sections. The *Chayei Adam* follows this approach with much success. A third approach is to organize the laws entirely by topic, based on contemporary experience rather than Shabbos chronology or technical labor categories. As we shall see, most guides today follow one of these last two approaches.

The third consideration is depth. A Shabbos guide that teaches detailed law after detailed law can serve as an excellent reference work but makes for dry reading. It is too boring to read from cover to cover. An overview that teaches general principles may oversimplify. Every author must find a balance between comprehensiveness and readability.

IV. Hebrew Shabbos Guides

Rav Yehoshua Neuwirth's *Shemiras Shabbos Ke-Hilkhasah* was a groundbreaking and lasting contribution for a number of reasons. The book follows a topical order and provides overviews of sub-topics followed by comprehensive detail. Written in Modern

Hebrew, its footnotes provide ample resources for scholars plus—importantly—a plethora of oral rulings from the important scholar, Rav Shlomo Zalman Auerbach, that for decades were unavailable elsewhere. Additionally, Rav Neuwirth dealt with many technological issues that arose in the mid- to late-twentieth century. His book was not only accessible to a broad readership but also valuable to scholars, leading it to become a classic that has survived for decades.

In contrast, Rav Yaakov Posen's *Kitzur Hilkhos Shabbos*, originally published in 1974, is brief and follows the order of the thirty-nine labors. His language is concise but remarkably precise, offering many details to scholars that novices will not even notice. He focuses on applications of the laws to contemporary life (of the 1970s), addressing technological developments as well. This short book seems to have been largely forgotten, despite its sustained value.

V. English Shabbos Guides

The first detailed English treatment of the Shabbos laws of which I know is Rav Shimon Eider's *Halachos of Shabbos*. Similar to Rav Neuwirth's Hebrew book, Rav Eider's organizes the laws according to topic and contains many otherwise (at the time) unknown rulings by important authorities. Personally, I always found the book a boring but important tool for both laymen and scholars. It has largely been surpassed by newer English books.

Rav Simcha Bunim Cohen's seven-volume series on the laws of Shabbos follows a combination of topical and labor organization.[23] Generally speaking, within each topic the author arranges

---

23. *The Radiance of Shabbos* (Artscroll, 1986); *The Sanctity of Shabbos* (Artscroll, 1988); *Shabbos Kitchen* (Artscroll, 1991); *The Shabbos Home Vol. 1* (Artscroll, 1995); *The Shabbos Home Vol. 2* (Artscroll, 1995); *Muktzeh: A Practical Guide* (Artscroll, 1999); *The Aura of Shabbos* (Artscroll, 2013).

material by labor. He presents overviews of each subject and then detailed laws. However, unlike Rav Neuwirth and Rav Eider, Rav Cohen provides (to my recollection) very few unpublished rulings of famous authorities. This makes his volumes less valuable to scholars, despite his extensive footnotes. On the other hand, he addresses technology of the late twentieth and early twenty-first centuries. His language is also very readable.

Rav Gersion Appel's second volume of his *Concise Code of Jewish Law*, published in 1989 and updated by Rav Daniel Goldstein in 2016, remains unique among English Shabbos guides. This book follows primarily the topics. What Rav Appel innovated was a way to be both comprehensive and interesting. His main text is a straightforward explanation of the detailed laws, which can become dry. Unlike other books in this genre, the *Concise Code*'s footnotes are intended for the general public and discuss issues of popular interest. The text has the details and the easily identifiable footnotes contain the highlights, i.e., the practical applications. You can flip through the book and the footnotes will answer many of your questions. Detailed sources are then provided in endnotes.[24]

Another unique aspect of Rav Appel's book is his canon of authorities. The books already discussed quote almost exclusively from Ashkenazic Charedi halakhic authorities. Rav Neuwirth's selection is somewhat broader. In contrast, Rav Appel quotes extensively from Rav Yitzchak Herzog and Rav Chaim David Halevy (and Rav Joseph B. Soloveitchik, when available), in addition to standard Charedi scholars like Rav Moshe Feinstein, Rav Yitzchak Weiss, and Rav Moshe Stern. The updated edition includes citations from Rav Hershel Schachter, Rav Yaakov Ariel, and others.

---

24. I was heavily involved in the 2016 updated edition, particularly with the endnotes.

VI. A Different Hebrew Guide

Rav Eliezer Melamed has published two volumes of *Peninei Halakhah* on Shabbos, part of a larger series on Jewish practice. Like some other works, Rav Melamed arranges the laws by topic. However, in my opinion, his organization of topics surpasses all others, allowing for extremely easy navigation.

Additionally, unlike the other books mentioned, he has very few footnotes. His book is meant to be a popular guide. Instead of footnotes, he took the unusual step of publishing an additional volume with essays discussing the sources and explaining his line of reasoning at length (he calls it *harchavos*, "expansions"). In my opinion, this substitution is a great improvement content-wise on footnotes but it causes logistical difficulties. When I use his book, I have to take two with me off the shelf—one with the text I am using and another with the sources. Significantly, Rav Melamed engages extensively with Religious Zionist and Sephardic authorities whose voices are often inexcusably ignored in guidebooks. The text, without the expansions, has been translated into English for publication.[25]

VII. Conclusion

I realize that I have only discussed some of the many available books. I selected those that I believe are excellent and with which I am sufficiently familiar to describe them. However, even from this limited selection we can see the ingredients for a successful halakhic guide in a crowded market.

As any educator knows, in order to teach a subject you have to be organized. Writing about a complex topic like the laws of Shabbos requires not just expertise but also organization. You need a successful lesson plan on how you want your readers to learn both the big picture and the intricate details. You also need

---

25. *Peninei Halakha: Shabbat* (Maggid, 2016), 2 vols.

to balance between speaking to experts and novices. Dayan Posen's book succeeded solely on his excellent pedagogy.

You also need to address contemporary issues. You cannot teach the laws of Shabbos as if we are still living in eighteenth century Lithuania. And if you provide original material, new rulings by respected authorities, or even citations from important but often ignored authorities, you will add enduring value.

When Is a *Kiddush* Not a *Kiddush*?

The common shul *kiddush*, the food served in synagogues after Saturday morning services, presents a puzzling halakhic case because it seems to contradict a basic rule. *Kiddush*, the blessing on the wine, must be part of a meal. However, the shul *kiddush* is generally not a meal as classically defined in Jewish law because it lacks bread/*challah*. A Shabbos meal should contain two loaves of *challah*, yet most people eat no *challah* at all at a shul *kiddush*.

In itself, this is not problematic. We could call it a "*kiddush*" with quotation marks, tacitly smirking at the misnomer. However, another law forbids eating before (real) *kiddush*. Therefore, unless the shul *kiddush* is halakhically proper, you are not allowed to eat it. We will examine three very different approaches from important halakhic authorities of the twentieth century, each with surprising implications.

I. Eat Before *Kiddush*

The *Shulchan Arukh* (*Orach Chaim* 273:5) quotes the opinion of the Geonim that, while a meal for *kiddush* should preferably include bread, if it includes cake (an olive's size, *ke-zayis*) or wine (a *revi'is*) then it counts as a meal. However, the Vilna Gaon (*Ma'aseh Rav* 122) rejects this leniency. Rav Joseph B. Soloveitchik (quoted by Rav Hershel Schachter, *Eretz Ha-Tzvi*, p. 47) takes the Vilna Gaon's view into account and is therefore puzzled by the common practice of the shul *kiddush*.

Rav Soloveitchik points to the debate between the Rambam and Ra'avad (*Mishneh Torah, Hilkhos Shabbos* 29:10) whether you may eat before *kiddush* on Shabbos day. The consensus follows the Rambam. However, Rav Soloveitchik suggests, common practice must rely on a combination of the Ra'avad's and the Geonim's leniencies. While each is insufficient, when combined together, the double-leniency allows this common practice. The *kiddush* in shul, according to the Ra'avad, is no *kiddush* and the food is no meal. But we eat anyway, relaxing the rule forbidding eating before *kiddush* in combination with the Ge'onim's view that this is a valid *kiddush*.

II. Cake is *Kiddush*

Rav Shlomo Zalman Auerbach, as reported by Rav Avigdor Nebenzahl (*Yerushalayim Be-Mo'adeha, Shabbos*, vol. 2 pp. 114-125), goes in a different direction. He accepts the Geonim's leniency that eating cake or drinking wine constitutes a meal for *kiddush. Kiddush* in shul is *kiddush.*

However, this position has interesting consequences. Rav Auerbach encouraged people to say the *mezonos* blessing on two pieces of cake.[26] Since we consider the cake to take the place of *challah*, you should have two pieces of cake as the two loaves of *challah*.[27] Additionally, if you forget the *retzeih* addition to *birkas ha-mazon* in the first two meals of Shabbos, you must repeat the entire prayer. However, if the shul *kiddush* counts as a meal, then your subsequent lunch is the third meal. According to Rav Auerbach, if you forget *retzeih* at lunch after eating at a shul *kiddush* with the intent that it count as a meal, you need not repeat.[28]

---

26. Following *Kitzur Shulchan Arukh* 77:17.

27. This is unrelated to the issue of eating two pieces to make sure you consume a minimum required amount (*ke-zayis*).

28. Quoted by Rav Nebenzahl, ibid., pp. 149-151. Rav Yaakov Yisrael Kanievsky, *Kehillas Ya'akov, Berachos*, no. 46 also rules similarly, unlike Rav Yehoshua Neuwirth in *Shemiras Shabbos Ke-Hilkhasah*, ch. 54 n. 63.

III. Two Types of *Kiddush*

Rav Moshe Feinstein (*Iggeros Moshe, Orach Chaim* 4:63) sees two elements of *kiddush*. One is that you must recite *kiddush* at your meal; the other is that before you eat, you must recite *kiddush*. He does not consider the shul *kiddush* a meal. However, since you recite *kiddush* before you eat, it is valid.[29]

IV. Implications

Do you have to eat cake at a shul *kiddush*? What I see at *kiddush* is a mad rush toward the cake. I charitably assume that this is due to a desire to eat a *ke-zayis* (minimum required amount) in order to have *kiddush* at a meal (although the rush aspect is worthy of separate discussion). If I understand correctly, Rav Feinstein would not require you to eat cake at a shul *kiddush* (although he would not object). According to him, only *challah* creates a meal. For Rav Soloveitchik, eating before *kiddush* is acceptable, but you must still eat cake to achieve the double leniency. For Rav Feinstein, this eating constitutes eating after *kiddush* but does not constitute a meal. However, Rav Auerbach requires you to eat a *ke-zayis* of cake (or the halakhic equivalent) in order to have *kiddush* at a meal.

Do you have to repeat *kiddush* at lunch if you already said it or heard it earlier? According to Rav Soloveitchik, yes, because the earlier *kiddush* did not count according to one leniency (although according to the other it did). According to Rav Feinstein, yes, because you still have to say *kiddush* at a meal. According to Rav Auerbach, no, because you already fulfilled the requirement earlier. However, he personally repeated *kiddush*.[30]

---

29. See also *Derekh Ha-Chaim*, Kiddush in synagogue Shabbos night, par. 3 in explanation of the view of the Sar from Coucy.
30. Rav Nebenzahl, ibid., p. 124.

Good Shabbos Afternoon

Should you say "Good Shabbos" (or "Shabbat Shalom" or "A Gutten/Gitten Shabbos") on Shabbos afternoon? Especially after it starts to get dark, it seems awkward to wish people Shabbos greetings. This is particularly so on my walk to shul at the end of Shabbos, when it is already dark out and some people may have already ended Shabbos. However, until I say *havdalah* in my prayers or as a blessing, it is still Shabbos for me.

A custom exists to refrain from offering Shabbos greetings on Shabbos afternoon. But just become a custom exists does not mean that it is or should be my custom. Rav Simcha Rabinowitz (*Piskei Teshuvos*, second series 292:8) quotes Rav Yair Chaim Bacharach (*Mekor Chaim* 270) as a relatively early source for this custom not to extend greetings close to, or during, twilight on Shabbos. Rav Rabinowitz explains that this custom is due to mourning over Moshe, David, and Yosef, all of whom died on Shabbos afternoon. Mourning over their death is the reason for reciting "*Tzidkasekha*" at the end of the Shabbos *Mincha* afternoon prayers.

Rav Avigdor Nebenzahl (*Yerushalayim Be-Mo'adeha*, Shabbos vol. 2 p. 196) says that some people refrain from offering Shabbos greetings on Shabbos afternoon. However, those who do so refrain the entire afternoon, beginning with mid-day. His language implies that this is a minority practice.

Rav Shlomo Aviner (Commentary to *Kitzur Shulchan Arukh*, vol. 3 75:1 p. 48) quotes from *Derekh Sichah* (vol. 1 p. 271) that Rav

Chaim Kanievsky says that his father, known as the Steipler Ga'on, followed this practice beginning (presumably, says the younger Rav Kanievsky) with the time of *minchah ketanah*, about halfway through the afternoon.

Rav Aviner quotes from *Divrei Meir* (p. 60) that the following great Torah scholars did not follow this custom and offered Shabbos greetings all day: Rav Yosef Shalom Elyashiv, Rav Shlomo Zalman Auerbach, Rav Yisrael Yaakov Fischer, and Rav Eliezer Fischer. *Divrei Meir* says that Rav Moshe Sternbuch told him he was unaware of a source for this practice.

From all of the above, this seems like a nice, legitimate practice but one that is only observed by those for whom it is their custom. If it isn't your custom, you need not observe it and should instead offer people the proper Shabbos greeting.

Pass the *Challah*

There is a debate about the proper way to cut *challah* bread for a group of people sitting at the table. May you cut pieces for everyone at first, or must you cut only for yourself, eat a little, and then cut for everyone else? And then there are variations in between. A neighbor of royal Bobov ancestry told me that his father has a letter from the previous Bobover Rebbe saying that, based on kabbalistic sources, one may initially cut an extra piece for one's wife. Others cut a bunch of pieces and then the leader takes the last piece, implying that he had to cut all those pieces just to get to the one that he wants. And so on, with many variations.

I. Who Eats First?

The Gemara (*Berakhos* 47a) states that when one person is reciting the *ha-motzi* blessing on the bread for everyone at the table, the others may not eat until the one who recites the blessing takes his piece of bread. The implication is either that the others may not take bread before the leader takes his piece or that they may not eat until he eats first.

Tosafos quote the Sar (Rav Shimshon) from Coucy who rules the first way, that people should not take their pieces of bread before the leader. But if he hands the pieces out, they may eat first. However, the Rambam and others rule the second way, that they may not eat first.

The *Shulchan Arukh* (167:15) quotes the words of the Gemara without explanation, while the Rema adds that the leader may give out pieces of bread but others may not eat their pieces until the leader eats first. This is clearly following the view of the Rambam and not the Sar from Coucy.

II. Serving vs Eating First

The *Magen Avraham* (34) raises a question on the Rema's ruling: The Talmud Yerushalmi states that Rav would eat and pass out the pieces of *challah* at the same time. While it is clear that Rav was acting above and beyond the law by doing both at the same time, he seems to have been of the view that the leader must eat first before distributing the pieces. The *Magen Avraham* leaves this question open, but an answer can be found in the *Bi'ur Ha-Gra* (to *se'if* 17). The Gra explains this passage as meaning that Rav knew that if he handed out the pieces, no one would be able to eat them until he ate first (as above). In other words, Rav's actions were not because he could not hand out the pieces before eating but because the people could not eat until he ate first.

The *Taz* (15) also raises a question on the Rema's ruling. The *Taz* explains that only according to the Sar from Coucy may one hand out pieces of bread since, according to his view, the people may eat as soon as they receive it. However, according to the Rambam—and this is how we rule in practice—people may not eat until the leader eats first. Therefore, distributing the pieces of bread is a needless wait before the eating may begin. In practice, we are very strict about any waiting time between the blessing and eating—even waits that are related to the meal and, therefore, technically permissible (see Rema, *Orach Chaim* 167:6). Therefore, passing out bread that no one can immediately eat is a needless wait and should be forbidden. This *Taz* is the starting point for anyone who wants to argue that one may not even cut bread for others, the argument being that cutting extra bread should be equivalent to handing it out.

III. Proper Procedure

However, the *Taz*, who is arguing based on the Rambam, seems to be against that very Rambam. The following is the Rambam's language in *Mishneh Torah* (*Hilkhos Berakhos* 7:5):

> The leader (*ha-botzei'a*) gives a piece to everyone and the other takes it in his hand. The leader does not put it in the eater's hand unless he is a mourner (*avel*). And the leader stretches out his hand first and eats. And those sitting down [to eat] may not taste until the one who recited the blessing eats first.

It seems clear that, according to the Rambam, the leader places pieces in front of each person and then takes his own piece and eats it first. The only other way I can see reading this Rambam is according to the version which the Rema himself quotes and dismisses in *Darkhei Moshe*, that the word *avel* (mourner) should read *okhel* (eating). In that version, the Rambam states that the leader may not distribute bread unless he is already eating. Otherwise, though, the Rambam—who is supposed to be the source of this whole stringency—seems to explicitly allow not only cutting pieces of *challah* for everyone but also giving it out.

The *Bach*, the *Taz's* father-in-law, recommends not giving out pieces to everyone because people will likely eat before the leader, which we rule is improper. That is my practice. But the *Taz* disagrees with his father-in-law, saying that it is prohibited to do so rather than just inadvisable. The *Taz*, and not the *Bach*, is what can lead to the stringencies regarding cutting pieces.

Medicine on Shabbos

I. Outdated Prohibition?

Medical technology has changed so dramatically over the past century that we can barely imagine the healing process of past years. Presumably, Jewish law should reflect that change, relating to current medicine rather than that of the past. In particular, the prohibition against taking medicine on Shabbos (absent pressing need) seems ripe for reevaluation. While *halakhah* is not changing, the appropriate rule for the new circumstances must be invoked.

We are forbidden to take medicine on Shabbos out of a concern that we might grind, which is biblically prohibited (*Shulchan Arukh, Orach Chaim* 328:1). However, medicine today is manufactured commercially and/or mixed at a pharmacy. We do not grind our own medicines, but instead take the liquids and pills professionally prepared. If so, does this prohibition still stand?

To be clear, someone with a serious need for medication may certainly take it on Shabbos. There are numerous other exceptions (we'll briefly mention some below) and you should discuss your personal situation with your rabbi. Good health is unquestionably a religious value. However, sometimes you just have a minor headache or need a little ointment or some other minor medical need that is not pressing. In ancient times, you might have ground yourself some herbs to relieve your pain. Must we retain this outdated concern?

I can imagine some people thinking that raising this question borders on heresy, revealing a lack of faith in the halakhic system. Quite the opposite! This is an excellent question that the greatest halakhic authorities of recent times have asked.

II. Permissible Today

Rav Avraham Chaim Na'eh (*Ketzos Ha-Shulchan* 134 n. 7.2) considers the above logic to permit taking medicine in pill form on Shabbos. Since the rabbinic concern for grinding no longer exists, perhaps the prohibition no longer applies. He bases his argument on the Rema (*Orach Chaim* 339:3) who, quoting Tosafos (*Beitzah* 30a s.v. *tenan*), permits clapping on Shabbos because we are no longer concerned that this might lead to fixing a musical instrument. Once the reason for the rabbinic decree ceases, the prohibition falls aside. However, because there are still some people somewhere in the world who grind herbal medicine (at the time of his writing and still today), Rav Na'eh was not willing to rule leniently.

This general approach is very difficult because the view of the Rema and Tosafos seems to contradict explicit talmudic passages. While resolutions have been proposed, none are particularly satisfying. As Rav Joseph B. Soloveitchik is quoted as saying (*Nefesh Ha-Rav*, p. 173), we don't understand the initial permission, so how can we expand it to others cases? (See also *Pischei Teshuvah*, *Even Ha-Ezer* 13:4, 9; *Iggeros Moshe*, *Orach Chaim* 2:100.) For this reason, most later authorities reject Rav Na'eh's permissive theoretical view.

III. Two Approaches

Rav Eliezer Waldenberg (*Tzitz Eliezer* vol. 8 15:15) takes a different path toward leniency. He argues that two general approaches exist to the prohibition against (non-essential) healing on Shabbos. Rashi (*Shabbos* 53b s.v. *gezeirah*) believes that the Sages enacted a general (obviously rabbinic) prohibition against any type of healing on Shabbos. While the underlying concern was grinding on Shabbos, the prohibition itself is not directly related. We see this in a number of cases, such as the permission to place a plaster on your eyes on Shabbos, which would be forbidden because of healing except that it looks like cleaning your eyes (Rashi, *Shabbos* 108b s.v. *ve-nosein*). And similarly, Rashi (*Shabbos* 111a s.v. *aval*) explains that you may not anoint with rose oil because you are clearly doing it solely for medical purposes. None of these examples involves a concern for grinding medicine but are still forbidden because of the general prohibition.

On the other hand, Rambam (*Mishneh Torah*, *Hilkhos Shabbos* 21:31) permits certain acts of healing, implying that the prohibition was specifically against taking medicine to treat an illness that is generally healed with privately ground medicine. While commentators debate the Rambam's intent, Rav Waldenberg believes Rambam rules that even if you do not grind the medicine, taking it is forbidden because grinding is generally involved in treatment.

According to Rashi and those who agree with him, the change in medical technology does not undermine the Sages' general prohibition. While they may not have enacted such a prohibition today, their ancient enactment remains in force. However, according to the Rambam as explained above, this enactment is specifically about grinding medicine on Shabbos that you normally grind during the week. Since we do not personally grind medicine anymore, the prohibition should no longer apply.

IV. Qualified Leniency

Significantly, the *Shulchan Arukh* (ibid.) adopts the Rambam's approach. If we follow this view, then today when we do not normally grind medicine for any illness, we may presumably freely take medicine on Shabbos. However, Rav Waldenberg is cautious, because some people do grind homemade remedies and because there are other interpretations of the Rambam's position. He therefore decides to be as lenient as possible without being entirely permissive.

He notes that some quote Rav Shlomo Kluger as permitting continuing taking a medication on Shabbos that you have already started taking prior. While Rav Waldenberg disagrees with Rav Kluger, he permits continuing taking medicine if failing to do so will cause severe discomfort. He additionally allows relying on Rav Kluger's view because of the above argument to permit taking medicine in general.

Similarly, Rav Ovadiah Yosef (*Yalkut Yosef* 328:52) finds Rav Na'eh's reasoning convincing but, without dismissing the prohibition, allows for great leniency. For example, he permits someone accustomed to swallowing pills to take medicine to relieve pain. Rav Eliezer Melamed (*Peninei Halakhah*, *Shabbos* 28:5 and in *harchavos*) also allows someone who is suffering from pain, even if severe but not life-threatening, to take medicine on Shabbos, because of the lenient views. See also *She'arim Metzuyanim Ba-Halakhah* (*Beitzah* 5a s.v. *kol*).

V. Stricter Views

However, other authorities disputed Rav Waldenberg's lenient conclusion, which is based on his original interpretation of the Rambam. As mentioned above, Rav Joseph B. Soloveitchik opposed leniency on this subject. Similarly, Rav Moshe Feinstein (*Iggeros Moshe, Orach Chaim* 3:53) forbids taking pills on Shabbos. Rav Yehoshua Neuwirth (*Shemiras Shabbos Ke-Hilkhasah* 34:3) and Dr. Avraham S. Avraham (*Nishmas Avraham, Orach Chaim* 328:5) also maintain the talmudic prohibition against taking medicine.

Working Out on Shabbos

A perennial challenge to communal unity has been the question of whether Jewish Community Centers should be open on Shabbos. This raises a number of interesting historical and halakhic issues. For now, I will set aside the historical aspects and address only one of the many halakhic issues: may one exercise on Shabbos? I used to attend early Shabbos services (7 a. m.) and I would see one person jogging who would later come to shul for the late/regular services. Is this allowed?

I. Two Opinions

The Mishnah in *Shabbos* (147a) states: "One may anoint with oil and massage [lightly] but not hard (*lo misam'lin*)" and the Tosefta in *Shabbos* (17:16) states: "One may not run on Shabbos in order to exercise (*lehisamel*) but one may travel normally and need not worry." Rashi explains that a hard massage is prohibited because of "*uvda de-chol*," meaning it is a weekday, non-Shabbos activity. The Rambam, however, in *Mishneh Torah* (*Hilkhos Shabbos* 21:28) explains that the problem is that one tires oneself out to the point of sweating (cf. Rabbenu Chananel on the Gemara). The *Shiltei Ha-Gibborim* (*Shabbos* 62b in the Rif, no. 2) explains that according to Rashi, any kind of heavy exercise is prohibited while according to the Rambam, only exercise that leads to sweating is prohibited.

This leaves us with two different distinctions regarding exercise:

1. Heavy vs. light exercise
2. Exercise that makes you sweat vs. that doesn't make you sweat

Everyone agrees that light exercise that does not make you sweat is permitted. Light exercise that makes you sweat (is there such a thing?) would be forbidden according to the Rambam but allowed according to Rashi. Heavy exercise that does not make you sweat would be forbidden according to Rashi but allowed according to the Rambam. And everyone agrees that heavy exercise that makes you sweat is prohibited.

II. Exercise at Home and in School

Rav Yosef Kafach, in his edition of *Mishneh Torah* (ibid., n. 83) deduces from the Rambam's language in an earlier *halakhah* that he only forbids exercise that sick people do but something that a healthy person does regularly is allowed. Based on this, he allows (within the Rambam's opinion, which is what he follows) someone to do on Shabbos his regular daily routine of running or exercise. However, I think there might be room to distinguish between what healthy people do to maintain their health and what they do for fun. The former would, possibly, be prohibited, while the latter would be permitted (see below).

The *Shulchan Arukh* first rules like Rashi (*Orach Chaim* 327:2) but then later rules like the Rambam (328:42). In other words, we have to be strict and observe the stringencies of both opinions.[31]

31. It is interesting that in explaining the above Tosefta, the *Minchas Bikkurim* writes: "In order to exercise: to sweat, which is medicinal, but for pleasure it is permissible." However, Rav Yechezkel Abramsky writes in his *Chazon Yechezkel*: "In order to exercise: which is medicinal and forbidden because of grinding herbs, but for pleasure it is permissible." In other words, he removed the phrase "to sweat." Thus the *Minchas Bikkurim* explained the Tosefta according to the Rambam while the *Chazon Yechezkel* explained it according to Rashi (or both Rashi and the Rambam).

However, what if one exercises for fun and not for health (or weight-loss) purposes? The *Shulchan Arukh* (*Orach Chaim* 301:1) writes that young men who run around for fun may do so on Shabbos. The *Taz* writes that if one does not enjoy running but only does so to help one's appetite (or presumably also one's digestion) then it is forbidden.

Apparently, someone who truly enjoys running or jogging would be allowed to do so. Since we are strict for both Rashi's and the Rambam's views, running must be considered light exercise and therefore only forbidden if it is done for health reasons (and causes sweating). But heavy exercise would be forbidden regardless of one's intentions.

Rav David Zvi Hoffmann (*Melammed Le-Ho'il* 1:53) was asked about some sort of exercise on Shabbos that I believe was done in secular schools on Shabbos. He rules that one should not permit this exercise. However, in a place where people already do this, one should not forbid it because it all depends on the type of exercise and one's intentions (and there is an additional consideration of causing anti-Semitism).[32]

III. Contemporary Views

Rav Eliezer Waldenberg (*Tzitz Eliezer* 6:4) addresses whether one may use some sort of home gym equipment on Shabbos. He considers this to be heavy exercise that induces sweat, which is prohibited according to both Rashi and the Rambam. He also adds the view of the Ramban (Commentary to Lev. 18:21) that there is a positive commandment of "*Shabbason*"—to rest on Shabbos— and such exercise is contrary to that commandment.

Rav Yehoshua Neuwirth writes in *Shemiras Shabbos Ke-Hilkhasah* (24:22):

---

32. See *Responsa Maharshag* 2:93 and *She'arim Metzuyanim Ba-Halakhah* 90:1 that if you are forced to do it in school, it is assumed that it is not fun for everyone.

a. One may not do strenuous physical exercises on Shabbos.

b. Nor may one engage in muscle-building exercises with the aid of spring-fitted, physical-training apparatus.

c. One may do simple exercises with one's hand, even if one's purpose in so doing is to relieve or alleviate pains.

Rav Gersion Appel writes in *The Concise Code of Jewish Law* (vol. 2, 2016 edition, p. 316, n. 3):

> You are permitted to go walking, but not running or jogging. Young children who enjoy jumping and running may do so on Shabbat, as this is their enjoyment. You are not permitted to do exercises on the Sabbath that involve physical exertion and are intended to work up a sweat and tire yourself. Some permit a person to follow a daily routine of calisthenics intended to maintain physical fitness, but this is a minority opinion and not commonly practiced. You may do breathing exercises to correct impairment. You may use a small, hand exerciser to strengthen the hand and the fingers.

Disposable Diapers on Shabbos

To my knowledge, there are three or four trends in disposable diapers that are relevant to their use on Shabbos.

I do not know whether disposable diapers ever required the use of safety pins. Regardless, the majority of *posekim* rule that there is no problem in using safety pins on Shabbos if you do it normally (i.e., piercing once in and then a second time out) and intends to leave the safety pin in for less than 24 hours.

The initial use of adhesive on disposable diapers was as follows: The diapers would have adhesive tabs that would allow you to close the diapers by using the tab. The adhesive tabs were covered with plastic in the factory and the user would remove the plastic and stick the tab to the other side of the diaper.

I. The Problem With Diapers

The potential problem, then, is the sticking and unsticking. Is that allowed on Shabbos? Generally speaking, most *posekim* allow this type of sticking and unsticking if it is of a temporary (i.e., less than 24-hour) nature, based on the *Magen Avraham*'s position (340:18) that sticking and unsticking of glue is only prohibited if it is/was intended to last (*le-hiskayyem*). Therefore, the sticking of the tab to the diaper is permissible since it is only intended to last for a few hours. However, the unsticking—the removing of the plastic from the adhesive tabs—is potentially more problematic. The plastic was put on in the factory and certainly remained there for days if not weeks. Therefore, removing the plastic might be prohibited.

Many *posekim* prohibit this (e.g., *Tzitz Eliezer* 16:6), while some permit this, since the factory workers/machine did not necessarily want the plastic to remain on for a long time; it just happens to be that way. The manufacturers would be perfectly happy to have the diapers sold and the plastic removed immediately. According to this second view, the plastic is considered to be stuck on temporarily (*Yechavveh Da'as* 6:24).

II. Solving the Problem

What many people used to do is remove the plastic from the adhesives before Shabbos and replace them, so that they will be on for less than 24 hours—i.e., temporarily—and permissible to remove on Shabbos.

This type of diaper was replaced with re-stickable adhesives that are made to be stuck, unstuck, and restuck again. This is significant because sticking and unsticking the adhesive becomes the normal way of using the adhesive, much like opening and closing a door is not considered building and destroying. According to most *posekim*, using these diapers is much less problematic and requires no pre-Shabbos preparation (e.g., *Shevet Ha-Levi* 5:31, 40). Other *posekim*, however, still require unsticking the adhesive once after its long stick from the factory.

Also, the *Minchas Yitzchak* (8:31) was very much against the use of any kind of adhesive in disposable diapers on Shabbos.

Nowadays, some manufacturers have entirely replaced the adhesive with velcro. This poses no problem at all.

Noteworthy is a very unusual footnote by Rav Yosef Kafach in his edition of *Mishneh Torah, Hilkhos Shabbos* 10:11. In an unnumbered footnote, Rav Kafach uncharacteristically argues that the phrase the Rambam (and *Shulchan Arukh*) uses for glue, "*kolan shel soferim*," implies glue that starts out liquid and then dries and connects two items. Therefore, he concludes, the adhesive on diapers does not fall under this definition and is entirely permissible.

The Candy Wrapper Dilemma

I. Candy Wrappers

Parents of small children have an embarrassing Shabbos secret. There is one act, which rabbis frequently warn against, that we all violate at one time or another. I cannot imagine raising children without committing this act. I will explain what it is and why it is disallowed, and offer an explanation on why doing it is permissible. I would not attempt to justify this on my own, but since one contemporary writer explicitly allows it and another implies it is permissible, I believe I have sufficient backing.

Writing and erasing are separate Shabbos prohibitions on a biblical level, consisting of the opposite of each other. What you may not write on Shabbos, you may not erase. You are not allowed to print a label on Shabbos with words on it because that constitutes writing. Similarly, you may not destroy the writing on a label because that constitutes erasing. Tearing a label so that the letters are destroyed erases the words printed on the label. Therefore, you may not tear open a candy wrapper if you rip through the lettering.

Anyone with children knows the difficulty of standing between them and candy. Parents need to take strong stands on eating habits, but they also need to choose their battles wisely. A detail in the laws of Shabbos makes the candy wrapper issue even more difficult.

In general, an incidental violation is not necessarily forbidden. On Shabbos, we distinguish between a *davar she-eino miskaven* and a *pesik reisheih*. The former is a contingent unintended consequence—it may or may not happen—and is therefore permissible. The latter is inevitable and forbidden. Translating this into candy wrappers: If you can open it without tearing through letters, then you may open it even if you accidentally tear through letters. The erasing was entirely unintended. But if it is impossible to open the wrapper without tearing through letters, it becomes a *pesik reisheih*. You may not even try because you will inevitably erase the letters.

II. Erasing Letters

This means that when your child asks if he can have a specific candy, you have to inspect the wrapper before answering. You have to raise his hopes and then, if the wrapper fails inspection, dash them. Observant parents do this in the supermarket when checking for kosher certification. But when children are used to eating a specific candy during the week, refusing them on Shabbos becomes more difficult.

What often ends up happening is that you tell the child to open the candy himself. In other words, you let him commit the sin. After a certain age, when the child is old enough to know it is wrong, this becomes problematic. And if he can't open it himself and needs parental assistance, you have to decide whether you want to use your parental capital to say no. After you have already said yes and the child has spent a few minutes trying to open the wrapper, saying no at that point risks a tantrum. Of course, sometimes you have to say no to your children. But you usually want to save those occasions for when you really need it.

Realistically, many parents look the other way. This is a judgment issue. Can you open the wrapper without tearing through letters? Well, if you try really hard, and use all your motor skills, maybe you can. That justification, usually false, assumes you have even tried to think it through. I suspect most parents don't even get that far and simply tear open the wrapper to avoid the uncomfortable situation.

III. Incidental Erasing

The Rema (*Orach Chaim* 340:3) quotes from the Mordekhai in the name of Rav Meir of Rotenberg that you may not cut letters on a cake. This is a common Shabbos problem. If letters are written in frosting on a cake, according to the Rema you may not slice through the letters because that constitutes erasing. This ruling serves as the source against all incidental erasing of letters, including on candy wrappers. When you open the wrapper and rip through letters, you erase the writing like on a cake.

However, the *Noda Bi-Yehudah* (*Dagul Me-Revavah* 340) boldly argues, based on technical details, that the Rema misunderstood Rav Meir of Rotenberg's ruling. Medieval authorities debate the status of a *pesik reisheih de-lo nicha leih*, an incidental violation that you do not care about. If you benefit from the incidental violation, there is room to say that you really wanted it to occur. But if you honestly do not care that it happened, the *Arukh* permits the act. While most authorities forbid it, when the incidental violation is only rabbinically prohibited, additional authorities are lenient. Going one step further, when an act is only prohibited rabbinically for two reasons, meaning it is two steps below a biblical prohibition, most authorities permit it when done as a *pesik reisheih de-lo nicha leih*.

If that was too theoretical, cutting food with writing serves as an excellent practical example. If the writing contains a personal secret you want destroyed, then that is a *pesik reisheih de-nicha leih*—you want the incidental violation. If the cake just just wishes someone a happy birthday, you do not care if the words are erased and might even be upset that the nice greeting is destroyed. That is a *pesik reisheih de-lo nicha leih*. Therefore, the *Arukh* would permit cutting a cake, unless you specifically want the word erased.

Additionally, erasing is only biblically forbidden if you erase with intent to rewrite—*mochek al menas likhtov*. That is certainly not the case with cutting a cake. You intend to eat the cake, not write on it. That would be a *pesik reisheih de-lo nicha leih* with one rabbinic level. The *Noda Bi-Yehudah* adds that cutting a cake is erasing in an usual way, which is also only rabbinically forbidden. Therefore, says the *Noda Bi-Yehudah*, cutting cake with words is a *pesik reisheih de-lo nicha leih* with two rabbinic levels and is permitted. This is certainly so if you eat the letters, rather than cut them, which is a very unusual way of destroying letters.

The *Noda Bi-Yehudah* suggests that Rav Meir of Rotenberg was discussing when a young child eats letters on a cake as he begins to learn the Hebrew alphabet. You want him to destroy the letters because his eating them is a metaphor for his future acquisition of knowledge. In such a case, you intend to erase the letters and, therefore, may not do so on Shabbos unless the child is very young. That is an entirely different situation than tearing a candy wrapper.

IV. Tearing Wrappers

The *Mishnah Berurah* (340:17) and other authorities follow the *Noda Bi-Yehudah* and permit eating cake with letters. However, they do not permit cutting letters on cake. Similarly, they forbid cutting through letters on a wrapper or piece of paper (e.g., *Shemiras Shabbos Ke-Hilkhasah* 9:12; Rav Gersion Appel, *Concise Code of Jewish Law* vol. 2, 2016 edition, p. 206). They take the *Noda Bi-Yehudah*'s leniency but do not extend it beyond the specific case he discussed.

However, his arguments are compelling. The *Arukh Ha-Shulchan* (*Orach Chaim* 340:23) writes that the law (*ikar ha-din*) follows the *Noda Bi-Yehudah* but it is good to be strict for the Rema.

While not quoting these sources in this way, Rav Eliezer Melamed (*Peninei Halakhah, Shabbos, Harchavos* 18:3:4) reaches the same conclusion about tearing letters on wrappers. If at all possible, you should be strict like the Rema and avoid tearing through letters. But if you cannot be strict like the Rema and you need to open the wrapper, you may tear through letters. Fundamentally, the law follows the *Noda Bi-Yehudah* and we may extend it to similar cases.

Rav Simcha Bunim Cohen (*The Shabbos Home*, vol. 1 p. 52 n. 18) writes in a footnote that the *Noda Bi-Yehudah*'s argument should also apply to tearing through letters while opening a wrapper. Since the *Noda Bi-Yehudah*'s specific ruling is generally accepted, this extension seems to implicitly permit the act.

What emerges from our study is that parents are doing the right thing. Try to open it without tearing the letters. If you can't, let a child open it. And if he can't, then—according to the view discussed here–open it yourself.

Is This Switch Kosher?

As technology changes, the proper application of *halakhah* may require changing practice to remain in step with the new reality. However, when evaluating new technology we have to look at reality and not hype. The new KosherSwitch® is billed as a game-changer that will radically redefine the practice of Shabbos.[33] In truth, it is a next-generation "Gerama Switch" that seems to fall short of the requirements of many major authorities. To fully understand the product and why its halakhic implications are probably minimal, we have to wade through some background.

I. *Gerama*

Over a century ago, halakhic authorities debated the status of a standard light switch. Rav Yechiel Mikhel Epstein, author of the highly influential *Arukh Ha-Shulchan*, published an article in a 1903 Torah journal arguing that lights may be turned on and off on Yom Tov. Part of his calculations was the incorrect scientific

33. This essay was originally published September 18, 2011. Not long after this was published, Rav Yehoshua Neuwirth wrote that he did not approve this product and Rav Nachum Rabinovich communicated the same. Other rabbis who were supposedly supporters also claimed they were misrepresented. Rav Osher Weiss published a long responsum on the KosherSwitch®, concluding that it is forbidden (*Responsa Minchas Asher*, vol. 3 no. 25). The people behind KosherSwitch® responded on their website to this essay, to which I published a response. See my article "In Defense of the Kosher Switch," *Torah Musings*, September 26, 2011.

understanding (as pointed out by Rav Yehudah Borenstein in a rebuttal in that journal) that electric current is fire running through the wires. Another of his arguments was that flipping a switch is considered *gerama*, indirect action. While *gerama* is generally forbidden, it is allowed when extinguishing a fire on Yom Tov. In a similar fashion, Rav Tzvi Pesach Frank, the Chief Rabbi of Jerusalem, published an article in a 1934 Torah journal arguing that flipping an electrical switch is *gerama*.

However, the overwhelming consensus of subsequent authorities rejected this approach. In 1935, the young Jerusalem scholar Rav Shlomo Zalman Auerbach dared to disagree with the two aforementioned scholars and devoted chapter three of his monumental study, *Me'orei Eish*, to this issue. He argued at length that flipping a switch is considered direct action, rather than *gerama*. He obtained for his book a glowing approbation from the eminent authority, Rav Chaim Ozer Grodzinski of Vilna. Rav Grodzinski also penned a responsum arguing the same, later published as *Achiezer* vol. 3 no. 60. Rav Eliezer Waldenberg, also a young scholar in Jerusalem, after studying Rav Auerbach's book and a copy of Rav Grodzinski's responsum (which he obtained from Rav Auerbach), wrote a responsum of his own disagreeing with details of argumentation but agreeing with the conclusion (*Tzitz Eliezer* vol. 1 no. 8). Others, both before and after, have concurred that flipping a switch is direct action. The reasons offered impact greatly both the Gerama Switch and the KosherSwitch®.

II. Un-*Gerama*

Halakhic engineers attempt to avoid issues like *gerama* through creativity. Examining their proposals and the objections they face will offer us insight into potential objections to the KosherSwitch®. The Zomet Institute bases its solutions on the concept of modulating currents. This interesting but controversial approach is irrelevant to our current discussion. The Institute for Halacha and Science developed a Gerama Switch based on the concept of obstruction removal (*meni'as meni'a*) that serves as a basis of the KosherSwitch®. There is a certain amount of rivalry between the institutions which I do not fully understand. I suspect that I may be oversimplifying the distinctions between their approaches, but this should suffice for our purposes. However, both work with the assumption that turning electricity on and off is forbidden on Shabbos. Their goal is to find workable solutions by avoiding the user's closing and opening circuits.

The Gerama Switch is poorly named because it is designed to avoid *gerama*. The switch contains an optical signal that closes or opens a circuit through an impulse light sent at random intervals. If the light is received, the circuit closes and if not, it is opened. The switch, in the off position, blocks the impulse light and prevents the circuit from closing. By moving the switch to the on position, you merely stop preventing the circuit from closing. You are neither directly nor indirectly closing the circuit, just removing the obstruction. Because this is not even *gerama*, moving the switch should be permissible on Shabbos even to perform an act indisputably prohibited.

Why isn't this *gerama*? Conflicting passages in the Talmud describe *gerama* as either permitted or forbidden. Placing bottles of water to break when hit by fire, thereby extinguishing the fire, is permitted. Tossing grain into the air so the wind separates the wheat from the chaff is prohibited. Some early authorities forbid all *gerama* except where explicitly permitted, and others permit it except where explicitly forbidden. The Rema codifies what is essentially a compromise position: We forbid *gerama* on Shabbos except in cases of great need (*Shulchan Arukh, Orach Chaim* 334:22). However, he does not define the boundaries of *gerama*, leaving that task for later authorities.

There are four main theories explaining the difference between permitted and forbidden indirect actions.[34]

1. A time delay between a person's action and the subsequent action makes the first permissible
2. If the second action will not definitely occur, then the first is allowed
3. If this is not the normal way of performing the act, then it is permitted
4. If the second action is not already in motion, then the first is allowed

The Gerama Switch does not rely on the rejected views of Rav Epstein and Rav Frank because its user only removes an obstruction. It also entails a time delay, until the next light impulse. However, this is only permissible according to the first approach to *gerama*. According to the other three, it is still forbidden. For another important reason, which we will discuss later, the designers of the Gerama Switch only allow it in exigent circumstances—for the needs of the infirm and security reasons—when the Rema would allow *gerama*.

III. Kosher Un-*Gerama*

The KosherSwitch® adds uncertainty to the Gerama Switch. Every time the device is supposed to send a light impulse, it calculates a random number below 100 and only sends the impulse if the number passes a threshold (usually over 50). The receiver also calculates a similar random number and only receives the light impulse if the number passes a threshold. These two levels of uncertainty separate the action of moving the switch to the on

---

34. Rav Dovid Miller explains these views nicely in a lecture: "Grama Machines," January 26, 2011. Available on YUTorah.org.

(or off) position from the closing (or opening) of the circuit. The first impulse may not change the circuit, and the second and third may not as well. There is a statistical possibility, albeit remote, that the person may have to wait days or even months until the light impulse is sent and received.

This improvement to the Gerama switch is an important step forward. It renders the device permissible also according to those authorities who follow the second approach above. However, those who follow the third and fourth still do not allow it. This is particularly significant because those authorities are highly influential.

IV. Not So Kosher

Rav Joseph B. Soloveitchik, as reported by Rav Hershel Schachter (*Nefesh Ha-Rav*, p. 169), follows the fourth approach. See also Rav Schachter's *Be-Ikvei Ha-Tzon*, ch. 7 ("*Ma'aseh U-Gerama Bi-Melekhes Shabbos*"). Because the KosherSwitch® functions constantly, waiting for the switch to be moved so it can close the circuit, Rav Soloveitchik would presumably forbid its use.

Rav Chaim Ozer Grodzinski (ibid.) follows the third approach, as does the *Tzitz Eliezer* (ibid.) based on the *Eglei Tal* (*zoreh* n. 4). So do Rav Yechezkel Abramsky (*Chazon Yechezkel*, Shabbos 120b) and Rav Nachum Rabinovich (*Si'ach Nachum*, no. 25). Rav Yosef Shalom Elyashiv also reportedly follows this approach (*Shevus Yitzchak*, p. 138; *Orechos Shabbos*, vol. 3 ch. 29 n. 52). See also Rav Nissim Karelitz, *Chut Shani*, vol. 1 p. 206.

Because flipping a switch is the normal way of closing a circuit (e.g., turning on a light), these authorities would not allow any type of Gerama or KosherSwitch®. If this switch becomes widely adopted, as its designers hope, then it will be the standard way of closing and opening circuits, turning lights on and off. This is precisely the situation that Rav Grodzinski and the others forbade.

Rav Shlomo Zalman Auerbach clearly followed this third approach in his *Me'orei Eish*, quoting Rav Isser Zalman Meltzer on the matter (*Me'orei Eish Ha-Shalem*, p. 217). He restated it in an early responsum on milking cows on Shabbos (ibid., p. 612ff.) and a later responsum on telephones (*Minchas Shlomo*, vol. 1, no. 9; *Me'orei Eish Ha-Shalem*, p. 576). A manuscript was posthumously published in a memorial book for Rav Auerbach, *Kovetz Ateres Shlomo*, which seems to contradict this approach but his son, Rav Shmuel Auerbach, insists that his father maintained his original attitude (*Orechos Shabbos* vol. 3 ch. 29 n. 52).

However, Prof. Zev Lev (*Ma'arkhei Lev*, p. 241) reports an important ruling from Rav Shlomo Zalman Auerbach. Rav Auerbach ruled that if an action is performed in a specific way only on Shabbos, that does not constitute the normal way the action is done. The KosherSwitch® has a weekday mode and a Shabbos mode, which function differently. According to this ruling of Rav Auerbach, turning lights on with the switch in Shabbos mode is not the normal way of turning on the lights and is therefore permissible.

I find this difficult to understand. This is a switch that is designed to work this way, functions the same way as other switches (from the user's perspective), and performs in the same way once a week plus holidays. I make no claim to expertise but that seems to me to be the normal way the action is done. From what I have seen in the name of Rav Elyashiv, he disagrees with Rav Auerbach's ruling and forbids all types of *gerama* (or un-*gerama*) devices. I think this aspect of the issue requires further elaboration and evaluation by halakhic decisors.

V. Publicity and Endorsements

The KosherSwitch® has reportedly received numerous rabbinic endorsements, including from Rav Yehoshua Neuwirth, Rav Nachum Rabinovich, Rav Moshe Sternbuch, and Rav Yisroel

Belsky. It is not clear, however, whether those endorsement are for use in exigent circumstances or in every home. I suspect it is the former, particularly given Rav Rabinovich's strict ruling on electric switches (*Si'ach Nachum*, no. 25).

However, the device's promoters claim that it is appropriate for every home. Indeed, in their halakhic defense of the innovation (sec. 12), they claim that the device will eventually become standard in all homes, thereby enabling universal Shabbos observance and the arrival of the messianic redemption. Are the endorsements also exaggerated PR? It was quickly discovered that many of the endorsers disavowed any supposed endorsement.[35]

VI. Confusion

The Institute for Science and Halacha, the designers of the Gerama Switch, only allow its use in exigent circumstances for the following reason (Rav Levi Yitzchak Halperin and Rav Dovid Oratz, *Shabbat and Electricity*, pp. 32-33):

> The difference between a *gerama* switch and a standard switch is not readily discernible to a layman. A person seeing someone using a *gerama* switch might conclude that the action is permissible with any switch. As a result, people could mistakenly permit many prohibited Shabbat actions, resulting in mass desecration of Shabbat. Under such circumstances, it is appropriate not to permit actions that should otherwise be permitted.
>
> To prevent such misunderstanding, the use of the *gerama* switch is limited to uses where an ordinary *gerama* would be permitted, hence the name *gerama* switch and not *meni'at hameni'ah* switch... Accordingly, the Institute uses the *gerama* switch only under those conditions in which ordinary *gerama* can be permitted.

---

35. Such as Rav Yisroel Belsky and Rav Nachum Rabinovich.

The designers of KosherSwitch®, in their halakhic defense (sec. 7), argue that this is unnecessary for a number of unconvincing reasons. Among them is that the KosherSwitch® looks very different from regular switches. I cannot speak for the situation in Israel, but in the US switches come in very different shapes and sizes. I compared the KosherSwitch® to four different switches in my house. The KosherSwitch® did not look particularly different to me. While it carries a KosherSwitch® logo, that is hardly sufficient, as the designers of the Gerama Switch acknowledged.

In addition to the issue of confusion, there are other issues that enter this discussion, such as *zilusa de-Shabbos*, diminishing the Shabbos experience, and *shevisah ha-nikkeres*, resting in a manner noticeably different from the rest of the week. I leave that for another time but wish to emphasize that they are also significant Shabbos values.

The KosherSwitch® is an important step forward in Shabbos technology and will improve the devices designed for security and health situations. However, I struggle to see how it satisfies the requirements of many important authorities and how it could possibly become a standard feature in Shabbos-observant homes.

Electronic Sensors on Shabbos

Halakhic authorities and common practice have unanimously accepted that Shabbos regulations forbid, at least on a rabbinic level, actively using electric appliances. This includes turning these appliances on or off. However, debate was recently renewed in an Israeli journal over passively adjusting these devices. As the world becomes more automated, as video cameras become ubiquitous and energy-conserving censors become commonplace, the ability to even minimally function on Shabbos demands closer consideration of the halakhic viability of this technology.

I. Rav Knohl

In 2003, Rav Elyashiv Knohl published an article in the journal *Techumin* (no. 23) suggesting that you may trigger an electronic sensor[36] in specific circumstances. He first discusses whether triggering a sensor is an indirect act—*gerama*—which is permissible in a situation of need. He concludes that this is a minority view of the *Magen Avraham* which may only be followed in a time of great need. His example is an automatic door into a hotel when no one else is around who will trigger it and you will otherwise be left outside for a long time. In a footnote, Rav

36. I used the term "electronic sensor" here in a general sense to include thermal, proximity, and other types of sensors that are triggered by human motion and/or presence. According to Rav Rosen, as mentioned in this essay, the details of the technology are largely irrelevant.

Yisrael Rosen, the journal's editor, disagrees that this can even be considered *gerama* and rejects the lenient ruling.

More generally, though, he builds on a responsum by Rav Shmuel Wosner (published in that journal and later in *Shevet Ha-Levi* 9:69) permitting walking past a sensor that turns on a light. If you do not want the light to turn on and do not intentionally trigger the sensor, then, Rav Wosner rules, you cannot be considered someone who commits an act. You are merely walking on your way as events happen without your consent. Rav Knohl feels that this can be generalized as long as you do not intentionally trigger the sensor.

II. Rav Fixler and Rav Reif

In the past decade, Rav Knohl's article has had little impact in halakhic literature. Recently, Rav Dror Fixler and Rav Eli Reif published an article going even farther (*Emunas Itekha*, 104). They similarly base their view on Rav Wosner's responsum, albeit finding additional bases for it in the Talmud and codes. For example, Rambam (*Mishneh Torah*, *Hilkhos Shabbos* 21:2) rules that you may walk on spit that is on a dirt road, even though you will be violating a biblical prohibition, since you are merely walking on your way. Similarly, Ritva (*Shabbos* 140a s.v. *mahu*), regarding rubbing a garment to soften it while also cleaning it, writes that we look at the permissibility of an action's primary purpose, regardless of whether the forbidden aspect is also intended.

Rav Fixler and Rav Reif conclude that triggering a sensor is different than flipping a switch. If you walk past a sensor, even though you will definitely trigger it, you are not committing a forbidden *pesik reisheih*[37] because you are not doing any act. According to them, if you are walking on your way for any

---

37. An act that necessarily leads to another act. In this case, walking past the sensor necessarily turns on the light.

purpose and trigger a sensor, even if you want to trigger it, you are not liable for the result. You are legitimately walking and the sensor's activity is not your concern—even if you want to trigger it. However, if you approach the sensor solely to trigger it, and you are not walking on your way with another purpose in mind, then you are liable for the result.

They add that even if you reject this logic and consider triggering a sensor to be a *pesik reisheih*, it should still be allowed. Many authorities permit a *pesik reisheih* when the prohibition is only rabbinic. When it comes to electricity, most activities are only rabbinically forbidden. They quote this rabbinic prohibition in the name of Rav Yosef Eliyahu Henkin. While many other authorities can be cited, this particular citation will be important.

III. Rav Rabinovich

Most signficantly, this lengthy article is followed by a brief article by the authors' teacher, the noted authority Rav Nachum Rabinovich. Rav Rabinovich explicitly agrees with their conclusion, also citing Rav Henkin. He repeats the argument of Rav Fixler and Rav Reif that a person does nothing when triggering a sensor; the sensor acts on its own, responding to what occurs around it. Rav Rabinovich writes, "Essentially, the person does not act on the sensor but the sensor acts on the person."

Rav Rabinovich quotes the Rambam (*Mishneh Torah, Hilkhos Shabbos* 11:4) who allows someone, while walking on his way, to step on a pest (i.e., an insect). Ramban (*Milchamos Hashem, Shabbos* 45b in the Rif) explicitly states that this includes intentionally stepping on the pest. Triggering a sensor is less problematic because the person does not commit any act, unlike stepping.

Rav Rabinovich concludes that in past generations, rabbis forbade activities that were similar to forbidden acts to prevent Shabbos from becoming like a weekday. However, the revolution of automation is different and cannot be treated in the same way. Automation will free people from work and allow them to enjoy Shabbos more.

IV. Rav Rosen

Rav Yisrael Rosen, head of the Zomet institute, responds negatively to both these articles. He has previously written a lengthy article on this subject, in *Emunas Itekha* (no. 102), subsequently published in his recent book, *Be-Chatzros Beis Hashem*, and he wrote a specific response to the above articles. To Rav Rabinovich's last point regarding turning Shabbos into a weekday, Rav Rosen points out that sensors can easily be used to do just this. You can set your lights to turn on as you enter a room, your stereo to play your favorite music when you step near it, your oven to cook when you stand in a specific place, etc. You can even arrange for your fields to be plowed and seeded at your control, all through electronic sensors.

Rav Rosen states that he does not believe that automation is inherently problematic. The halakhic issues arise when the work is done based on human interaction. Automation must be completely automatic, without need for human action.

However, this is not Rav Rosen's main objection. Once upon a time, rabbis questioned whether a person who plows with a tractor is considered having plowed the field. After all, he did not touch the field and merely manipulated a machine. The *Chazon Ish* ruled, to great acceptance, that the tractor is only a tool for the person to plow. Similarly, when an electronic sensor is the normal way to perform a forbidden action, it becomes a human tool. The exact technology of the sensor is irrelevant. We have to look at the results. If a person's actions trigger an electronic reaction, then it is as if the person flipped a switch.

Consider a gun connected to an electronic sensor. As you approach, it shoots in the other direction. Imagine if you wait for someone to stand directly in the gun's sights and then you intentionally walk to your car, causing the gun to shoot the person. Are you exempt? You intentionally activate the gun so it shoots. Rather, Rav Rosen argues, triggering a sensor is like flipping a switch or pulling a trigger. .

He additionally points out that Rav Fixler and Rav Reif base their approach on Rav Wosner's responsum. However, Rav Wosner clarified, as an addendum to the end of the responsum when published as *Shevet Ha-Levi* 9:69, that he was only discussing a case in which you do not intentionally activate the sensor. Even if you benefit from a light turning on as you pass the sensor, Rav Wosner contends that if you do not intend to turn it on you are innocent. This is debatable because you benefit from the light. Regardless, Rav Wosner's ruling cannot be extended to a case in which you intentionally activate the sensor, which he explcitly forbids.

V. Rav Eitam Henkin

Rav Rabinovich, Rav Fixler, and Rav Reif quote Rav Yosef Eliyahu Henkin, particularly some recently published *teshuvos*. Rav Henkin's great-grandson, Rav Eitam Henkin, published an article in response in the latest issue of *Emunas Itekha* (no. 105), which he says has his father's (Rav Yehuda Herzl Henkin) agreement. The younger Rav Henkin's article contains almost everything I want to say on the subject, only better than I could have said it.[38]

Rav Henkin's first point, which Rav Rosen mentions briefly, is that this discussion is not new. Home thermostats, operating on the functional equivalent of heat sensors, have existed for decades. The question of opening refrigerator doors, and thereby likely

---

38. This essay was originally published on December 1, 2014. On October 1, 2015, Rav Eitam Henkin and his wife Na'ama were shot and murdered by terrorists in front of their children. Their martyrdom for the Jewish homeland is a terrible loss for their family and the entire nation. We mourn the loss of these young, brilliant lives.

triggering the motor as the temperature rises, was addressed years ago. While the technology has grown in complexity, the halakhic question remains largely the same.

In all those discussions, no authority suggested that the ovens, refrigerators, or thermostats acted independently. Those who ruled leniently found other reasons. We are not dealing with autonomous machines but automation triggered by human intervention. Rav Henkin quotes the Rambam (*Mishneh Torah, Hilkhos Shabbos* 1:6), who says that any forbidden action that could not be done without a prior action is considered a *pesik reisheih*. The Rambam focuses on the inevitability of the actions, not the reason for their connection. The only remaining question is whether a person benefits from the inevitable work he causes (*nicha leih*).

Consider the extensive discussions of riding an elevator on Shabbos. One of the questions is whether standing in an elevator is forbidden if doing so causes forbidden work. This is even less causative than triggering a sensor through movement, yet is still forbidden according to many.

Rav Henkin also points out that the permission to step on a pest is extensively discussed by the commentators. Some believe it is permitted because the action is not intended for itself, a *melakhah she-einah tzerikhah le-gufah*, which is normally rabbinically prohibited but permitted here due to the need. Others suggest that we are dealing with life-threatening pests. Regardless, it is irrelevant to the case of turning on a device through a sensor.

Additionally, Rav Fixler and Rav Reif argue that using a sensor is allowed because it is a *pesik reisheih* on something otherwise rabbinically forbidden, which some authorities permit. However, Ashkenazim do not follow this permissive ruling. Some permit a *pesik reisheih de-lo nicha leih* that is otherwise rabbinically forbidden—meaning, it is a *pesik reisheih* whose result is not desired on a rabbinic prohibition. Otherwise, we require two levels of rabbinic prohibitions—meaning even more permissible than something rabbinically forbidden—in order to allow a *pesik reisheih de-lo nicha leih*. Certainly, normative Ashkenazic practice does not allow a regular *pesik reisheih* that provides a benefit, even if only rabbinically forbidden.

VI. Other Discussions

Rav Rosen and Rav Henkin both point out that the issues surrounding electronic sensors have been discussed both explicitly and implicitly for decades.See, for example, Rav Shlomo Zalman Braun, *She'arim Ha-Metzuyanim Ba-Halakhah*, second edition, 80:2 (automatic door); Rav Gedaliah Felder, *Yesodei Yeshurun* vol. 5, pp. 160-161; Rav Yehoshua Neuwirth, *Shemiras Shabbos Ke-Hilkhasah* 23:53; Rav Gersion Appel, *The Concise Code of Jewish Law*, vol. 2 p. 214; Rav Mordechai Eliyahu, *Responsa Ha-Rav Ha-Roshi*, no. 73; idem., *Responsa Ma'amar Mordekhai* 4:166; Rav Levi Yitzchak Halperin, *Responsa Ma'aseh Chosheiv* 1:12; idem., *Shabbat and Electricity*, chs. 7 (alarm system) & 9 (automatic door); Prof. Zev Lev, *Ma'arkhei Lev*, pp. 387-388; Rav Shalom Yosef Gelber & Rav Yitzchak Mordechai Rubin, *Orechos Shabbos*, 26:26-33 and notes; Rav Eliezer Melamed, *Peninei Halakhah*, *Shabbos* 17:14 and *Harchavos*.

From what I can tell, the permissive position is unique and unsustainable.

Combat Exoskeletons on Shabbos

I. Bionic Men

Reports, albeit somewhat dubious, are circulating regarding Russian development of combat exoskeletons that can mechanically increase the strength and endurance of soldiers. Worn like body armor, these artificial extensions of the body are expected, within five years, to receive direction through brain waves. When a soldier thinks about moving his arm or leg, the mechanical extension will move, thereby multiplying the soldier's strength. While combat is almost always a case of life-threatening danger that overrides the rules of Shabbos, the tantalizing reports still raise the question of whether such technology can be used on Shabbos in non-combat situations.

The basic technology already exists. Computers have already been developed that can receive instructions through brain waves. This Brain Computer Interface (BCI) technology currently requires direct contact with the skull, but the possibility of remote connection—a sort of brain wifi—is certainly conceivable. I'm hardly an expert so it may already exist and I just do not know about it. I see three questions related to Shabbos with this technology.

First, can we use BCI to perform a forbidden labor? Can I command, through my thoughts, a plow to work my field or a coffee maker to brew me fresh coffee? Second, can I use this technology to utilize a machine to do something that is not otherwise forbidden, such as turning the page in a book or lifting a fork full of food? (We'll get to the third question later).

II. Thinking Labor

Rav Shlomo Zalman Auerbach was asked this question, apparently multiple times. He believed that there is a talmudic precedent for prohibiting an activity on Shabbos that is done through thought (beyond thinking about business and similar thoughts, which is a separate issue). Rav Zalman Menachem Koren, the editor of Rav Auerbach's writings on electricity (*Me'orei Eish Ha-Shalem*, vol. 2 pp. 765-766), discusses Rav Auerbach's oral response. Rav Auerbach pointed to the prohibition against designating food as *terumah*—the portion given to priests and forbidden to others (Tosafos, *Gittin* 31a s.v. *be-machashavah*)—on Shabbos. Even an activity that consists of thought can be forbidden.

In one of his earliest writings (*Me'orei Eish*, ch. 4), Rav Auerbach quotes a responsum by Rav Avraham Walkin (*Zekan Aharon* vol. 1 no. 15), in which the author argued that someone who miraculously cooks through thought or speech violates a biblical prohibition. Rav Walkin proves this from the *man* (manna) that the Jews ate in the Desert. The Torah (Ex. 16:23) forbids cooking the *man* on Shabbos. However, the *man* required no preparation—you merely thought about what you want and it tasted that way. Clearly, Rav Walkin argues, cooking through thought is biblically forbidden. Rav Auerbach rejects this entire line of argument (although not necessarily the conclusion) because the Torah only forbids cooking with fire, not miraculous cooking. Whatever you may be doing wrong by thinking *man* to be cooked, it isn't cooking.

Rav Yisrael Rosen (*Be-Chatzros Beis Hashem*, p. 90) writes that he asked Rav Auerbach the same question and received the same answer about designating *terumah*. However, Rav Rosen challenges this proof. He points out that designating *terumah* violates the rabbinic prohibition of fixing an object, *tikkun keli*. If so, it is not a Shabbos rule that thought can violate the prohibition but a function of designating *terumah*. Since the rules of *terumah* allow thought, the food is "fixed" and the Shabbos rules are thereby violated. There is no general rule here to be extracted that Shabbos can be violated by thought.

Rav Rosen quotes Rav Meir Dan Plotzki (*Keli Chemdah, Beshallach*) who also attempts to prove from the cooking of the *man* that a forbidden labor caused by thought is prohibited. However, Rav Auerbach's above objection should apply similarly. Rav Plotzki also gets philosophical. He points out that on Shabbos, we rest like God did after creating the world. Since God created the world through thought, a labor that is caused by thought is also forbidden. Although one can counter that God created the world through speech, it is not clear to me whether divine speech and divine thought are distinct.

III. Miraculous Labor

Rav Rosen briefly raises the idea that performing a forbidden activity through thought is comparable to performing it using supernatural powers. Consider, for example, killing someone by invoking God's name or writing by asking a question of the *Urim Ve-Tummim*. If directly causing a labor by speaking is allowed, then certainly causing it by thinking is permitted. Rav Shay Schachter advances this argument in a lecture, citing many more examples.[39] He quotes a responsum by Rav Chaim Palaggi (*Lev Chaim*, vol. 2 *OC* 188), in which the author permits extinguishing a fire on Shabbos supernaturally (with a *segulah*), such as reciting Psalm 98.

I believe his father, Rav Hershel Schachter, implies such a position in an article. In *Be-Ikvei Ha-Tzon* (p. 47), the senior Rav Schachter writes in regard to *gerama* and what is required for an act to be forbidden on Shabbos:

---

39. "Urim V'Tumim & BCI Technology on Shabbos," February 26, 2015, available on YUTorah.org.

Even though we need a human action—as opposed to sitting doing nothing and thinking—we do not need human power

Maybe I am overreading this brief phrase, but I think it might permit otherwise forbidden activities caused by thought.

IV. Natural Labor

However, Rav Osher Weiss (in an online essay), rejects the comparison to miracles offered by the younger Rav Schachter.[40] Rav Weiss argues that miraculous and supernatural actions are inherently different from natural causation. A supernatural activity is really caused by God, not man, and therefore is permitted. But when a person directly causes a forbidden activity, even if just by thinking, then it makes sense to say that he has effectively pushed the plow himself.

However, lacking a definitive proof, Rav Weiss hedges, saying that at best causing a forbidden activity by thinking constitutes *gerama*, which is rabbinically forbidden except in exigent circumstances. He concludes that whether this constitutes direct or indirect labor requires more study, but it is definitely forbidden under normal circumstances.

V. Extended Human

However, this discussion only answers the first question— may you use thought to perform a forbidden action? Regarding an electronic prosthetic limb, the issue turns to whether you may use thought to move an electronic device. It is not entirely the same for two reasons.

First, electronic motion may be only rabbinically prohibited. Second, and perhaps more importantly, the device itself might be

---

40. "An Act Performed By Speech Or Miraculous Manner" (Hebrew) on Tvunah.org.

considered part of the person, which brings us to the third question: What is the distinction between a person and the machines he uses? Some today argue to an extreme that computers are an extension of your own mind. More moderate thinkers suggest that artificial appendages become part of you. Is a hearing aid distinct from the person whose hearing is improved? A pacemaker? An artificial heart? If an artificial limb is considered part of you, then you may use it on Shabbos like you use your arm.

Personally, I believe that if it's organic then it is part of you, even a donated organ and even if grown in a laboratory. If it is inorganic, even partially, then it is not part of you. If and when they make completely organic computers, then maybe that can become part of you, as well. I am not a halakhic authority so my opinion is not conclusive. But it would seem that this line of thinking implies that artificial body parts that violate rabbinic Shabbos prohibitions (absent the considerations of thought, discussed above) may only be used by someone who would otherwise be defined as ill but not life-threatening. Similarly, artificial body parts that violate biblical prohibitions may only be used by someone who would otherwise be in a life-threatening situation. I am not aware what halakhic authorities have said on this subject. (In short, the Bionic Man is *asur* according to some authorities.)

When it comes to exoskeletons, we have to ask whether they are external to the human body. If they are, as I suggest, then we arrive at the dispute above. According to Rav Shlomo Zalman Auerbach and Rav Osher Weiss, they are forbidden. According to Rav Shay Schachter and possibly his father, Rav Hershel Schachter, this might be allowed (I did not hear the younger Rav Schachter reach a definitive conclusion). Rav Rosen also seems to lean toward leniency but does not reach a final conclusion.

Pocketwatches on Shabbos

In the evolution of *halakhah*, the debates that eventually become settled and codified, not all leniencies stay in place. The idea sometime bandied about that the talmudic phrase "*ko'ach de-hetteira adif*, the lenient position is stronger" means that lenient rulings take priority is not only incorrect but disproven by history. In reality, many combinations of circumstance, personalities, and the force of arguments determine where *halakhah* ends up. One such example is the pocketwatch.

I. Pocketwatch on Shabbos

From the time of its development in the sixteenth century until the rise of wristwatches after World War I, pocketwatches were the most common type of watch. The question naturally arose whether you may wear a pocketwatch on Shabbos where there is no *eruv* and therefore carrying is not allowed. Is the way people use a pocketwatch considered wearing or carrying?

A pocketwatch contains a watchpiece and a chain. The chain is typically clipped to clothing, whether a jacket, vest, or pants. The watch is kept tucked into a pocket on the jacket, vest, or pants. Sometimes the watchpiece has a cover on it, further obscuring it from view. Often, a pocketwatch is worn as a fashion statement. However, in older times, wearing a pocketwatch was the only way to carry a timepiece.

II. Functional Jewelry

Before we engage the question of wearing a pocketwatch in public on Shabbos, we first have to determine whether a watch is *muktzeh*. If it is, you would not be able to wear/carry it even indoors. While opinions differ, the majority of authorities rule that a mechanical watch (as opposed to a sand clock) is not *muktzeh*. In the course of a discussion of this subject, Rav Raphael Meyuchas (Jerusalem; 1701-1771) writes that most people wear a gold or silver pocketwatch as jewelry (*Peri Ha-Adamah*, vol. 4, 25:2). This places a pocketwatch into a category of items that serve as both jewelry and a useful function. Rav Meyuchas quotes the *Shulchan Arukh* (*Orach Chaim* 301:11), which quotes a view that forbids wearing such an item where there is no *eruv* because people might think you are wearing it for the functional use. However, some permit if the jewelry is made of silver.

Effectively, Rav Meyuchas permits wearing a pocketwatch in public on Shabbos even where there is no *eruv*. This ruling of Rav Meyuchas to permit wearing a pocketwatch is quoted approvingly by Rav Daniel Tirani (Florence; ca. 1770-1814; *Ikkarei Ha-Dat*, vol. 1 12:2) and Rav Chaim Palaggi (Turkey; 1788-1869; *Lev Chaim*, vol. 3 no. 84).

III. Early Codes

Rav Avraham Danzig (Vilna; 1748-1820; *Chayei Adam*, *Hilkhos Shabbos* 56:2; *Zikhru Toras Moshe* 45:21) rejects the premise of the question. A pocketwatch is carried, not worn. It is like anything else placed inside your pocket. The chain, whether ornamental or for safekeeping, does not change the process of carrying the watch into an act of wearing. Therefore, Rav Danzig forbids "wearing" a pocketwatch on Shabbos where there is no *eruv*.

Following Rav Danzig's important code, Rav Shlomo Ganzfried (Hungary; 1804-1886) similarly prohibited wearing a pocketwatch on Shabbos (*Kitzur Shulchan Arukh* 84:2). However, he seems to have been uncertain about this ruling because he sent this and another question to the leading halakhic authority of his day, Rav Yosef Shaul Nathanson (Ukraine; 1810-1875). Rav Nathanson replied permissively (*Responsa Sho'el U-Meishiv*, 1st series, vol. 3 no. 31). Apparently, in his question, Rav Ganzfried notes that Rav Tzvi Ashkenazi (known as the *Chakham Tzvi*; Amsterdam; 1658-1718) personally would not wear a pocketwatch where there is no *eruv*. However, Rav Nathanson disagrees. He argues that if you wear the pocketwatch on your clothing, particularly if the chain is gold, then it constitutes jewelry and is permitted.

Interestingly, at the end of his life, Rav Ganzfried made corrections to his *Kitzur Shulchan Arukh*. However, he never changed this ruling despite this responsum to him from Rav Nathanson.

IV. Ornamental Watches

What if the watch is worn as a pin and not tucked inside a pocket? In theory, that would make it more a piece of jewelry. Rav Chaim Halberstam of Sanz (Poland; 1797-1876) rules against wearing a watch, whether tucked in a pocket or pinned on clothing (*Responsa Divrei Chaim*, vol. 2 *Orach Chaim* no. 33). He argues that even if worn on clothing, the watch does not become an article of jewelry. He also expresses concern that men will remove the watch because it is embarrassing for a man to wear it that way.

Rav Shlomo Ganzfried (ibid.) seems to refrain from outright forbidding an ornamental watch. He writes that you may not wear a watch connected to a chain around your neck, even though it is jewelry. But, he continues, a pocketwatch is not even jewelry and is forbidden. Rav Shlomo Zalman Braun (*She'arim Metzuyanim Ba-Halakhah* 84:3) infers from this difference in language that Rav Ganzfried considered an ornamental watch a matter less clearly forbidden, but still something he believed should not be worn.

V. Later Authorities

Rav Shalom Schwadron (Galicia; 1835-1911) discusses pocketwatches in four places. In two responsa (*Responsa Maharsham* 3:369, 5:34) and in his glosses to *Shulchan Arukh* (*Orach Chaim* 301:7) he permits wearing a pocketwatch as long as the watch is permanently connected to the chain. However, in one responsum (4:127) he seems to lean to the strict side.

Rav Yisrael Kagan (Belarus; 1838-1933) forbids both ornamental watches and pocketwatches (*Mishnah Berurah* 301:45; *Bi'ur Halakhah*, ad loc., s.v. *ba-zeh*). Because pocketwatches are hidden from view, they are not jewelry. Additionally, they are not secondary to the chains but more important. Even ornamental watches are worn primarily for timekeeping, not as jewelry. As he points out, nobody wears a broken watch as jewelry. One could counter that jewelry does not need to be seen. Women frequently wear rings and bracelets underneath gloves. Additionally, some people do, indeed, wear pocketwatches as a fashion statement. Something which is worn as both jewelry and a utensil is precisely the subject of the discussion in that paragraph of *Shulchan Arukh*.

Rav Yechiel Epstein (Belarus; 1828-1908) has a reputation as a lenient authority, particularly one who justifies common practice. However, he also forbids wearing pocketwatches and ornamental watches (*Arukh Ha-Shulchan, Orach Chaim* 301:62). He goes so far as to say that anyone who acts leniently "is destined to give judgment" in heaven for his transgression. This harsh language implies that he was trying to stamp out the practice. Similarly, Rav Kagan's lengthy discussion also implies that he was trying to convince people to stop wearing pocketwatches on Shabbos where there is no *eruv*.

Despite the earlier permissive rulings, normative *halakhah* forbids wearing a pocketwatch on Shabbos where there is no *eruv*. At one time, this was a matter of debate. However, *halakhah* has evolved and the matter has been closed.

An additional, relevant source is a responsum by Rav David Tzvi Hoffmann that I have not seen mentioned elsewhere in this context. Rav Hoffmann was asked whether there is any permission to carry items over your shoulder, where they are clearly more than ten *tefachim* from the ground. In *Melamed Le-Ho'il* (no. 64), Rav Hoffmann analyzes the question, which revolves around a passage in the beginning of *Shabbos* (5a).

He shows that commentators debate whether the prohibition to carry above ten *tefachim* is biblical or rabbinic. He concludes with an interesting suggestion:

> Those who are lenient to carry a watch with a gold chain or other types of jewelry, or wear a belt on which each side is connected by a key rather than a buckle, and similar leniencies that were permitted for them in times of need, they should try to carry those things at least above ten *tefachim*, which is 95 centimeters. Then they have another support for leniency, particularly in a *karmelis* [in which carrying is only rabbinically forbidden].

This is not a ringing endorsement of wearing a pocketwatch. If anything, Rav Hoffmann is forbidding it. However, recognizing that sometimes people act differently for a variety of reasons, he recommended an additional practice to lessen the prohibition.

Home Fires in Jewish Law

I remember once as a teenager walking with some friends one Friday night in our small suburb. We somehow got to talking with gentile (African American) teenagers around our age who were also walking at that time. We explained some of the rules we follow and one asked us: "So if you find a twenty dollar bill on the street, you won't pick it up and take it with you?" We answered in the negative, to their dumbfounded and a little impressed response. To all of us suburban teenagers, this seemed like a massive sacrifice in the name of religion. It is nothing compared to what is demanded of us. God gives us everything in our lives and we must be ready to give back some of those gifts if necessary. This is a hard lesson to accept in today's age.

If you see an uncontrolled fire in your house on Shabbos, standard halakhic codes today tell you to put out the fire if you can or call the fire department immediately. This is noteworthy because it is the opposite of what the Talmud says to do. I find the story of this development fascinating, as it takes us through both precedent-setting rulings and changes of circumstances that impact halakhic conclusions.

I. The Talmudic Response

The Talmud (*Shabbos* 115a-122b) dedicates a whole chapter to the proper response to a home fire on Shabbos. In short, the Sages were concerned that a person whose house is burning on Shabbos may, in his concern, violate the Shabbos rules. Therefore, they instituted even stricter rules. Among the thirty-nine forbidden Shabbos labors is extinguishing a fire. Because someone who sees all his earthly belongings burning into oblivion is likely to attempt to stop it directly, the Sages added protective measures to prevent you from extinguishing the fire. You are only allowed to remove enough food for the remaining Shabbos meals from the house, and you are only allowed to take the clothing that you wear and the few sacred texts you own. You may call a gentile over to help but you may not ask him to extinguish the fire. However, you are not required to discourage him; you may say, "whoever extinguishes this fire will not lose." You are allowed to indirectly extinguish the fire by placing barrels of water around the fire so the fire eventually opens the barrels, causing the water to spill out onto the fire.

This means, for example, that if in talmudic times a small fire started burning in a corner of your house on Shabbos, you could take a limited amount of items out of your house. You could ask a gentile to come but you could not ask him to extinguish the fire. And you could try to indirectly place water in the path of the fire. In sum, this was a very challenging law to follow. Even if you had water in your hand, you would have to watch your house burn down. That takes an incredible amount of devotion and faith.

Granted, in ancient times people had less "stuff." But whatever stuff you had and couldn't wear got destroyed while you watched. All this is because of the concern that you might extinguish the flame in your understandable concern for your property (*Shabbos* 117b). But Shabbos is more important than property. As difficult as that is to accept in the realm of reality rather than theory, it is an important lesson to keep with us at all times. As we chase after more things in life, we need to keep our perspective and our priorities straight.

What is perhaps most remarkable is that according to R. Shimon in the Talmud, which is whom most authorities follow, you only violate the biblical prohibition if you extinguish a fire in order to use its remains, i.e. the charcoal. Otherwise, it is forbidden only rabbinically. The Talmud Yerushalmi (*Shabbos* 16:3) suggests that you may extinguish a fire to save a sacred text because this is only a rabbinic violation. However, the Babylonian Talmud seems to reject this leniency. Despite the rabbinic nature of the prohibition, we are required by talmudic law to rescue very few of our possessions in the case of a fire.

II. Expanding Leniencies

The first to offer a major leniency was Rabbeinu Tam (12th century, France). He made the quite compelling inference that the talmudic stringencies only apply to the people whose house is on fire (Tosafos, *Shabbos* 115a s.v. *kol*). Any neighbors who are concerned that the fire might spread may empty all their possessions from their house. The talmudic concern is that someone whose house is burning might extinguish the flames. Someone whose house is not yet burning lacks that specific concern and therefore is not subject to the stringencies.

Because it is so compelling, Rabbeinu Tam's leniency spread quickly without objection. It is widely quoted without dissent. Obviously, no one recommends rushing back and forth into a burning house. However, because we may not extinguish the fire, a small fire in one corner of the house or in a nearby house might allow time to remove items from other parts of the house before the entire building becomes enveloped in flames.

Rav Barukh of Mainz, a student of Rabbeinu Tam's nephew Ri, goes a step further (*Sefer Ha-Terumah*, Shabbos 245) and argues that the circumstances have changed, demanding a halakhic change. Since, as opposed to in talmudic times, today we do not have a public domain as halakhically defined (*reshus ha-rabbim de-oraisa*), carrying is permitted in the case of a fire. Even the house owner may remove his belongings from his burning house if there is an *eruv*. Any *muktzeh* that may not normally be carried can be carried together with something permissible, like a sacred text. In this way, a person can empty the house of his valuables rather than lose the house and everything in it.

From the perspective of legal theory, Rav Barukh's ruling is difficult. The reason for the greater stringency is the possibility of extinguishing the fire, not the possibility of carrying the belongings into a public domain. The absence of a public domain should have no impact on the risk of extinguishing a fire. However, from a pragmatic perspective, the ruling retains great emotional appeal.

Rav Yonah, the author of *Issur Ve-Hetter* (*Pikku'ach Nefesh*, no. 42) quotes earlier sources that he claims permit removing all items from a burning house as a leniency. The logic for the leniency is that if we do not permit people to remove their valuables, they may extinguish the fire. While the rationale seems appealing, it directly contradicts the Talmud's reasoning. The Talmud believes we should be strict for the very reason that Rav Yonah says we should be lenient. Additionally, the earlier sources he quotes do not say what Rav Yonah claims they do. The *Chayei Adam* (*Shabbos* 45:8) points out this difficulty in the *Issur Ve-Hetter*.

III. Dangers

Rav Yitzchak of Vienna (13th century) adds a completely different reason to permit extinguishing a house fire on Shabbos (*Or Zaru'a, Eruvin* 149). In Europe, the gentiles would riot and kill people when there was a large fire. To avoid this life-threatening danger, the Jews had to quickly extinguish any fire. Rav Yisrael Isserlein (15th century, Austria; *Terumas Ha-Deshen*, part 1 no. 58) agrees and adds that he heard some people saying that the problem is that the gentiles would kill a Jew in whose house a fire started. Therefore, if a Jewish house catches fire from someone else's house, you cannot extinguish that fire. Rav Isserlein disagreed. The problem is not the punishment but the lawlessness and riots, even if a riot is only a remote possibility.

According to this view, the circumstances had changed. Living among the gentiles, allowing your house to burn down on Shabbos endangered your life. Therefore, you must extinguish a house fire. However, Rav Isserlein added, if you live in a place with a strong government that will enforce law and order and and thereby prevent the murder of Jews, the talmudic rule returns in force and you may not extinguish a house fire on Shabbos. Significantly, Rav Moshe Isserles (16th century, Poland) ruled according to this approach in his glosses to *Shulchan Arukh* (*Orach Chaim* 344:26).

However, a further step was taken in the seventeenth century. Much earlier, the *Hagahos Mordekhai* (Germany; *Shabbos*, no. 393) pointed out that many people extinguished fires on Shabbos, claiming that it was in order to save children. The author was unconvinced and concluded that it is better not to object so people sin unintentionally. Surprisingly, Ritva (14th century, Spain; *Shabbos* 115a) quotes this ruling verbatim. Centuries later, Rav Chaim Benveniste (b. 1603, Turkey) adopted an approach similar to what the others rejected. He ruled that because fire spreads quickly from house to house, and every place has elderly and sick people who have trouble evacuating, any house fire is a life-threatening danger. Therefore, we violate Shabbos and extinguish any fire to avoid the potential threat to life (*Sheyarei Keneses Ha-Gedolah, Orach Chaim* 334, *Hagahos Beis Yosef* 11). This is a broad permission that quickly became standard. Rav Eliyahu Shapiro (b. 1660, Prague) rules similarly (*Eliyah Rabbah, Orach Chaim* 334:24). Perhaps this is an overly historicist speculation, but I cannot help but notice that a great fire burned down London in 1666. I wonder if this created awareness of the danger of quickly spreading fire in modern cities that influenced these halakhic authorities.

IV. Modern Times

More recently, the *Mishnah Berurah* (334:73), *Arukh Ha-Shulchan* (334:43), *Kaf Ha-Chaim* (334:131), and *Chazon Ish* (quoted in Rav Chaim Kanievsky, *Shoneh Halakhos* 334:36) accept this broad, lenient approach. Rav Osher Weiss (*Responsa Minchas Asher*, vol. 1 no. 27) asks whether this should still apply in Israel today, when so many houses are made of stone. He investigated and concluded that the danger of fire spreading through electrical wires is very strong. Additionally, gas pipes and tanks can explode. If high-voltage lines fall, they can be very dangerous. Therefore, given modern conditions, any house fire can threaten many lives beyond the house itself and must be extinguished on Shabbos.

Despite all this change, the Talmud's lesson seems more necessary than ever. The self-control and commitment required to watch your house burn down while you refrain from saving it is awe-inspiring. We should never see such loss in our lives. However, we can learn from this the proper priorities in our lives. We need to value "stuff" less, value lives more, and recognize that the religious life can sometimes demand great sacrifice. And those sacrifices are worth it.

Driving Under the Influence of Coffee

Questions of kosher status sometimes mask larger dilemmas that, when uncovered, demonstrate the complexity of applying straightforward laws. Principles are easy. Life is messy.

The rabbis of Kosharot, an Israeli kosher supervision agency associated with Mechon Ha-Torah Ve-Ha-Aretz, were asked a complex question that is unique to Israel: Is it religiously problematic to buy coffee at a gas station that remains open on Shabbos? Across the globe, Jews can safely assume that gas stations, tankers, and convenience stores are operated by gentiles, who are not bound by Shabbos regulations. However, in Israel, Jews often perform the gas station work. If you buy gas or goods at a gas station, particularly Saturday night, are you benefiting from or encouraging Shabbos desecration?

The rabbis of Kosharot broke down the question into its different parts and concluded that it is best to buy at a gas station that is closed on Shabbos. However, if there is a great need and no better option, you are permitted to buy from a gas station that is open on Shabbos. One example they gave is a driver who is tired and needs a cup of coffee to stay awake. This need overrides any of the other concerns discussed (*Emunas Itekha*, no. 98 p. 35).

In a letter to the editor (ibid., no. 100, p. 183), Uriel Banner takes issue with the "permission" to buy coffee. He argues that it is an obligation. You should not be strict in one area of *halakhah* (possible benefit from or support of Shabbos violation) if it will lead to a greater violation (endangering oneself and others). Driving while tired is a life-threatening danger. He quotes a responsum by Rav Shmuel Wosner (*Shevet Ha-Levi* 8:301) about someone who fell asleep in the middle of a long drive from New York to Montreal and got in an accident. Rav Wosner ruled that the driver was negligent for driving without sufficient sleep beforehand.

Rav Mordechai Walnow of Kosharot responded with an even stronger stance (ibid., p. 185). Coffee will not help someone who is too tired to drive. Its effect is temporary and otherwise limited. If you feel so tired that you might fall asleep at the wheel, you must pull over to the side of the road and rest, and perhaps splash cold water on your face. If, after this, you still feel like you need coffee, then you may buy it from a gas station even if it is not closed on Shabbos.

All this raises the question of how tired is too tired to drive? Many of us are constantly on the move and always tired. It is easy to say "Don't drive when you are too tired" but much harder to define the parameters. Especially when you have young children in the car, it is difficult to make the decision to pull over to the side of the road and rest your eyes. You usually do not know you are so tired that your eyes are closing until they are closing, at which point it might be too late. I don't have an answer to the dilemma other than recommending resting in advance (often impractical), opening your window (weather permitting), and drinking coffee.

One thing this issue makes clear is that even if a state is subjective, it is still real. We may not know the precise boundary, but it is clear that you can be too tired to drive. Some people argue that if a boundary cannot be defined, the state is meaningless. For example, if you can dispute the precise definition of heresy then nothing is heresy. Exhaustion is one of many examples that demonstrate that gray areas do not undermine the state. Some people really are too tired to drive.

PART 4: JEWISH HOLIDAYS

Seder on the Rooftops

Some modern thinkers—mainly Jewish universalists—express discomfort with the *seder* recitation of "*Shefokh chamasekha* – Pour out Your wrath." In this passage of the Haggadah, we call on God to punish the heathens who do not recognize Him and who destroyed the Temple in Jerusalem. While this is a direct biblical quote (Ps. 79:6-7), and addresses specifically the gentile nations that destroyed the Temple, it seems at a superficial reading to be directed at all gentiles, which makes some uneasy. Some have revised this text, substituting a more positive version for the biblical passage. The Schechter Haggadah (Jerusalem, 2009, p. 268) quotes this nineteenth-century German alternative text: "Pour out Your spirit on all flesh / May all nations come to serve You / Together in one language / Because the Lord is the Sovereign of Nations." This entire attempt not only misreads the biblical text as anti-gentile rather than anti-destroyer, it fails to ask why this passage is placed right after the meal, as we open the door before we continue Hallel.

Many possible explanations have been offered. *Or Zaru'a* explains that we have largely completed the extensive discussion of Egypt and now we curse their evil. Meiri connects the four cups of wine to the four exiles we have endured. As we pour the fourth cup, we ask God to avenge the persecution we have endured in those exiles. The Rema (*Orach Chaim* 480:1) says that we open the door as a show of faith in God's protection. We recite "Pour out Your wrath" to show our faith that God will bring the final redemption. (All these and more are brought in Rav Menachem Kasher's *Haggadah Shelemah*, pp. 179-180.)

In his recently published *Haggadah Yesamach Av*, Rav Eliyahu B. Shulman offers a simple but fascinating history-based explanation. The Gemara (*Pesachim* 85b-86a) says that in the time of the Temple, Hallel split the roofs of Jerusalem. Even though people were not allowed to eat the Pesach sacrifice on their roofs, they would eat the meal inside their homes and then go onto their roofs to sing Hallel. Imagine the entire city full of families singing on their roofs.

Rav Shulman quotes Rav Shmuel Baruch Eliezrov, who in his *Devar Shmuel* (*Pesachim* 86a) says that his grandfather, Rav Yosef Salant, used this historical practice to explain our current practice of opening our door for "Pour out Your wrath." The Pesach sacrifice has to be eaten in the home, with the group. Therefore, people would close their doors to ensure that everyone ate the food in the correct place. After they finished eating, they opened their doors to go up to their roofs and sing Hallel. We open our doors in commemoration of the ancient practice of singing Hallel on the rooftops.

Rav Shulman adds that nowadays we open our doors and see that we are in exile, not Jerusalem, and in our grief ask God to avenge our plight. He further explains why Hallel is interrupted with the meal.

The Mishnah (*Pesachim* 116b) records a debate over how much of Hallel to recite before the meal. According to Beis Shammai, just the first paragraph (Ps. 113); according to Beis Hillel, also the second paragraph (Ps. 114, "*Be-tzeis Yisrael mi-Mitzrayim*, When Israel went forth from Egypt"). On the one hand, we need to recite Hallel over the Pesach sacrifice, which was the meal. On the other hand, people wanted to say Hallel on the roofs. Therefore, we start Hallel before the meal, say a little, eat the meal, and then finish Hallel (in Temple times on the rooftops). According to Beis Shammai, one paragraph suffices for starting Hallel. According to Beis Hillel, we include the second paragraph which discusses the Exodus so we finish the Maggid (story) section of the evening on the second cup of wine, before the meal.

When we think about how the *seder* progressed in ancient times, our current practice seems like a faint shadow of its former glory. Each family conducted its own *seder* and then joined with the community for glorious Hallel. Today, we open the door to start the communal phase, only to realize in frustration that due to our exile we must return to our tables and forego the experience. Modern revisions of the *Shefokh Chamasekha* passage completely fail to express this frustration of exile and the hope for rebuilding the Temple and reinstituting the sacrificial system.

Buying Clothes During *Sefirah*

The period between Pesach and Shavuos contains a mourning period—different days depending on one's custom—during which certain joyous behaviors are forbidden (commonly called *Sefirah* because this period also includes the counting—"*sefirah*" in Hebrew—of the *Omer*). These mourning customs have developed over time. However, I often hear confusion about the permissibility of buying new clothes during this mourning period. The short answer is that it is allowed. The long answer is that it might not be allowed.

During the mourning period prior to the summer fast day of Tisha B'Av, we experience an intense mourning over the destruction of the Temple in Jerusalem. Among the activities forbidden by custom is reciting the "*Shehecheyanu*" blessing on new fruits or new clothes. Some early authorities, such as the author of *Keli Yakar* (*Olelos Efraim* 2:107) and the *Eliyah Zuta* (593) in the name of Rabbeinu Yerucham (1:5), rule that this also applies to the *Sefirah*. *Yosef Ometz* (845), Rav Chaim Palaggi (*Mo'ed Kol Chai* 6:12) and his son Rav Yitzchak Palaggi (*Yefeh La-Lev* 2:493) say that the custom is to refrain from wearing new clothes during *Sefirah*. However, the vast majority of authorities make no mention of this custom to refrain from reciting the blessing of "*Shehecheyanu*" during *Sefirah*.

Four customs seem to have developed about this issue:

1. **No *Shehecheyanu*:** Some people are strict and do not do eat new fruits or buy new items that would necessitate a

Shehecheyanu blessing. Rav Mordechai Eliyahu (*Ma'amar Mordekhai Le-Mo'adim U-Li-Zemannim* 20:55) says that some have this practice (*yesh nohagim*).

2. **Yes *Shehecheyanu*:** Some have no such practice whatsoever and feel free to eat new fruits and buy new clothes. Rav Eliyahu (ibid.) says that this is the standard practice (*ve-khen nohagim*). *Kaf Ha-Chaim* (593:4) and *Mishnah Berurah* (593:2) take this approach, as well.

3. **Only On Fruits:** Rav Ovadiah Yosef (*Yechavveh Da'as* 1:24) distinguishes between reciting a *Shehecheyanu* on new fruits and on buying new things. He argues that the practice of refraining from reciting *Shehecheyanu* on new fruits is a mistake and should not be observed. You do not even need to annul your custom before discontinuing it because it is an error. However, he suggests refraining from wearing new clothes during *Sefirah*, based on the comments of Rav Chaim Palaggi and others (mentioned above). If there is a need to wear new clothes, wear them for the first time on Shabbos, when there is no mourning and therefore no problem in reciting "*Shehecheyanu*."

4. **If Necessary:** Some desire to act strictly and refrain from doing anything that necessitates reciting a "*Shehecheyanu*" during *Sefirah*. However, when a need arises—such as a sale or a young man returned for a brief yeshiva break who needs to go shopping—you buy the clothing and wear it for the first time on Shabbos or at a mitzvah celebration like a circumcision (*Peninei Halakhah, Zemanim* 3:11 says that this should be the practice for those who are strict).

If someone asks me whether they may buy clothes during *Sefirah*, I tell them the second view above, adopted by the *Mishnah Berurah* and *Kaf Ha-Chaim*. But really there are more views. When it comes to customs, custom is as custom does. They evolve over time organically. I suspect that the strict opinion is slowly gaining ground because of confusion with the Three Weeks. Eventually, people will observe the two mourning periods in the same way. Perhaps this will become the standard custom. Until then, we still have the *Mishnah Berurah*.

Staying up Most of the Night

I. Learning and Sleeping

On Shavuos, many stay up all night learning Torah and go to sleep after early morning services. When the holiday follows Shabbos, most people have time to rest before the learning marathon. Other years, some of us rush from a full day of work straight into the holiday. In those years, staying up all night is more of a challenge. What if you can't make it through the night?

Rav Osher Weiss (*Responsa Minchas Asher*, vol. 2 no. 6) addresses the proper approach to prayer on Shavuos morning after studying Torah throughout the night. Some people are so exhausted that they can barely pray, much less with deep intent. Should they go to sleep and wake up for later services? Is this even allowed? Normally you are not allowed to go to sleep when the time for a mitzvah approaches (generally within half an hour of the beginning time for that mitzvah). If so, within half an hour of dawn, you should not be allowed to go to sleep even if you plan to pray later.

II. Napping and Sleeping

Rav Weiss quotes Rav Ya'akov Emden (*Siddur*) as forbidding taking a nap within half an hour of the time for the afternoon *minchah* prayers. In contrast, Rav Yitzchak Isaac Chaver (*Responsa Binyan Olam*, no. 1) permits afternoon naps. He distinguishes between daytime naps, which are short, and nighttime sleeping, which

145

is long. There is little danger that a nap before mincha time will prevent you from praying. However, a full night's worth of sleep can last the whole time for morning prayers, preventing you from fulfilling the mitzvah. Therefore, Rav Chaver permits daytime naps but forbids someone who stayed up all night from sleeping before his morning prayers.

The *Siddur Ha-Gra* (by Rav Yitzchak Moltzen) quotes Rav Yehoshua Leib Diskin and Rav Shmuel Salant as saying that someone who wakes up in the morning after sunrise but before his normal time for waking up may not stay in bed and go back to sleep. He is obligated to pray and may not avoid this obligation by going back to sleep. However, the *Chazon Ish* (*Dinim Ve-Hanhagos* 4:13) says that you may go back to sleep. Rav Weiss quotes all this and adds that in his opinion you obviously may return to sleep. We find no mention of this prohibition in any early source. Why would we be concerned that you won't wake up at your regular time just because you woke up earlier also?

III. Reawakening

Similarly, continues Rav Weiss, if you have an alarm clock that normally wakes you up, you may go to sleep after sunrise and rely on the clock to wake you up for services. While Rav Shlomo Zalman Auerbach did not allow use of an alarm clock in the place of a person, Rav Weiss disagrees. Whatever works for you suffices.

Regarding Shavuos, Rav Weiss says that a man's wife or children can be trusted to wake him up for morning prayers. Even if you don't ask them, if that is their regular practice then you can assume they will do it on Shavuos also. Therefore, you may go to sleep after learning all night and then wake up for the later services.

IV. Learning Through Shavuos Night

Rav Weiss adds that the custom of learning throughout Shavuos night comes from the *Zohar* (*Emor*) which specifically mentions the *entire* night. Therefore, Rav Weiss recommends that someone who gets too tired to pray should learn until after sunrise, go to sleep, and wake up for services later. However, he points out that the *Seder Ha-Yom* says that you should learn on Shavuos the entire night *or most of it*. Based on this, Rav Weiss recommends to people who are old and weak that they should learn Torah until after midnight, at which point the majority of the night has passed.

I find Rav Weiss' reasoning difficult. Yes, if I go to sleep at a normal hour, then my wife, children, or alarm clock can wake me at my normal hour or a little later. But if I am up all night and only go to bed at 4:30 or 5 a.m., nothing will wake me up in time to get to synagogue by 9 a.m. What works for me in a normal situation will not work for me in that highly unusual circumstance.

Maybe Rav Weiss can function on such little sleep—maybe most people can—but I can't. But as Rav Weiss wrote, if it works for you then feel free to do it.

Learning Torah on Shabbos Erev Tisha B'Av

One of the prohibitions of Tisha B'Av is learning Torah, which brings you joy. You may only learn certain sad parts of the Torah. The Rema (*Shulchan Arukh, Orach Chaim* 553:2) records a custom to refrain from learning Torah on the afternoon before Tisha B'Av. Presumably, if you enter the mournful day with these Torah thoughts on your mind, the joy will linger with you. He adds that when the observance of Tisha B'Av falls out on Sunday, we maintain this practice and refrain from studying *Pirkei Avos* on Shabbos afternoon.

Mishnah Berurah (ad loc., 8) points out that this must only merely be a stringency. On the afternoon before Tisha B'Av, we are allowed to eat, drink, wash, and do other practices forbidden on the day itself. Certainly, on a technical level we are allowed to learn Torah. He also quotes a number of authorities who felt this was a bad stringency, including Maharshal, Vilna Gaon, and *Chayei Adam*. The *Mishnah Berurah* concludes that whoever wishes to act leniently may do so.

Another important view on this was expressed by Rav Yosef Dov Soloveitchik, the author of *Beis Ha-Levi* and namesake of his famous American great-grandson. The story is told[41] that one time when Rav Soloveitchik was visiting Minsk, a wealthy businessman associated with a group of *maskilim* ("enlightened" religious

---

41. I am utilizing the report in the *Haggadah Shel Pesach Mi-Beis Ha-Levi* (Jerusalem, 1983), pp. 308-309.

reformers) approached him. This gentleman told Rav Soloveitchik that their generation requires rabbis to rule leniently, in order to prevent Jews from leaving the path of observance (some arguments never change). Rav Soloveitchik replied sarcastically that, indeed, he agreed and rules leniently on a number of matters. The businessman asked for examples and Rav Soloveitchik provided the following seven, all of which are really stringencies formulated as leniencies:

1. Some rule that if you fail to pray by halakhic midnight (*chatzos*), you have lost the opportunity to fulfill the mitzvah (this is the view of Rabbenu Yonah). Rav Soloveitchik said that he rules leniently, that if you failed to pray by midnight, you may pray any time throughout the night.

2. Some only allow people to wear two pairs of *tefillin* (Rabbenu Tam in addition to the standard Rashi) if the individuals are extremely pious (this is the view of the *Shulchan Arukh, Orach Chaim* 34:3). Rav Soloveitchik is lenient and allows anyone who wants to wear the second pair of *tefillin*.

3. Some people are careful not to recite *piyyutim* (liturgical poems) during the regular prayer service because the poems serve as interruptions (*Shulchan Arukh, Orach Chaim* 68:1). Rav Soloveitchik permits these additions to the prayers.

4. Some forbid learning Torah on Shabbos afternoon before Tisha B'Av (the Rema, discussed above). Rav Soloveitchik rules leniently and permits learning any kind of Torah until Tisha B'Av begins.

5. Some forbid fasting on Rosh Hashanah (see *Shulchan Arukh, Orach Chaim* 596), even for the sake of repentance. Rav Soloveitchik permits penitent fasting.

6. Some forbid people from fasting two consecutive days of Yom Kippur (*Shulchan Arukh, Orach Chaim* 624:5), as we observe

all other holidays in the Diaspora. Rav Soloveitchik permits observing two days of Yom Kippur.

7. Some rule that if you forget to count one night of the *Omer*, you cannot count future nights with a blessing (*Shulchan Arukh, Orach Chaim* 489:8). Rav Soloveitchik rules that even if you miss one night, you can continue with a blessing.

Of course, these were not the kinds of leniencies the *Maskilim* desired. They wanted a life less bound by *halakhah*, allowing more personal freedom. Rav Soloveitchik did not believe in watering down religion in an attempt to keep people from drifting away.

Deodorant on Tisha B'Av

The digest of Tisha B'Av laws in *The Koren Mesorat HaRav Kinot*[42] specifically mentions that one may apply deodorant to oneself on Tisha B'Av (p. 787 par. 17). While it would normally be considered anointing oneself, one of the forbidden activities of Tisha B'Av, it falls under an exception:

> One is allowed to anoint oneself for any purpose that is not pleasurable (S.A., O.H. 554:15). This includes medical ointments and deodorant (B.H. 554:15).

I wrote this section of the book and specifically this passage, but it does not solely represent my personal view. It was reviewed by both Rav Menachem Genack and Rav Hershel Schachter, as well as others, prior to publication. I would like to explain the background behind this decision.

While anointing oneself is forbidden on various occasions, this is only when anointing for pleasure. Doing it for medical reasons is allowed. But the in-between cases that aren't clear include anointing oneself with perfumed oil for reasons that are neither medical nor pleasurable, such as to remove an unpleasant odor. In the laws of Yom Kippur, the *Shulchan Arukh* (*Orach Chaim* 614:1)

---

42. Published by Koren and OU Press (Jerusalem, 2010) with commentary on the *Kinos* adapted from Tisha B'Av tapes of Rav Joseph B. Soloveitchik.

forbids rubbing oil on yourself even to remove an unpleasant odor. Only anointing for medical purposes is allowed.

However, in the laws of public fasts, when discussing a fast day declared in a severe drought, the *Shulchan Arukh* (*Orach Chaim* 575:3) writes that anointing is forbidden but is allowed to remove an odor. Regarding Tisha B'Av, the *Shulchan Arukh* (*Orach Chaim* 524:15) does not specify whether anointing to remove an odor is allowed. This leaves us the question whether Tisha B'Av is like Yom Kippur in this regard or like a public fast. Is any non-pleasurable anointing allowed or only medical anointing?

The *Mateh Yehudah* (ad loc.) quotes the Gemara (*Pesachim* 54b) which says that the only difference between Tisha B'Av and Yom Kippur is that the doubtful time is forbidden on the latter and permitted on the former. Evidently, the rule of anointing is the same for both days. Therefore, the Mateh Yehudah rules that anointing to remove an odor is forbidden on Tisha B'Av.

However, the *Mishnah Berurah* (*Bi'ur Halakhah* 554:15 s.v. *sikhah*) argues that the *Mateh Yehudah* is reading that passage overly literally. Not only does the Talmud Yerushalmi (quoted in *Bi'ur Ha-Gra* on *Orach Chaim* 614:1) say explicitly in multiple places that Tisha B'Av follows other fast days and not Yom Kippur in this respect, but the Gemara (*Ta'anis* 30a) says that all the rules of mourning (*shivah*) apply on Tisha B'Av. Since the Gemara (*Ta'anis* 13b) explicitly permits a mourner during *shivah* to anoint himself in order to remove an odor, by implication this permits it also on Tisha B'Av.

The *Mishnah Berurah* therefore rejects the *Mateh Yehudah*'s ruling and permits anointing oneself on Tisha B'Av in order to remove an odor. This is the equivalent of applying scented deodorant, which is allowed even on Tisha B'Av.

Sheva Berakhos in a Sukkah

I. A *Chuppah* in a *Sukkah*

After a couple is married, they celebrate with family and friends for a week.[43] Each celebratory meal is accompanied with special blessings during the grace after meals, traditionally called *Sheva Berakhos*. However, the form of celebration has changed significantly since talmudic times, requiring a reevaluation of the practice. The holiday of Sukkos highlights the transformation of post-wedding practices and the resulting halakhic implications.

The Gemara (*Sukkah* 25b) says that a groom and his attendants are exempt from eating in a *sukkah*. In talmudic times, a newly married couple would have a *chuppah* canopy in their home in which they would celebrate for a week with friends (and/or attendants). The Gemara explains that their joy must be at a meal in the *chuppah*. The *chuppah* cannot be placed in a *sukkah*, either because a normal *sukkah* with only three walls lacks privacy, or the possibility of the bride remaining alone with male guests if the groom has to leave to use the facilities. Due to these logistical problems in relocating the *chuppah* to a *sukkah*, the *Sheva Berakhos* were held indoors.

---

43. However, interestingly, the *Arukh Ha-Shulchan* (*Orach Chaim* 640:14) writes that the custom in turn-of-the-twentieth century Poland was not to have a meal each of the seven days of the week. See also *She'arim Metzuyanim Ba-Halakhah* (*Kuntres Acharon* 149:3) from the *Levush*.

II. What Is a *Chuppah*?

Tosafos (ad loc., s.v. *ein*) infer quite reasonably that if a couple leave their *chuppah* for a meal, they do not recite *Sheva Berakhos* at that meal. If they would, then there would be no exemption from *sukkah*. However, the Rosh (*Sukkah* 2:8) quotes another opinion which holds that the Gemara only discusses the case of a couple leaving temporarily for a meal and then returning to their *chuppah*. In such a case, the celebration must take place in the *chuppah*. If a bride and groom leave their *chuppah* permanently, such as they move to another house or even another city, then the celebration follows them. The Ran (ad loc.) goes even further, explaining the Gemara to mean that the main celebration of a bride and groom is in the *chuppah*, but we can still have a lesser celebration elsewhere. He adds that the common practice in Spain of his time was to recite *Sheva Berakhos* wherever the couple are, although he thinks they should be strict and not allow this.

The *Shulchan Arukh* (*Even Ha-Ezer* 62:10) rules like the Rosh, the middle opinion, that if a couple moves to a new place, their new home is considered their new *chuppah*. According to this opinion, you do not need a canopy to have a *chuppah*. The *chuppah* is the couple's primary residence, where the celebrations should take place. The *Taz* (ad loc., 7) disagrees with this explanation of the Rosh. He interprets the Rosh as saying that as long as the couple plans on returning to their home, wherever they eat a wedding-type meal is called a *chuppah*.

However, the *Taz* adds an even more important historical concern. He points out that in modern times, we no longer have a canopy beyond the actual wedding ceremony. Is the reference to a *chuppah* literally to the canopy or does it refer to the couple's home? If it refers to the home, then the lack of a canopy is halakhically irrelevant. The *Taz* believes it refers specifically to a canopy. Therefore, the question remains how *halakhah* must address the changed situation. During talmudic times, the post-wedding celebrations took place in the *chuppah*. Today, there is no *chuppah* and the post-wedding celebrations take place in a variety of locations. The *Taz* explains that the *Sheva Berakhos* are a function of the celebration and therefore are recited at any celebratory meal for the bride and groom.

This is quite a radical step, although the *Taz* mitigates it somewhat by pointing out that the Ran's view allows *Sheva Berakhos* in other houses. And even though the Ran concludes that we should be strict for the other opinions, the practice in Spain in his time was like this lenient view. The *Taz* adds this lenient view to his historical argument.[44]

III. Moving a *Chuppah*

Today, two practices dominate. Rav Shlomo Zalman Auerbach (*Minchas Shlomo* 3:103:20) writes that Sephardim generally follow the old practice and only recite *Sheva Berakhos* in the couple's home, although some Sephardim are more lenient. Generally, they believe that a *chuppah* refers to the couple's home, not specifically the canopy. They also reject the *Taz*'s explanation that wherever the couple celebrates with a meal is called a *chuppah*. Therefore, the original rules remain in place. Ashkenazim follow the *Taz* and recite the *Sheva Berakhos* at any celebratory meal for the newlywed couple. As long as the meal has extra food, drink, and joy for the couple, Ashkenazim can recite *Sheva Berakhos*.[45] Additionally, the

---

44. Many other Ashkenazic authorities agree with this ruling. The *Taz* quotes the Maharal of Prague as ruling similarly. The *Beis Shmuel* (ad loc., 13) and *Yam Shel Shlomo* (*Kesubos* 1:20) also agree.

45. This is the language of Rav Auerbach, ibid. Rav Gershon Zaks (*Mo'adei Ha-Gershuni*, ch. 31) says in the name of his father, Rav Mendel Zaks (son-in-law of the *Chafetz Chaim*), that any place in which there are special preparations for the bride and groom is called a *chuppah*.

Magen Avraham (640:11) points out that today we usually build a *sukkah* with four walls (and invite both men and women to a *Sheva Berakhos*), so the Gemara's concerns about relocating a *chuppah* to a *sukkah* no longer apply.

How does this affect *Sheva Berakhos* in a *sukkah*? The Rambam (*Mishnah Torah, Hilkhos Sukkah* 6:3) follows the Gemara above that a groom is exempt from *sukkah*. However, the Rosh (ibid.) points out that R. Zeira in the Gemara ate in a *sukkah* and then rejoiced in a *chuppah*, fulfilling both requirements when he was a groom. While this could imply an allowance for stringency, the Rosh believes this is the conclusion of the Gemara, requiring a groom to eat in a *sukkah* without *Sheva Berakhos*. The *Mishnah Berurah* (640:33) concludes that a groom is obligated to eat in a *sukkah* without reciting a blessing on the *sukkah*. However, the *Piskei Teshuvos* (640:9 n. 29) quotes the *Arukh Ha-Shulchan* (ad loc., 14), Rav Auerbach (*Shemiras Shabbos Ke-Hilkhasah*, ch. 68 n. 115), and others who rule that a groom is obligated in a *sukkah* and should recite its blessing.

Therefore, despite the explicit ruling in the Gemara, Ashkenazim (and some Sephardim) today celebrate *Sheva Berakhos* in a *sukkah*, with *Sheva Berakhos* and a blessing on the *sukkah*.

Women Dancing with Torah Scrolls

I don't like dancing, not on Simchas Torah, nor at bar mitvahs, nor even at my wedding. It's a chore I've learned to deal with. Looking over the *mechitzah* on Simchas Torah, I am both troubled and envious.

Many of the women I see look very bored. Why should they sit bored on this holiday? On the other hand, they do not have this communal, family, and customary obligation to dance. They can sit in the women's section and open a *sefer* and learn. I can't do that without being reprimanded.[46] In many synagogues, the women watch the men dance, some with great delight, others bored and others just talking with each other and ignoring the dancing. To level the field and give women more options, decades ago some synagogues began women dances and even introduced Torah scrolls into the women's dances. This was, and remains, controversial.

In 2014, the Beit Hillel organization in Israel published a responsum permitting women to dance with Torah scrolls on Simchas Torah.[47] They base their view on Rav Nachum Rabinovich's ruling in *Si'ach Nachum* (no. 40), which some mistakenly claim permits this practice. Without detracting from the men and women of Beit Hillel, I cite here contrary opinions.

---

46. Yes, I've been reprimanded for failing to help create a festive atmosphere.

47. http://eng.beithillel.org.il/responsa/women-dancing-with-torah-scroll/

Primary among them is Rav Joseph B. Soloveitchik. He is quoted by his nephew, Rav Moshe Meiselman, as deeming the practice impermissible (he does not say forbidden). While Rav Meiselman's assertions in the name of his uncle can sometimes be questioned, readers should note that the following quote appeared in a book published in 1978 as part of Rav Norman Lamm's Library of Jewish Law and Ethics. I am not suggesting that Rav Lamm agrees with everything in this book (he indicates in his Foreword that he does not). I am suggesting that if an explicit quote in this book in Rav Soloveitchik's name was incorrect, in all likelihood he would have made it known. I am not aware of any claim that this specific depiction of his view is inaccurate.

Rav Moshe Meiselman wrote (*Jewish Woman in Jewish Law*,[48] p. 146):

An associated issue, although technically totally different, is the permissibility of women dancing in the synagogue with Torah scrolls during hakafot on Simhat Torah. This practice has been opposed by all contemporary rabbinic authorities. My revered teacher, Rabbi Joseph B. Soloveichik, told me that he opposed this practice when questioned by synagogues in Brookline, Massachusetts, and New York City. The basis for this ruling, he told me, is the Talmud in Berakhot (63a) which says that just as there is an etiquette that regulates one's behaviour when visiting someone else's home, so too there is a tradition that regulates behaviour in the synagogue. Thus, for example, eating in the synagogue is not permitted. An element of proper synagogue behaviour, such as the prohibition against eating in the synagogue, is explicated in legal detail by the Talmud and by subsequent codes of Jewish law. The

---

48. Ktav, 1978

same applies to the introduction of innovations which our ancestors considered to be in conflict with the feeling of respect and awe owed to the synagogue. Proper synagogue behaviour is determined by practice and tradition. Since it has been the age-old practice of synagogues that women do not dance with Torah scrolls during hakafot, the introduction of this practice would be a violation of synagogue etiquette.

Rav Menachem Schneerson, the late Lubavitcher Rebbe, wrote a 1975 letter to Rav Shlomo Riskin, voicing his opposition to women's dancing with a Torah scroll on Simchas Torah.[49] He argues that:

1. We may not create new synagogue customs
2. We may not change existing synagogue customs
3. The Rema only permits menstruating women to attend synagogue and pray with the community—responding "*Amen*" and "*Yehei shemeih rabbah*" because of "great sadness" if they are prevented from attending synagogue. Rav Schneerson infers that only attending synagogue is permitted and not other changes.

More recently, Rav Yaakov Ariel opposes women dancing with a Torah scroll.[50] He points out that celebrating the Torah does not require dancing with a Torah scroll. Some communities have the tradition that even men do not dance with Torah scrolls. Women are right to want to celebrate the Torah but they should do so creatively, finding their own way to do so rather than imitating how (some) men celebrate.

---

49. http://www.haoros.com/Archive/index.asp?cat=11&haoro=7&kovetz=902#ftnref37
50. http://www.yeshiva.org.il/ask/1197

Rav Dov Lior writes that throughout the generations women have not danced with Torah scrolls.[51] The differences between men and women are real, each with their own religious roles. When women act in ways that men traditionally have, they detract from the respect due their own roles. Therefore, women certainly should not dance with Torah scrolls.

I don't claim that this list is comprehensive. In the end, it is up to the synagogue rabbi to consult with his *posek* and decide what is permissible and appropriate.

---

51. http://www.yeshiva.org.il/ask/379

Is Every Day Thanksgiving?

Thanking God is an integral part of Jewish life. We receive so much from God—from the time we wake up each morning with our full physical and mental abilities, as we go through our busy days of ups and downs, until we go to sleep with our families in our homes—that praise should naturally flow from our mouths as we recognize our good fortune. Recognition of our dependence on a higher power, the humility of human awareness, forms a crucial basis of the religious personality. The *Chovos Ha-Levavos* (*Sha'ar Avodas Hashem*, introduction) builds this gratitude into a philosophical foundation of mitzvah observance: We owe God so much, the least we can do is follow His rules. For an observant Jew who prays and recites blessing throughout each day, every day is Thanksgiving.

However, the Talmud (*Shabbos* 118b) seems to reject this idea when it states that anyone who says Hallel every day is a blasphemer. Apparently, thanking God daily is an inappropriate response to our divine gifts. This startling idea challenges not only the prayers and blessings we recite but the mitzvah observance that the *Chovos Ha-Levavos* says should stem from our gratitude. If we are not expected to thank God every day, why should we show gratitude by observing *mitzvos*?

Clearly, there is something special about *Hallel* that distinguishes it from other, expected praise. The Gemara itself says that *Pesukei De-Zimra*, part of the morning prayers, is an appropriate daily recitation. With the over 100 blessings we recite daily, our lives are filled with expressions of gratitude to God. *Hallel*, however, should not be recited on a daily basis. Why not?

Rashi (ad loc, s.v. *harei*) explains that *Hallel* was established for specific days—holidays. If you recite it daily, if you remove it from its proper context and treat it like a song or rote recitation, you don't understand its significance. *Hallel* is reserved for special occasions, for days of extra joy and praise. It is intended to commemorate great miracles, not everyday events. If we fail to distinguish between different reasons to praise God, if we ignore context and instead equate all divine gifts, we fail to truly appreciate all that God does for us.

This is a surprising message. We normally associate religious enthusiasm with a higher level of worship. We aspire to pray with inspiration and intention, with uplifting tunes and soulful tears. However, the Talmud is telling us that everything has its right place and time. When we turn regular days into holy days, we give lip service to the Lord. How can this be? How can honest, well-intentioned praise be turned away? How can prayerful songs be rejected?

Rabbenu Yonah (*Berakhos*, 23b s.v. *ve-ha-amar*) explains that our prayers reflect our beliefs in how God runs the world. In Judaism, not just behavior but also belief is important. Judaism teaches a worldview, an understanding of how God interacts with the world. When we pray improperly, even if inadvertently, we may be reflecting an improper religious worldview.

God runs the world in a hidden manner. Nature is a divine creation through which God's plan is enacted every day, every moment. The religious observer sees the divine hand everywhere, hiding in our daily lives, moving events behind the scenes. Every day we thank God for the natural gifts He gives us, the successes we achieve with His help, the wise choices we make with His guidance.

These are miracles but of a natural kind—hidden, constant, bound up with human action.

Then there are supernatural miracles. They dazzle us with their wonder, demonstrating God's power to all who are willing to see. A miracle is rare, an occurrence about which legends are told, stories we transmit for generations. We celebrate miracles on our holidays and discuss them in our sacred texts. Miracles sometimes—rarely—occur even in the post-biblical world, and when they do we recite a special blessing commemorating it (*Shulchan Arukh*, *Orach Chaim* 218) and say *Hallel*.

Every day we thank God for the everyday miracles, the natural course of providence in which the divine hand runs the world. On holidays, we thank God for the supernatural miracles, the wonders that have come to define Jewish history. Confusing this order by reciting *Hallel* daily, singing about miracles rather than praying about ordinary life, risks confusing how God runs the world (*Meshekh Chokhmah*, Lev. 26:4). It reflects a misunderstanding that can lead to denial of God's role in the everyday world. If we only care about miracles, we neglect the divine role in everything else that happens, mistakenly relying on our own, limited abilities.

The American celebration of Thanksgiving is traditionally about thanking God for the bounty He has given us—for our sustenance, health, and family. In Jewish thought, every day is that type of Thanksgiving for natural gifts. Note that this does not imply that there is anything within Jewish law opposing the celebration of Thanksgiving, which is a separate discussion. Celebrating the daily Thanksgiving once a year, in the fall, risks reducing the thankful praise we offer God every day. However, if done right, it may serve as a teaching moment, an example of the gratitude we must show every day.

Is the Yom Ha-Atzma'ut Liturgy for Everyone?

The additional prayers for Yom Ha-Atzma'ut (Israel's Independence Day) are standard in Religious Zionist synagogues in Israel but much less so in America. I believe the reason reflects different ideological priorities outside of Israel, which can best be understood by examining the early documentation of the prayers' origin.

I. History

The most comprehensive study of the origins of the Yom Ha-Atzma'ut liturgy is Rav Shmuel Katz's extensive article in the three-volume series in honor of the seventieth anniversary of the Israeli Chief Rabbinate (*Ha-Rabbanut Ha-Rashit Le-Yisrael: Shivim Shanah Le-Yisudah*,[52] vol. 2, pp. 804-966). A translated and highly condensed summary is published in the recent *Koren Mahzor for Yom Ha-Atzma'ut and Yom Yerushalayim*, which in addition to the full liturgy for the days includes extensive commentary and a large collection of important essays. Rav Katz studied the Chief Rabbinate archives as well as contemporary newspapers, particularly *Ha-Tzofeh*, the Religious Zionist organ, in order to recreate the discussion and evolving practices. The date and liturgy for a celebratory day was subject to debate and contradictory pronouncements.

At the time, the State was at war, Jerusalem was under siege, and the Chief Rabbis were dealing with numerous critical issues,

---

52. Heikhal Shlomo, 2002

including the arrival of Holocaust survivors, many of them widows with uncertain information about their husbands' deaths. Despite all this, the historical significance of renewed Jewish sovereignty in the land of Israel was overwhelming. When Israeli troops conquered parts of Jerusalem and raised an Israeli flag over the city, Rav Yitchak Herzog, the Ashkenazic Chief Rabbi, drove around and told anyone who asked him that this was the beginning of the Redemption (using the terminology of the Talmud (*Megillah* 17b) that the *Aschalta Di-Ge'ulah*, beginning of the Redemption, will be war) (Katz, p. 814).

Despite the contradictions in how to observe the day that would eventually be called by the Knesset "Yom Ha-Atzma'ut," I see one consistent thread throughout the proclamations of the Chief Rabbis: They declared the onset of the "*Aschalta Di-Ge'ulah*." After the UN vote approving a Jewish state in Israel, the Chief Rabbinate Council issued a proclamation declaring the Shabbos of *Parashas Vayeishev* of that year a day for prayer and thanksgiving. The proclamation concluded with a prayer that God grant them continued success as he did with the "beginning of the Redemption" (Katz, p. 816). In the first official communication by the Chief Rabbis about Yom Ha-Atzma'ut, a letter to the Chief Rabbinate Council sent three weeks after the Knesset declared the national holiday, the Chief Rabbis called it "the day of joy of the beginning of the Redemption of the Jewish people" (Katz, p. 833). Indeed, Rav Katz highlights this term in his quotations because it is highly significant.

II. Whose Prayers?

Years ago, I differentiated between Messianic Zionists and Hopeful Zionists.[53] The former believe, as the Chief Rabbis declared, that

---

53. See my e-book, "The Religious Zionism Debate," avavilable on my Academia.edu page: https://independent.academia.edu/GilStudent.

we are experiencing the beginning of the Messianic Redemption, even though the messiah has not yet appeared. Following Rav Tzvi Hirsch Kalischer, they see a messianic chronology in which the messiah arrives midway through the Redemption. In contrast, the latter group consciously refrains from interpreting current events in prophetic terms. We can't say with certainty what cosmic significance the events we are witnessing may have but we know that Jewish sovereignty in Israel is a good thing for both religious and practical reasons.

The Yom Ha-Atzma'ut liturgy was collected and composed from a Messianic Zionist perspective. For whatever reason, in 1949 the Chief Rabbis had difficulty settling on a liturgy for the day. Therefore, Rav Shaul Yisraeli and Rav Isser Yehuda Unterman—two formidable Torah scholars, the latter to eventually become Chief Rabbi—took the initiative to compose a service and present it to the Chief Rabbis for approval. With a few significant changes by Rav Bentzion Meir Chai Uziel, the Sephardic Chief Rabbi, this liturgy was approved and became standard for Yom Ha-Atzma'ut.

The liturgy for Yom Ha-Atzma'ut is unapologetically messianic. While many passages can be read as referring to redemption from danger, others clearly refer to the final Redemption. The commentary in the *Koren Mahzor for Yom Ha'atzmaut and Yom Yerushalayim* (Koren, 2015) points this out in places. The evening service includes selections from *Lekha Dodi*, commonly recited on Shabbos eve. As the commentary indicates, the paragraphs included refer to the Redemption: "The prayers of the current service were carefully chosen to express our acknowledgment that Yom HaAtzma'ut is only the beginning of the redemption process." This is a modest and restrained messianism but certainly not something a Hopeful Zionist would declare.

Toward the end of *Ma'ariv*, the congregation recites an adaptation of a passage from the blessing of Rosh Chodesh

(Koren, p. 112). The Yom Ha-Atzma'ut version declares that God redeemed us (not just our ancestors) from slavery to freedom and requests a complete redemption. This, too, indicates the beginning of the final Redemption.

Quite explicitly, after hearing shofar at the end of *Ma'ariv*, the congregation states: "May it be Your will, Lord our God and God of our fathers, that as we have merited to witness the beginning of redemption, so may we merit to hear the sound of the shofar of our righteous anointed one, swiftly in our days" (Koren, p. 114). You don't need a subtle reading to see the messianism here.

The *Al Ha-Nissim*, *Shehecheyanu*, and Hallel that some say (the Koren Machzor, pp. 88-91 explains the different views) do not, in my opinion, express messianic themes. They can equally refer to thanksgiving for military victory. The special *Haftarah* reading that some include is arguably messianic (Koren, p. 385ff from Jer. 10:32-12:6). While those of us in the Diaspora read this passage about the messiah on the eighth day of Pesach as a message of hope, its inclusion on Yom Ha-Atzma'ut seems like a messianic declaration. However, it could be plausibly interpreted as a hopeful reading. The prayer for the State of Israel, which many congregations read every Shabbos but is particularly important to Yom Ha-Atzma'ut, is explicitly messianic in referring to the State as "the first flowering of our redemption" (Koren, p. 387).

III. Why Pray?

What is a Hopeful Zionist to do? I see two reasons to recite the Yom Ha-Atzma'ut liturgy. One is as an expression of Messianic Zionism. While I was not educated in the Messianic Zionism path, which is mostly centered in the Hesder and other pro-army yeshivas, as I grow older I find myself more sympathetic to their theology, albeit not to their politics. This is somewhat contrarian, since the Disengagement from Gaza has caused this ideology to lose favor among many. While I am going in the opposite direction, I'm not there yet.

But there is another reason a Hopeful Zionist would recite the messianic liturgy of Yom Ha-Atzma'ut—as an act of patriotism. The Chief Rabbinate instituted these services. A patriotic Religious Zionist may view following the Chief Rabbinate's ruling a civic duty. What more appropriate way can there be to celebrate the establishment of a Jewish country than by following its official ceremonies and rituals? Put slightly differently, reciting the liturgy is an act of unity with all Israelis and all people who support the State of Israel—except that most Israelis do not go to synagogue on Yom Ha-Atzma'ut. It is more an act of affiliation with Religious Zionism. Yom Ha-Atzma'ut is the Religious Zionist day, for both Messianic and Hopeful Zionists, and therefore its liturgy is the text for all Religious Zionists. Viewed in this way, reciting the Yom Ha-Atzma'ut prayers is an act of religio-political affiliation, no small matter.

Some may put it more halakhically: The Chief Rabbi is the *Mara De-Asra* of the country, its official halakhic decisor. Therefore, his decision about the liturgy is binding even if its language and underlying worldview makes you uncomfortable. Rav Shaul Yisraeli (*Amud Ha-Yemini*, ch. 6) argues that the Chief Rabbi is the *Mara De-Asra*, but many find that really he is merely a figurehead. Additionally, those of us who, for whatever (usually insufficient) reason, live outside Israel are not subject to the Chief Rabbi's authority.

Is patriotism or religio-political affiliation enough of a reason to recite Messianic Zionist liturgy that you do not believe? For some, it may be. Others may not even consider the issue. Others may simply be comfortable reciting prayers that don't completely conform to their beliefs. But there are some Hopeful Zionists who reject the liturgy, following the example of Rav Joseph B.

Soloveitchik, who denounced the official Yom Ha-Atzma'ut liturgy in the harshest terms.[54]

Be that as it may, Koren's *Mahzor for Yom Ha'atzmaut and Yom Yerushalayim* is a fascinating study guide, full of important essays, insightful commentary, and sensitivity to the many ways of celebrating renewed Jewish sovereignty in the Holy Land.

---

54. See *The Rav Thinking Aloud: Transcripts of Personal Conversations with Rabbi Joseph B. Soloveitchik* (Holzer Books, 2009), p. 194ff.

Dirty Laundry on Chol Ha-Moed

Does the prohibition against washing dirty clothes on Chol Ha-Mo'ed, the intermediate days of the holiday, still apply today when doing laundry is relatively quick and easy?[55] In theory, washing laundry always should be allowed on Chol Ha-Mo'ed. Generally speaking, simple work needed for the day is allowed. If you run out of clean clothes, you need to do laundry so you can wear clean clothes on the holiday.

However, the Sages enacted a special prohibition forbidding the washing of laundry on Chol Ha-Mo'ed to ensure that we wash our clothes before the holiday (*Mo'ed Katan* 14a). Built into this rabbinic prohibition are specific exceptions, including someone with only one garment. Even if he washes it before the holiday, he will have to wash it again in Chol Ha-Mo'ed.

Times have changed since the Talmud. In olden days, washing laundry took hours. You had to take the clothes to a water source (river or stream), hand wash every item, hang them to dry and then press them. It was common to wear clothes for many days before placing them aside for laundry. Today, plumbing and technology have turned laundry into a relatively quick experience. The washing machine and dryer do all the work. We just have to carry and fold, and perhaps iron shirts if necessary. Most people today wear clothes once and then place them aside for laundry,

---

55. Note that this essay benefited from input of members of a private list with whom I discussed this issue.

particularly undergarments. Do we still have to follow this ancient enactment? If so, we need enough undergarments to last every day of the holiday without washing.

The simple answer is yes; the enactment remains in place because we cannot remove it. However, to some degree, the reason for the enactment still applies despite the advances in technology. With all the preparations for Yom Tov, it would be easy to delay work like laundry. But that would leave us entering Yom Tov without newly laundered clothing (see Rav Yekusiel Farkas, *Chol Ha-Mo'ed Ke-Hilkhaso* 5:3 n. 8). We must prepare for the entire holiday by washing our clothes rather than waiting until Chol Ha-Mo'ed.

However, given the changed behavior patterns regarding clean clothes, perhaps another leniency applies. On the one hand, we change our clothes every day, certainly our undergarments. Technology makes laundry much quicker and easier. On the other, clothing is less expensive. If for whatever reason, a person runs out of clean undergarments on Chol Ha-Mo'ed, he usually can buy plenty of new undergarments for less than $20. Most people will find that a minor expense. For people who can easily afford new undergarments but run out of clean undergarments on Chol Ha-Mo'ed, can they do a quick laundry or should they pop into a store (or shop online with overnight delivery)?

Among the exceptions to the prohibition of laundry on Chol Ha-Mo'ed, the Mishnah (*Mo'ed Katan* 14a, 18a) includes a person's only outergarment and hand towels, which get dirty very quickly and even in ancient times could not be reused on multiple days. The *Chayei Adam* (110:2) extends this to handkerchiefs used for blowing your nose, which also get dirty quickly. Do undergarments today have the same status as hand towels and handkerchiefs?

Rav Ovadiah Yosef (*Yalkut Yosef, Yom Tov*, p. 198, cited in Rav David Brofsky, *Hilkhot Mo'adim*, p. 658 n. 25) rules that because undergarments are changed every day, you may wash them on

Chol Ha-Mo'ed if you run out. Similarly, Rav Asher Bush (*Sho'el Bi-Shlomo*, no. 31) rules that if you prepare for Yom Tov properly by doing laundry but run out of clean undergarments, you may wash dirty undergarments (but nothing else) on Chol Ha-Mo'ed.

However, Rav Dovid Zucker and Rav Moshe Francis, the authors of *Chol Hamoed: A Comprehensive Review of the Laws of the Intermediate Days of the Festivals*, sent a number of questions to various authorities. Among the responses from Rav Moshe Stern is a ruling on this subject (p. 184, no. 22). Rav Stern writes that he does not want to permit it outright because clothes are inexpensive in this country. But if there is a great need, people should be advised to ask their rabbi who can permit based on the above reasons. Rav Zucker and Rav Francis summarize this ruling (p. 47): "If the supply of a particular item does become depleted on Chol HaMoed, usually the only recourse is to purchase whatever is needed for the festival. (If purchasing is difficult or unduly expensive, competent Rabbinic opinion should be sought.)"

Interestingly, Rav Yekusiel Farkas, in his *Chol Ha-Mo'ed Ke-Hilkhaso* (5:11 #3) rules that someone who runs out of clean socks can wash them on Chol Ha-Mo'ed. As a source for this leniency, he quotes Rav Moshe Stern's response to the authors of the book, *Chol Hamoed*. Rav Stern was actually less lenient, which is why the authors advised purchasing new clothes over washing dirty clothes.

Rav Farkas also quotes Rav Yehoshua Neuwirth, who permits washing socks on Chol Ha-Mo'ed if you run out of clean socks (*Shemiras Shabbos Ke-Hilkhasah* 66:66). However, Rav Neuwirth (n. 260) points out that we know how long the holiday lasts and roughly how much clothing we will need. If you fail to prepare in advance by cleaning them before the holiday, you may not wash them on Chol Ha-Mo'ed. That is precisely how the original enactment was set up, to ensure we prepare for the holiday in advance.

When Is *Kiddush Levanah?*

Rosh Chodesh Elul marks the end of the Jewish summer and the beginning of the autumn holiday season. Throughout the month, we engage in customs that grow as we approach Rosh Hashanah, preparing us for the annual judgment day. In accordance with this mood, the *Mateh Ephraim* (582:1) writes that we should be particularly careful to recite *Kiddush Levanah*, the blessing on the renewal of the moon, at the best time. This poses a halakhic challenge to determine which time is best. There are at least three different opinions on the subject.

The Gemara (*Sanhedrin* 41b) asks when the latest time is to say *Kiddush Levanah*. Rabbi Yochanan says until the moon's concavity is filled. One opinion in the Gemara is that this means until seven days; another opinion is until sixteen days. The Gemara does not say anything about the earliest time for *Kiddush Levanah*, but Rashi (ad loc., s.v. *ad kamah*) says that you can recite the blessing on the first day of the month. Similarly, Rambam (*Mishneh Torah, Hilkhos Berakhos* 10:17) writes that if you do not recite *Kiddush Levanah* the first night, you can say it until the sixteenth. According to Rashi and Rambam, the best time to recite *Kiddush Levanah* is the first night of the month. Others disagree.

Masekhes Soferim (20:1) says: "We do not recite the blessing on the moon except on Saturday night, when he is happy (*mevusam*) and wearing nice clothes." *Talmidei Rabbenu Yonah* (*Berakhos* 21a in the Rif) quote this but without the phrase "*Motza'ei Shabbos*

— Saturday night," and offer two interpretations of the word "*mevusam*," which we just translated as "happy." The first is that it refers to Saturday night, when we recite a blessing on spices (*besamim*) in *Havdalah*. Maybe the words "*Motza'ei Shabbos*" were written on the side of the text by a commentator and mistakenly added into the text by a copyist. The second explanation is that the moon, not the man, should be *mevusam*, like a canopy, which takes two to three days after the new moon. Rabbenu Yonah rejects the first interpretation, effectively requiring you to wait three days—until the fourth night—before reciting *Kiddush Levanah*, so the moon is large enough to make an impact with its light. *Avudraham* (*Hilkhos Berakhos*, ch. 8) suggests that "*mevusam*" means sweet, i.e., when a person can enjoy the light of the moon. Similarly, the *Siddur Rav Saadiah Ga'on* (p. 90) says to recite *Kiddush Levanah* from the fourth night through the fourteenth night.

We have seen three views about when you may first recite *Kiddush Levanah*: the first night of the month, the first Saturday night, and the fourth night. Surprisingly, the *Shulchan Arukh* (*Orach Chaim* 426:4) follows a fourth view. It quotes a responsum of Rav Yosef Jikatilla in which he rules, based on Kabbalah, that you may only recite *Kiddush Levanah* after the seventh day, i.e., beginning on the eighth night. The *Bach* (ad loc.) strongly opposes that view. He points out that the Gemara records a debate about the last day to recite *Kiddush Levanah* but not the first day, implying they all agree on that subject. But one opinion is that the last day is the seventh day, which is impossible according to Rav Yosef Jikatilla. The *Bach* adds that he has a tradition from his teachers that you only wait three full days before reciting *Kiddush Levanah*.

The Rama Mi-Fano (Responsa, no. 78) defends the *Shulchan Arukh*. He explains that the two opinions in the Gemara actually agree. One is saying the earliest day for the blessing (after seven days) and the other the last day for the blessing (sixteen). The Chasam

Sofer (Responsa, *Orach Chaim* no. 102) praises this explanation and says that the custom is to wait seven days, if possible. However, the *Yeshu'os Ya'akov* (526:6) finds this explanation of the Gemara unlikely. (See Rav Ovadiah Yosef, *Yechavveh Da'as* 2:24 for more sources.)

Rav Eliezer Melamed (*Peninei Halakhah, Zemanim* 1:18) summarizes current practice as follows:

> The custom of Chasidim and Sephardim is not to recite the blessing before seven days in the month. The custom of Ashkenaz is to recite the blessing after three days. But in practice we recite *Kiddush Levanah* on Saturday night in order to say it with joy and nice clothes. So in practice, according to the custom of Ashkenaz and Morocco, we recite *Kiddush Levanah* on the Saturday night after three full days from the time of the *molad* (new moon). According to the custom of Sephardim and Chasidim, we recite *Kiddush Levanah* on the Saturday night after the seventh of the month.

However, the *Arukh Ha-Shulchan* (526:7), writing in Poland, says that during the winter the practice is not to wait until Saturday night because of the frequency of cloudy nights. Instead, they would recite *Kiddush Levanah* the first night possible after three full days. Since Elul is less cloudy, it seems that Ashkenazim should recite *Kiddush Levanah* the first Saturday night possible.

Electric Menorahs Throughout the Year

Around Chanukah time, we expect to see articles explaining why electric menorahs are invalid for the mitzvah of lighting Chanukah candles. However, a variation of that type of menorah raises a different question that reflects how we typically maintain memories of the destroyed Temple.

I. Temple Replicas

The Gemara (*Rosh Hashanah* 24a) learns from the verse "You shall not make with me gods of silver or gods of gold" (Ex. 20:20) that we are forbidden to make replicas of anything used to serve God. This includes replicas of the table or menorah in the Temple. The Gemara's precise language is relevant:

> A man may not make a house in the form of the Temple, or a porch (exedra) in the form of the Temple hall, or a courtyard corresponding to the Temple courtyard, or a table corresponding to the [sacred] table or a candlestick corresponding to the [sacred] candlestick, but he may make one with five or six or eight lamps, but with seven he should not make, even of other metals.

Tosafos (ad loc., s.v. *akhsadra*) note the lack of parallelism. You may not make a candlestick corresponding to the Temple candlestick, a courtyard corresponding to the Temple courtyard, or a porch corresponding to the Temple hall. Why is a porch forbidden?

Ancient porches had three walls, with one side completely open. The Temple hall had four walls. Shouldn't this be similar to a candlestick with eight lamps, in contrast to the Temple's seven-lamp menorah? Tosafos answer that the Temple hall's doorway was so wide, and open because it had no actual doors, that to the casual observer it looked like it had only three walls. The appearance of a Temple element is sufficient to forbid replication. However, an obvious difference serves to permit replication.

II. Inexact Replicas

Rav Yosef Kolon (*Responsa Maharik*, no. 75) deduces from Tosafos that even an inexact replica is forbidden if it looks like the original. However, Rashi (*Avodah Zarah* 43a s.v. *beis*) says that a porch is only forbidden if it has the exact same measurements as the Temple's hall—even a small change renders it permissible. Maharik suggests that Rashi only permits a porch that has slightly different measurements because such a porch is not an obvious replica of the Temple's hall. After all, people build homes and porches all the time. However, a menorah is obviously patterned on the Temple utensil even if it has different measurements than the sacred menorah. (He adds that even if you disagree with this interpretation of Rashi, we should be strict because it is a debate between Rashi and Tosafos on a biblical prohibition.)

Rav Tzvi Ashkenazi (*Chakham Tzvi*, no. 60) finds Maharik's dismissal of Rashi's concern regarding a menorah unconvincing. He argues that a menorah that is exactly like that of the Temple but of a different size is permissible. He further argues that Tosafos did not intend to forbid a porch even though it has only three walls. Rather, the number of walls does not affect the permissibility because they are not part of the porch. Tosafos were merely explaining how someone could confuse a porch for the Temple hall.

According to *Chakham Tzvi*, a replica must be exactly like the original to fall under this prohibition. According to Maharik, it must merely look like the original. Both agree that a menorah with any number other than seven branches is permissible. What other changes to a menorah render a replica permissible?

III. Invalid Replicas

The Temple menorah had cups, knobs, and flowers (Ex. 25:31). Can you make a menorah replica with seven branches if you omit the cups, etc.? Maharik rules that any change that would invalidate the menorah for use in the Temple renders the replica permissible. The Gemara (*Menachos* 28a) says that a golden menorah must have the cups, etc. Otherwise it is invalid. However, a menorah of any other metal is valid even without cups, etc. Therefore, Maharik rules, followed by *Shulchan Arukh* (*Yoreh De'ah* 141:8), a golden replica of the menorah lacking cups, knobs, and flowers is permissible because it is invalid for use in the Temple.

Rav Alexander Schorr (*Bekhor Shor, Rosh Hashanah* 24a) reads the *Shulchan Arukh* as being stricter than Maharik. According to Rav Schorr, the minutiae of Temple acceptability are irrelevant to the issue of replicas. Any replica that looks like a Temple version, more or less, is forbidden. If a silver, seven-branched menorah is forbidden because it looks like what was used in the Temple, so is a similar menorah made of gold. However, the *Shakh* (ad loc., 36) reads the *Shulchan Arukh* as agreeing with Maharik (see glosses of Rav Akiva Eiger, ad loc.).

IV. Forbidden Replicas

Rav Yehudah Leib Graubart (*Chavalim Ba-Ne'imim*, vol. 3 no. 54) suggests that this debate revolves around the reason for the mitzvah. Is it because the broad prohibition against making idols extends to turning the Temple and its utensils into idols? Rambam (*Mishneh Torah, Hilkhos Avodah Zarah* 1:1-2) explains that idolatry originated from a desire to serve that which serves God. Similarly, the Temple and its utensils serve God and may be mistakenly used as objects of worship.[56] If so, only that which can be used in the Temple falls under the prohibition.

Alternatively, as *Sefer Ha-Chinukh* (254) suggests, the prohibition stems from the awe and respect we must show to the Temple. If it looks to the outsider like you are showing disrespect to the Temple's utensils, you violate this prohibition regardless of the technical requirements of the utensils.

Underlying this suggestion is the method in which we show respect for the Temple. In today's consumer economy, the approach to maintaining awareness is surrounding yourself with reminders. Visit; hang pictures in your home; make it your screensaver. In the halakhic tradition, we show respect by refraining from visiting and from mentioning. We do not say God's name out of respect. Similarly, we do not own Temple replicas out of respect. Holiness comes from rarity and separation, not familiarity. I find this meaningful to the contemporary debate over visiting the Temple Mount.

As a further point, some authorities argue whether we are only forbidden from making these replicas but may purchase them if already made. *Pischei Teshuvah* (*Yoreh De'ah* 141:12) quotes *Tiferes Le-Moshe* as permitting. However, the Vilna Gaon (*Bi'ur Ha-Gra* 141:22) and *Birkei Yosef* (*Yoreh De'ah* 141:8) forbid owning Temple replicas even if you did not make it.[57]

In conclusion, according to *Chakham Tzvi*, you are allowed to own a seven-branched electric menorah because it is slightly different from the Temple menorah. According to Maharik and *Bekhor Shor*, this is forbidden. Rav Ovadiah Yosef (*Yechavveh Da'as*, vol. 3 no. 61) rules leniently.[58]

---

56. I have greatly expanded Rav Graubart's argument here.

57. See *Darkhei Teshuvah* 141:52.

58. Rav Yosef does not quote Rav Graubart's responsum. This is one of the rare times when I have found a source that Rav Yosef missed. I later saw that Rav Shlomo Zalman Braun quotes it in his *She'arim Metzuyanim Ba-Halakhah*.

PART 5: PRAYER

Synagogue Dues: The Middle Path

As Jewish communal institutions suffer declining membership, synagogues continue to reevaluate their dues structure. On the one hand, an established organization must cover significant overhead. On the other, the financial burden scares away potential new members. Two models have been generally discussed but a third, popular in certain Orthodox communities, is often ignored.

I. Synagogue Dues

The primary model consists of dividing the costs among members. Take the annual budget and spread it out among the members, accounting for additional income from various fundraisers, including sales of high holiday seats. Many such synagogues offer a broad variety of services to the community beyond basic prayers and Torah classes (e.g., swimming pool, gym), which provide added value for the high membership fee but also increases the expense of the synagogue facilities and therefore the cost to the members. If followed simply, this dues model discourages young and/or less well-off families from joining because of the high cost. However, most synagogues are happy to offer discounts to those who cannot afford the full membership fee. The phrase "pay to pray" is sometimes used to deride such synagogues, but I seriously doubt many houses of worship would turn away someone due solely to lack of funds, occasional horror stories notwithstanding.

Another model, which was popularized by Chabad and has taken hold among others, is to charge no membership fee at all. Allow people to benefit fully from the synagogue's bare-bones facilities and provide the least amount of non-basic services. Synagogues that follow this approach rely on volunteers and focus on prayers and classes, which significantly lowers the synagogue's overhead. And they fundraise from individuals to cover the comparatively low costs. This is a risky dues model because it relies entirely on voluntary donations. It also places significant control in the hands of the largest donor(s). Some have argued that people find less value in a service for which they do not pay.

A third model takes a middle path which, I suggest, is roughly based on the financial management of the Temple in ancient Jerusalem. As we once discussed,[59] the final chapter of Leviticus seems oddly placed. The penultimate chapter concludes a lengthy, striking passage of blessings and curses that seems like a proper ending to the book. Why continue with another chapter about a variety of voluntary contributions to the Temple?

II. Historical Attitudes

Some commentators explain that the beginning of Leviticus describes the workings of the Tabernacle/Temple. However, the mandatory donation of one half-*shekel* per year, along with the various sin and other mandatory offerings, are insufficient to maintain the sacrificial system throughout the year. The voluntary offerings provide the additional income necessary. Therefore, like a bookend, Leviticus concludes the way it began, with a discussion of the Temple's sacrifices and finances. Note the financial arrangements: a combination of basic mandatory fees with substantial voluntary contributions. This is the middle path, which the Vilna Gaon suggests is the guide for normative practice. To explain this, we need to take a detour through history.

---

59. "Leviticus and the Rest of Us," *Torah Musings*, April 17, 2013.

The Gemara (*Bava Basra* 7b) discusses how a Jewish community collects money from its members, how it calculates individual taxes. In the case of building a city wall, should the community allocate costs based on headcount (everyone pays the same amount), based on wealth (the richer pay more), or based on usage (those closer to the wall pay more)? All commentators seem to agree that when we are dealing with life-threatening issues, everyone pays the same amount (e.g., Tosafos, ad loc., s.v. *lefi shevach*). In all other matters, the division of cost follows any of a number of models.

The method of this allocation seems to be a four-way debate. Rambam (*Mishneh Torah, Hilkhos Shekheinim* 6:4) rules that we charge only based on usage, without taking wealth into account. Rav Meir of Rotenburg (quoted in Mordekhai, *Bava Basra*, ch. 1 nos. 475, 479) rules that we tax based solely on wealth (part of his reasoning is that poor people can easily leave town because what little property they have is easily carried while rich people have deeper roots, therefore wealth is the same as usage). However, Rabbenu Tam (Tosafos, ad loc., s.v. *lefi kiruv*) and Ri Migash (quoted by Rosh, ad loc., no. 22) state that we use both measures. The wealthier pay more than the poor and those closer to the wall pay more relative to those in the same wealth bracket.

III. A Middle Ground

There is a fourth view, specifically regarding how to pay the cantor's salary. Apparently, Rav Meir of Rotenburg changed his mind and later ruled that this tax is partly based on headcount and partly on wealth (*Hagahos Maimoniyos, Hilkhos Tefillah* 11:1). He would spread equally the cost of a minimal cantor, one with the least talent and who leads the minimum amount of prayers. The rest is allotted based on wealth.

Somewhat similarly, Rav Meir of Padua (Responsa, no. 44) rules that part of the money for synagogue building should be raised with a means-based tax and part with a flat tax. He justifies the means-based portion with the logic that either poor people can easily leave or that they only require a mere shack and not a fancy building. However, payment for a cantor or rental of synagogue premises are based entirely on wealth.

The *Beis Yosef* (*Orach Chaim* 53) quotes Rav Hai Gaon as ruling the same as Rav Meir of Rotenburg regarding a cantor but offering a biblical rationale. The obligatory parts of prayer that a cantor leads are equally binding on all community members and are collected like the half-*shekel*. Most of the cantor's role revolves around customary prayers which are not technically obligatory. That part of the salary is paid based on wealth, like the voluntary contributions to the Temple.

Rav Yisrael Isserlein (*Terumas Ha-Deshen*, responsum 345) addresses a city whose Jews were asked to contribute to reinforce the city's defenses. How should the Jewish community tax its members to fund this effort? There are two main questions: 1) is this a life-threatening matter?, 2) do we rule according to Rabbenu Tam, either of Maharam Rotenburg's views, or Rambam? The *Terumas Ha-Deshen*'s final ruling is surprising and important. To the first question, he points out that while some people may die in battle, the defense is really a matter of which feudal lord governs the city. Therefore, it is primarily a financial matter, not one of life or death. To the second question, he seems to follow Rabbenu Tam and Ri Migash that we use both wealth and usage as measures.

However, the *Terumas Ha-Deshen* adds an important caveat, both at the beginning and end of his responsum. These matters, he states, are never clear within the law and therefore require the use of judgment. Instead, the community should reach an internal compromise and decide on its own how to tax its citizens for this matter.

IV. Halakhic Decisors

In at least three places, the *Shulchan Arukh* discusses how to tax community members. When a community needs to hire a cantor, the *Shulchan Arukh* (*Orach Chaim* 53:23) rules that this expense is paid from the communal general fund, which means that the rich pay more than the poor. Even though the need for a cantor is equal among the community members and therefore the burden should be shared equally, the poor simply cannot afford it.

On the other hand, when two people want to travel away for the High Holidays from a small town that will then lack a *minyan*, they have to share the cost of hiring replacements (*Orach Chaim* 55:21). This cost is shared part equally and part based on the ability to pay. Regarding the talmudic case above, the *Shulchan Arukh* (*Choshen Mishpat* 363:3) quotes the Rambam's and Rabbenu Tam's opinions.

The Rema (*Orach Chaim* 53:23) rules that the cantor's salary is always paid partly by a flat fee and partly based on wealth. The question remains why he adopted this position. Is it due to a compromise or because it is based on the biblical model? *Taz* (ad loc., 14) and *Arukh Ha-Shulchan* (ad loc., 23) state that it is a compromise. The latter adds that it only applies where the compromise has already been implemented and is the existing practice. Otherwise, argues the *Arukh Ha-Shulchan*, and presumably outside of unique cases requiring such a compromise, the ideal model is to allocate the cost entirely based on wealth. It is a communal expense that is not life threatening, and must therefore be paid based on ability.

However, the Vilna Gaon (*Bi'ur Ha-Gra*, ad loc.) seems to say that the Rema follows Rav Hai Gaon's biblical model. The bimodal fee structure is the ideal, not a compromise. It represents a correct allocation of the costs. If we follow this logic further, the costs of any part of a synagogue's services that are technically required should be equally borne by all members. This is a very small portion of the costs. The rest of the synagogue's budget should be paid based on ability.

V. Synagogue Fees Today

Today's synagogue dues differ from historical fees in a crucial way—they are voluntary payments rather than taxes. You can choose which synagogue to join, if any. You cannot choose whether to pay a synagogue tax. Therefore, it is questionable whether medieval tax assessment methodologies apply to the current situation. If membership is volitional, then your joining the synagogue is an acceptance of its fee structure, whatever it may be. It need not be fair or Torah-based because it is based on a voluntary contract. Additionally, according to the *Terumas Ha-Deshen*, these matters are never clear in Torah law anyway and should be determined based on communal compromise.

However, according to Rav Hai Gaon and the Vilna Gaon's conceptual model, we have an ideal that applies equally to contemporary synagogues. Like in the Temple, the minimal and mandatory functioning should be paid equally and everything else should be voluntary. In fact, today we may approach the biblical model more closely than in medieval times. The voluntary portion used to be assessed as a tax based on wealth but it is now entirely optional, like in Temple times.

Synagogues that follow this conceptual approach charge modest annual membership fees, as well as fees for using the synagogue's premises for personal celebrations. But they also seek donations in a variety of forms. They auction honors on Yom Tov (many *shtieblakh* do this on Chol Ha-Moed, as well), ask for donations in the *mi she-beirakh* after calling someone to the Torah (although most will accept an unspecified "gift," which can be just a penny) and constantly seek funding for programs throughout the year. As annoying as much of this may be, it keeps the annual membership fee very low. And if people cannot afford the few hundred dollars required, they can easily obtain a waiver.

As mainstream synagogues consider alternative fee structures, they may want to consider this middle path, the conceptual approach. Aside from being modeled after the Temple in Jerusalem, it strikes a balance between reliance on the entire community and affordability, and between fees and fundraising.

Why No *Tefillin?*

Why don't men wear *tefillin* all day long? The mitzvah is not just during morning services; it is throughout the day (*Tur, Orach Chaim* 37). So why don't we wear them all day?

The answer to this question is historical. It used to be that men wore *tefillin* all day, certainly in the times of the Mishnah and Gemara, but at some point the custom was changed to wearing them only during morning services. The good news is that we know exactly when that happened.

There is textual evidence that already in talmudic times there were many people who did not wear *tefillin*. The Gemara (*Shabbos* 130a) quotes R. Shimon ben Elazar as saying: "Every mitzvah for which the Jews submitted to death at the time of the royal decree, e.g., idolatry and circumcision, is still held firmly in their minds. However, every mitzvah for which the Jews did not submit to death at the time of the royal decree, e.g., *tefillin*, is still weak in their hands." In other words, granted they could not wear *tefillin* at a time of a royal decree not to wear it. However, even after the decree was rescinded the mitzvah was still "weak in their hands." The Gemara (*Rosh Hashanah* 13a) specifically condemns those who never wear *tefillin*.

This laxity by many in wearing *tefillin* continued into the Middle Ages. Tosafos (*Shabbos* 49a s.v. *ke-Elisha*) write that one should not be surprised that at that time people were lax in *tefillin*, since they were in the times of the Talmud also. This is attested to in many other places, and in the times of the Geonim there are even implications that almost no one in the land of Israel wore *tefillin*. The *Beis Yosef* (*Even Ha-Ezer* 65) quotes the *Kol Bo* who suggests that in some communities ashes are not placed on a groom's forehead because the community members do not wear *tefillin*. There was even a responsum by Rav Sherira Gaon, copied in many medieval works on *halakhah*, answering a question about whether it is *yuhara* (haughty) for a yeshiva student to wear *tefillin* when no one else does.

It seems that in order to defend this practice, some *rishonim* utilized the idea that one who wears *tefillin* needs a "*guf naki* – clean body." The *Shibbolei Ha-Leket* (Buber ed., p. 382) quotes one view that "*guf naki*" means that a person is clean of sins. In other words, only someone without any sins is allowed to wear *tefillin*. This view can be found in other *rishonim* that explicitly dispute it. For example, the *Sefer Ha-Chinukh* (no. 421) states that "*guf naki*" does not refer to someone who has no sins or impurity, implying that someone else had suggested that it did. The author explicitly condemns those who are strict on the holiness of this mitzvah and thereby deprive the masses of the mitzvah. Rather, "*guf naki*" refers to the ability to refrain from passing gas and thinking improper thoughts while wearing the *tefillin*.

Rav Moshe of Coucy (*Semag*, imperative, no. 3) tells of how he traveled around thirteenth-century Europe, preaching to people that they should wear *tefillin* during the morning prayers. Even if they cannot control themselves all day, people can certainly maintain a *guf naki* for the prayer services (that is the view of Tosafos;[60] *Rosh*[61] and *Beis Yosef*;[62] footnote 8 in the Schlesinger

60. *Pesachim* 113b sv. *ve-ein*.
61. *Hilkhos Tefillin*, no. 28.
62. *Orach Chaim* 37.

edition of *Semag* assumes the *Semag* agrees). Evidently, this practice of wearing *tefillin* only during morning prayer services took hold and the prior practice of widespread abandonment of the mitzvah slowly turned into minimal performance of it during the morning prayers.

However, someone who cannot control himself and cannot maintain a *guf naki* may not wear *tefillin*. Despite the biblical obligation, someone in a definite situation such as that should not wear *tefillin* at all (*Shulchan Arukh, Orach Chaim* 38:1). For this reason, the *Arukh Ha-Shulchan* (*Orach Chaim* 38:6) rules that those who are not obligated in the mitzvah of *tefillin*—such as women— should never place themselves in even a doubtful position of not maintaining a *guf naki*. For centuries, men who were obligated to wear *tefillin* refrained from doing so because of a concern for *guf naki* and, even today, we only wear *tefillin* for a minimal time. And even then, if we are certain that we cannot maintain a *guf naki* we do not wear *tefillin*. Women, who are not obligated to wear *tefillin*, should recognize the sensitivity surrounding this mitzvah and not place themselves in the position of even possibly lacking a *guf naki* while wearing *tefillin* without any obligation to do so.[63]

---

63. This is without considering other issues associated with women wearing *tefillin*. Rav Menachem Meier, my teacher and high school principal, told me that he once asked Rav Joseph B. Soloveitchik whether a female student from a Conservative home may wear *tefillin* for morning prayers in an Orthodox high school. Rav Soloveitchik told him not to allow it.

Dew's Disappearing Comma

After Pesach, as our prayers transition from winter to summer, I am reminded of an irate caller I once had to handle. During my brief stint at the OU, I quickly learned the downside of becoming friendly with the receptionist. Any caller with a question or comment in any way related to a book was directed to me. One caller conveyed his gratitude for the ArtScroll Chumash, which has no connection at all to the OU. Another was extremely upset about Koren's choice in vowelizing the seasonal addition in the second blessing of the *Amidah*. Since the prayerbook was co-published by the OU, he called us rather than Koren.

The Koren *siddur* vowelizes the winter addition as "*mashiv ha-ru'ach u-morid ha-geshem*." The last word, *geshem*, is vowelized as if it is in the middle of a sentence. Otherwise, it would be vowelized *gashem*, with a *kamatz* vowel. However, the summer addition (for *Nusach Sefard* and Israelis who tend to follow many of the Gra's versions of *Nusach Ashkenaz*) is vowelized with a *kamatz*, "*morid ha-tal*," as if it is at the end of a sentence. Why the inconsistency? Indeed, some vowelize the winter addition with a *kamatz*, as well.

I responded that this is standard practice and later confirmed with both the OU's in-house linguist and Koren's linguist that this is correct and is the way the best manuscripts and *siddurim* have the additions vowelized. However, I never received a good explanation for the difference.

I later saw that Rav Ya'akov Kamenetsky (*Emes Le-Ya'akov*, Gen. 3:19) explains the difference and adds an additional impact

190

this has on pronunciation.[64] The key lies in the themes before and after these additions. The second blessing is called *Gevuros* and discusses God's miraculous sustenance and revival of humanity. It begins with God's resurrecting people ("*mechayeh meisim attah rav le-hoshi'ah*") and then proceeds to His sustaining people ("*mechalkel chaim be-chesed*"). The winter addition is about wind and rain, which is part of the sustenance. Since it begins the next sentence, there should be a period before, rather than after, the winter addition.

However, the summer addition is about dew. Dew is connected to resurrection, as it says (Isa. 26:19), "Your dead will live... for your dew is a radiant dew." Similarly, the Gemara (*Shabbos* 88b) refers to the dew with which God will resurrect the dead. Therefore, the summer addition (for those who say it), is not a praise of God for dew. Rather, it cleverly transforms the praise over rain into a reference to the resurrection.[65] Since resurrection is the prior phrase, the summer addition is the end of the sentence, after which a period is appropriate.

Rav Kamenetsky adds that the placement of the period also effects the pronunciation of the word "*attah*." If it immediately precedes the final phrase of the sentence, it should have a comma after it: "*mechayeh meisim attah, rav le-hoshi'ah*." If it has that comma (the equivalent of an *esnachta*), the word's emphasis is moved to the penultimate syllable: "*AT-tah*" rather than the usual "*at-TAH*." If the sentence continues with an additional phrase then there is no comma and no change in pronunciation.

Therefore, concludes Rav Kamenetsky, in the winter, when "*mashiv ha-ru'ach*" is part of the next sentence, the word "*attah*" should be pronounced *mi-le'eil*: "*AT-tah*." In the summer, when

---

64. Following the Vilna Gaon's approach that prayer adheres to Biblical grammar.

65. It was pointed out to me that this interpretation is difficult because the *piyutim* for *tal* are clearly about dew and not resurrection.

"*morid ha-tal*" is a continuation of the prior sentence, there is no comma after "*attah*" and it is pronounced normally: "*at-TAH.*" (Plain *nusach Ashkenaz*, which does not include "*morid ha-tal,*" always has the word as "*AT-tah.*")

I found that Rav Yosef Eliyahu Henkin wrote a responsum to Rav Avraham Chaim Naeh on this subject, published in *Gevuros Eliyahu* (1:26). Rav Henkin distinguishes between words that are punctuated with a *segol* vowel and two-letter words with a *patach*. The former only change to a *kamatz* at a strong pause. The latter change at almost any pause. For example, we see in Ex. 16:13 that *tal* is punctuated with a *kamatz* due to the pause of a *zakef katon*, which is not a full pause because the *esnachta* (comma equivalent) is a few words earlier.

Rav Henkin explains that the pause at this part of the prayer is a small pause. The big pause comes at the end of the list, after the word *afar*. Since this is a small pause, *geshem* remains unchanged but *tal* is transformed with a *kamatz*.

Mispronouncing Hebrew

I. Mispronouncing Hebrew

The minority of Jews who have received sufficient Jewish education to allow proper prayer in Hebrew face a dilemma regarding their less well-trained co-religionists. Can a Jew who is incapable of properly pronouncing the prayers lead the community services? There are times when tradition, and even law, would demand it, such as on a *yahrtzeit* or a kohen leading *birkas kohanim*. If the Jew cannot pray in proper Hebrew, is he even allowed to pray silently in his garbled reading? And let us not forget those with speech impediments who, despite their adequate education, cannot pronounce Hebrew properly.

The Mishnah (*Megillah* 24b) raises the issue regarding leading prayers and *birkas kohanim*. People from Chaifah and Beis She'an may not lead because they confuse the *alef* and *ayin* sounds, along with the *heih* and *ches*. Rashi offers what could be understood as two reasons why they may not lead: 1) By using an *ayin* sound rather than an *alef* in *birkas kohanim*, they change the blessing into a curse. Additionally, 2) their mispronounced prayer is defective.

II. No One Else

Why does Rashi give both reasons? The *Divrei Chaim* (vol. 2, OC no. 10) suggests that Rashi is referring to someone who can pronounce the Hebrew properly when he tries hard. Such a person would not be allowed to lead the congregation in prayer because the length of the service makes it extremely unlikely that he will be able to maintain his focus throughout. *Birkas Kohanim* is much shorter and such a person would be allowed to lead, except that the possibility of his accidentally cursing the congregation forces us to prevent him from leading as well.

This fits with one of the views of Tosafos. The Gemara (*Megillah* 24b) says that R. Chiya mispronounced Hebrew. However, elsewhere the Gemara (*Bava Metzi'a* 86a) says that R. Yehudah Ha-Nasi appointed R. Chiya to lead prayers on a special fast day. How could R. Chiya lead prayers if he mispronounces Hebrew? *Tosafos* (*Megillah* 24b s.v. *ke-she-attah*) suggest that R. Chiya could pronounce Hebrew properly if he concentrated. In such a case, R. Yehudah Ha-Nasi allowed him to lead prayers.

However, *Tosafos* elsewhere (*Bava Metzi'a* 86a s.v. *achtinhu*) take a different approach. They explain that R. Chiya was the only person capable of leading prayers in that unique circumstance of the special fast. If there is no one else available, then even someone who mispronounces Hebrew may lead. Some later authorities (e.g., *Pri Chadash, Orach Chaim* 53:12) accept this view in practice.

III. His Way

Returning to Rashi, the *Turei Even* (ad loc.) offers a different explanation for the two reasons. He suggests that a mispronounced prayer is not defective for someone who normally speaks Hebrew in this improper way. That is how he pronounces the words. If this were not the case, then he would always need to find someone to recite prayers for him. However, when such a person leads the prayer services, which amounts to praying on behalf of others, then the mispronounced prayers are defective for the listeners. This does not apply to *birkas kohanim*, which is why Rashi needs another reason—turning the blessing into a curse—to disqualify someone who cannot pronounce Hebrew properly. The *Chelkas*

Yo'av (*Even Ha-Ezer* no. 17) rules this way regarding *chalitzah* when the man cannot pronounce Hebrew properly.

IV. Used to It / Normal There

The *Shulchan Arukh Ha-Rav* (128:48) also quotes two reasons for disqualifying such people from leading prayers, although slightly differently from Rashi's explanations: 1) they distract the public with their improper pronunciations, 2) their prayers are defective. The practical difference between these two views is significant. According to the former, when the public is used to the mispronunciation, such as by an established member of the community, there is no problem with him leading services. According to the latter, it is only allowed in a place where most people pronounce Hebrew that way. The *Shulchan Arukh Ha-Rav* rules strictly, like the second view.

A source for this second approach is a responsum of the Radbaz (Responsa 1:399). He was asked whether Greek Jews could recite *birkas kohanim* in Egypt, where their pronunciations sounded foreign and incorrect. He replied that while their pronunciation of the blessings was sufficient for Greece, where all the Jews spoke Hebrew that way, they could not do so in Egypt. The *Magen Avraham* (53:15) rules like the Radbaz and a similar responsum of the Maharit (1:16). The *Beis Shmuel* (169:28) and *Mishnah Berurah* (53:37) rule similarly.

However, the first view also has a precedent. The Rambam (*Mishneh Torah, Hilkhos Tefillah* 8:12) writes that a teacher may appoint a student who mispronounces Hebrew to lead prayers. Why this exception? The *Or Samei'ach* (ad loc.) explains that the reason for preventing someone who mispronounces the prayers from leading them is respect for the congregation. Therefore, when the congregation is familiar with the person and his speech, there is no slight to the congregation and he may lead. A teacher and students know each other and therefore the teacher may appoint a student to lead without concern (cf. *Taz, Orach Chaim* 128:30).

V. Today

Most Hebrew dialects today—both Ashkenazic and Sephardic—have apparent deficiencies. For their own communities, where most people speak that way, their pronunciations are sufficient. Even in other situations there are ample reasons to allow the alternate pronunciations, as above. However, other cases are more difficult.

Someone with a speech impediment or who lacks the education to properly pronounce Hebrew is still unable to lead services. He may only do so when no one else can. I can see a sympathetic halakhic authority stretching for leniency in defining such situations. For example, Rav Yechiel Ya'akov Weinberg (*Seridei Eish, Orach Chaim* no. 6 – in the new edition) deems a bar mitzvah boy to be the only person capable of leading services at his bar mitzvah. I suspect that a mourner and someone observing a *yahrtzeit* would also qualify, despite his mispronouncing Hebrew. This would explain the cases I have seen where a mourner who cannot properly pronounce Hebrew leads prayers throughout the year of his mourning. His courage is commendable and the congregation's leniency is, I suspect, due to the mourner being irreplaceable in that situation.

Bypassing *Kohanim*

I. Honoring the *Kohen*

Complicated situations require creative solutions, but sometimes they can be too clever. The Torah (Lev. 21:8) commands us to honor *kohanim*, members of the priestly family, by allowing them to go first (*Gittin* 59b). We let them go first in line and, by rabbinic decree, call them to the Torah for the first *aliyah*.

However, this system can cause tension in certain circumstances. Consider a synagogue with only one *kohen*, who receives the first *aliyah* each time the Torah is read—Monday, Thursday, Shabbos morning, and Shabbos afternoon. The Gemara (ibid.) states that on Shabbos morning, a *kohen* may not forgo his privilege and allow another to receive the first *aliyah*, even a great Torah scholar, because it might lead to fighting in the synagogue. However, at the other three Torah readings, which fewer people attend, the *kohen* may relinquish his right to go first.

This would seem to resolve many problems. If there are many people who need to receive an *aliyah* on a Monday or Thursday, a *kohen* may give permission to someone else to receive his *aliyah*. However, Tosafos (ad loc., s.v. *aval*) say that in the time of Talmud, not as many people attended synagogue during the week. However, in the Tosafist era, weekday synagogue attendance was high and the concern of fighting was sufficient to prohibit a *kohen* from forgoing his honor, even for a great Torah scholar. This is the standard ruling (*Shulchan Arukh, Orach Chaim* 135:4).

II. Communal Custom

There is another important ruling that affects our question. The *Beis Yosef* (*Orach Chaim* 135) and *Magen Avraham* (ad loc., no. 7) quote the Maharik (Responsa, no. 9) as permitting a congregation to forcefully remove a *kohen* when someone else buys the first *aliyah* in the Torah on the Shabbos of *Parashas Bereishis*. This could serve as an important precedent.

However, Rav Moshe Sofer (*Responsa Chasam Sofer*, vol. 1 nos. 24-25) makes some important points and corrections based on a careful reading of the Maharik's responsum. This *kohen* was asked to attend another nearby synagogue because this one time a year, the synagogue had a long-standing custom—accepted by the entire community including the *kohanim*—to raise money for the synagogue's upkeep by selling the first *aliyah*. The *kohen* was forcefully prevented from attending the synagogue, not removed. This is a very limited precedent. Even a communal custom that is accepted by *kohanim* can only be maintained if it is an occasional occurrence and for the sake of a mitzvah.

Rav Sofer's contemporary, Rav Elazar Fleckles (*Teshuvah Me-Ahavah* 1:91), makes similar points. Another contemporary, Rav Shmuel Landau (*Shivas Tziyon*, no. 6), writes similarly and adds that the Maharik was dealing with a custom that is intended to honor the Torah. The Torah's honor takes precedence over that of the *kohen*. Otherwise, a custom that is intended to undermine the commandment to honor a *kohen* must be discarded.

III. Allowing and Leaving

Rav Moshe Feinstein (*Iggeros Moshe, Orach Chaim* 2:34; 3:20) writes that our current reality is closer to that of the Talmud than Medieval times—significantly fewer people come to synagogue during the week than on Shabbos. Therefore, the original talmudic rule should apply and *kohanim* may relinquish their right to the first *aliyah*. He emphasizes repeatedly, though, that they must do so willingly. The Maharsham (Responsa 1:214) makes a similar point about times being different.

Rav Moshe Sofer's son, Rav Avraham Shmuel Binyamin Sofer (*Responsa Kesav Sofer* 1:36), offers two original arguments to allow *kohanim* to forgo their right on *mincha* of Yom Kippur in a community where that *aliyah* is sold and failure to do so will cause a fight. First, the *kohen* is not allowing anyone specific to take the *aliyah*. He is merely giving it to the highest bidder, without choosing an individual. Second, this will actually prevent an argument rather than cause one. The first reason would only apply in unique situations.

Rav Moshe Schick (*Responsa Maharam Schick, Orach Chaim* 61) writes that calling a *kohen* to the Torah for the first *aliyah* is a fulfillment of a biblical mitzvah. If no *kohen* is present, there is no mitzvah. However, asking a *kohen* to leave is plotting to avoid a mitzvah, which is hardly proper. We must strive to fulfill *mitzvos*, not actively avoid them.

IV. Two Grooms

But if we do not ask a *kohen* to forgo his privilege nor to leave the synagogue, what do we do if two *Yisra'elim* have *chiyuvim*, obligations to be called to the Torah? What do we do when we have two grooms, on their wedding day, in the synagogue on a Monday morning? If a *kohen* is present, only one groom may be called to the Torah.

We have to remember that the term "*chiyuv*" is misleading. The obligation is a matter of custom. In contrast, the commandment to honor a *kohen* is a biblical law (some of the above-quoted responsa discuss whether the obligation today is biblical or rabbinic).

Rav Tzvi Hirsch Grodzinski (*Mikra'ei Kodesh* 17:6 n. 8) rules that in such a case as described, we do not call one of them in the place of a *kohen*. Rather, the two grooms draw a lottery (the equivalent to flipping a coin), and the loser receives *hagbahah*, lifting the Torah, instead of an *aliyah*.[66] However, Rav Moshe Feinstein allows asking the *kohen* to leave. Similarly, Rav Eliezer Melamed (*Peninei Halakhah, Tefillah* 22:7) quotes Rav Ovadiah Yosef (*Yabi'a Omer* 6:23) as ruling that the congregation may ask the *kohen* to leave the synagogue for the first *aliyah*. I have never seen a *kohen* asked to leave but I'm told it sometimes happens.

---

66. Rav Joseph B. Soloveitchik used to tell a story about the author of the *Sha'agas Aryeh*, when two mourners asked him who had priority in saying *Kaddish* (back when only one person said it at a time). The *Sha'agas Aryeh* told them to draw a lottery. They pointed out that the *Magen Avraham* has a long list of priorities, with many rules and details. The *Sha'agas Aryeh* replied that this is precisely how the *Magen Avraham* compiled his list, by drawing a lottery (*Nefesh Ha-Rav*, p. 135).

Ebola and *Tefillin*

In an article in the Spring 2015 issue of *Jewish Action*, Rav Dr. Eddie Reichman discusses halakhic issues surrounding the Ebola scare that had briefly overtaken the nation. He quotes Rav Moshe Feinstein's ruling that you may not bring *tefillin* to a quarantined patient if subsequently the *tefillin* will have to be burned (*Iggeros Moshe, Orach Chaim* vol. 1 no. 4). While this is correct, I'd like to expand on the subject based on the treatment in *She'arim Metzuyanim Ba-Halakhah* (28:15).

During an infectious disease outbreak in 1933, halakhic authorities debated the subject. The *Imrei David* (no. 218) permitted bringing *tefillin* to a quarantined patient. The *Dovev Meisharim* (no. 99) and *Chazon Nachum* (no. 6) forbade it (like Rav Feinstein would later rule). This debate revolves around indirect causation (*gerama*) of the destruction of holy texts. Even though we may not directly burn a Torah scroll or *tefillin*, perhaps we may put the holy objects in a situation in which they will later be burned.

The *Chelkas Ya'akov* (*Orach Chaim*, nos. 17-19) points out that the possibility exists that the *tefillin* will be buried rather than burned. If that is a legitimate possibility, the bringing of the *tefillin* into the quarantine becomes an uncertain case of indirect causation (*safek gerama*), which should be permitted.

The *She'arim Metzuyanim Ba-Halakhah* (ibid.) adds that the *Chavos Ya'ir* (no. 16) concludes that having a gentile erase God's name is only rabbinically prohibited. Therefore, causing a gentile to destroy *tefillin* is also prohibited only rabbinically. The *She'arim Metzuyanim Ba-Halakhah* argues that the patient's fulfillment of the biblical mitzvah to wear *tefillin* should override this rabbinic prohibition. He further quotes the *Machazeh Avraham* (vol. 2 no. 10), who rules that you may indirectly cause God's name to be erased for the sake of a mitzvah.

I believe that Rav Feinstein's ruling is normative, at least in America. I am only pointing out the debate.

Three Steps Forward

Jews trained in prayer from youth often assume that the three steps before and after the *Amidah* prayer parallel each other. In fact, they are different, and the first three steps have a surprising history. The theories underlying these three steps forward have interesting practical implications.

I. A New Custom

Standard practice, as described in most prayerbooks and taught in most schools, is that you take three steps forward and put your feet together to recite the *Amidah*. Generally, you have to take three steps back to make room for the three steps forward. On conclusion of the prayer, you take three steps back while bowing. After a short pause, you return three steps forward and are done.

The three steps back are mentioned in the Gemara (*Yoma* 53a) as the proper way to take leave of a king. The three steps forward have no similar textual source. They originate with a single school, perhaps a single individual who may have been the first Jew to take three steps forward into prayer.

The *Shulchan Arukh* does not mention the three steps forward and only discusses the three steps back (*Orach Chaim* 123:1). Only the Rema, in his glosses (*Orach Chaim* 95:1), states that "some say" you should take three steps forward before the *Amidah*. This weak endorsement is all we have for what seems to be a very widespread practice. Nonetheless, dissenters can be found. *Piskei Teshuvos*

(95:2 n. 17) states that Rav Yisrael Ya'akov Kanievsky (the Steipler Gaon) and Rav Chaim Elazar Shapira (the *Minchas Elazar*) did not take three steps before praying. While the *Kitzur Shulchan Arukh* (18:2) quotes this custom, the *Chayei Adam* does not. Neither does Rav Chaim David Halevi in his edition of *Kitzur Shulchan Arukh*. In contrast, the *Kaf Ha-Chaim* (95:7) quotes kabbalistic sources, including the *Ben Ish Chai*, that require not only three steps forward before praying but three steps back before the three steps forward.

The earliest source we have for this practice is Rashi. *Machzor Vitri* (no. 29) offers two reasons for taking three steps forward. This text is repeated with minor differences in *Siddur Rashi* (no. 29) and *Sefer Ha-Pardes* (no. 57). The text reads like a midrash and may come from a lost passage. Or it may be Rashi's innovation. This is the key passage from *Machzor Vitri* (my translation):

> It says, "[I will go and return to My place,] until they acknowledge their guilt and seek My face" (Hos. 5:15) – Therefore one walks forward three steps and backward. As it says, "And their feet were a straight foot" (Ezek. 1:7) – there are three feet and three steps before prayer, afterward straight. [This] straightens their prayers. It also says, "Bring an offering and come before Him" (1 Chron. 16:29). In other words, when you pray before Him, make yourself as one who brings a gift to a king. When He arrives before you, hurry step three steps and then bow to Him in *Magen Avraham*.

II. Two Approaches

In the above text, Rashi offers two midrashic derivations of the practice. One is the two mentions of feet regarding angels (one plural implying two and another singular, 2+1=3). The other is the idea of approaching a king in respect. These two derivations are based on the idea of showing respect to God during prayer but are slightly different. The first has the three steps as part of standing still like an angel. The second has them as approaching God. The former is about standing before God, the latter about approaching Him. There may be a practical difference between these two opinions.

Sefer Ha-Manhig (no. 44) quotes slightly different midrashic derivations. First he compares the three steps forward to walking through the three camps in the desert—the camp of Jews, Levites, and the camp of Divine Presence. He then quotes a variation of the derivation from the angels' feet. These two approaches can also be split between approaching God and standing before Him.

Rokei'ach (no. 362) adds another derivation. In addition to the angels' legs, he points out that three times in the Bible a person is said to approach prayer (*va-yiggash*) – Avraham (Gen. 18:23), Yehudah (Gen. 44:18), and Eliyahu (1 Kings 18:21). These two can also be divided between approaching God and standing before Him.

III. Implications

There may be practical implications to these two understandings of this custom. When must the three steps be taken? If the three steps are about standing before God, part of keeping your feet together, then they must immediately precede the *Amidah*. However, if they are about approaching God, then perhaps you may take them even earlier.

The *Eliyah Rabbah* (95:3) points out that the *Levush* omits this custom. While his reason may have been that he does not consider it necessary, like the *Chayei Adam* and others mentioned above, the *Eliyah Rabbah* offers a different explanation. He suggests that the *Levush* believed that walking to synagogue suffices as taking three steps before prayer. If the reason for the three steps is that it is part of standing before God, this explanation is very difficult. However, it is more reasonable if the reason is to approach the King. Walking toward Him before the very beginning of the prayer services may also constitute approaching God before prayer.

On the other hand, if taking three steps is part of standing before God like an angel, maybe it is only necessary when we speak like an angel. During the *Kedushah* section of the *Amidah* repetition, we say the biblical praises of the angels. *Shibbolei Ha-Leket* (no. 20) quotes in Rashi's name that we must take three steps before *Kedushah*. While he presumably had a variant of the text from Rashi, his view makes most sense if we see the three steps as part of standing before God. *Kedushah* is the quintessential moment of standing before God like an angel.[67]

A question authorities discuss is whether the three steps may be taken after the closing blessing before the *Amidah* or that constitutes an impermissible break between the end of the blessing and the beginning of the *Amidah*. *Piskei Teshuvos* (95:2) quotes *Tehillah Le-David* (111:1) as saying that the three steps are necessary for the *Amidah* and therefore do not constitute a break. However, I found that the *Siddur Otzar Ha-Tefillos* (before "*Tzur Yisrael*") writes that the custom is to take the three steps forward before *Tzur Yisrael*. He then quotes the *Eliyah Rabbah* who says to take the three steps earlier, at *Tehillos le-Kel Elyon*. The implication is that the three steps would constitute a break. Similarly, Rav Eliezer Melamed (*Peninei Halakhah, Tefillah* 17:2) writes that one should take the steps before finishing the blessing to avoid a break between the blessing and the *Amidah*.

If the three steps are part of standing before God, then perhaps they do not constitute a break. The steps must be taken

---

67. Note that *Orechos Chaim* (*Tefillah* no. 25) and *Arugas Ha-Bosem* (ed. Urbach, vol. 1 p. 44) seem to have had the same text as *Shibbolei Ha-Leket*.

immediately before the *Amidah* and are an element of the prayer stance. However, if they represent approaching God, then they are a preparation for prayer and may constitute a break.

I find it interesting that this custom of taking three steps before prayer developed into extremes. As cited above, some do not observe it at all. The Rema only mentions it as "some say." In my experience, most people—including Sefardim—observe it. And some kabbalists have imbued the practice with sanctity and even required three steps backward before the three steps forward (note that the *Mishnah Berurah* [95:3] states that the steps backward are customary but unnecessary).

Pray with the Leader

The standard way to pray with a *minyan* is to arrive more or less on time and to pray together with everyone else. That way, you start the silent *Amidah* together with everyone else, praying as a quiet community. This is *tefillah be-tzibbur*, prayer with a community. What if you come too late to catch up? The answer to that question lies in disproven accusations of forgery.

In a letter to Rav Yehudah Aszod, Rav Moshe Sofer (the Chasam Sofer) writes that praying together with the leader (*shali'ach tzibbur*) is the primary fulfillment of *tefillah be-tzibbur* (*Iggeros Soferim*, part 2 no. 14; *Likkutei Teshuvos Chasam Sofer*, no. 3). Ideally, everyone should recite their own prayers word for word with the leader. However, we have a silent prayer first so the leader can prepare and then recite the prayer for everyone. When someone prays together with the leader, for whatever reason, that is the true *tefillah be-tzibbur*. Therefore, if you are running late you should start your silent prayer when the leader starts his loud repetition.

Rav Moshe Feinstein (*Iggeros Moshe, Orach Chaim* 3:9) disagrees with this conclusion. He points out that the Rema (*Orach Chaim* 109:2) says that if you are running late, preferably you should wait until the leader finishes *Kedushah* before starting your silent prayer; praying with the leader is only for emergencies. Clearly, Rav Feinstein argues, the Rema disagrees with Rav Sofer's thesis. After asking more questions, Rav Feinstein concludes that this letter is so mistaken that it must have been a forgery.[68] If only someone who prays with the leader achieves *tefillah be-tzibbur*, prayer with the community, then most people most of the time are praying by themselves in synagogue! This is an absurd conclusion. Rather, everyone praying silently together is a fulfillment of *tefillah be-tzibbur*.

Rav Feinstein was not the first to suggest that *Iggeros Soferim* is unreliable in the letters it contains. Rav Chaim Elazar Shapira (*Nimukei Orach Chaim* 243:1) objects strongly to this book for a number of reasons, among them the inclusion of pictures of rabbis from the Sofer family, which Rav Shapira finds improper. He also objects to a letter in which the *Chasam Sofer* rebukes the Kaliver Rebbe for refusing to allow the marriage of an *agunah* whom the *Chasam Sofer* permitted. Rav Shapira argues that this must be a forgery because the Kaliver Rebbe was a great *tzaddik*.

Rav Binyamin Shlomo Hamburger (introduction to *Zikhronos U-Masoros Al Ha-Chasam Sofer*, p. 15ff.) lists these and other accusations of forgery. He points out that each claim has been refuted conclusively. In Rav Feinstein's case, the *Chasam Sofer*'s letter was also published in *Likkutei Teshuvos* from a manuscript in which the author wrote that he copied from the original, which was written in the *Chasam Sofer*'s handwriting. Additionally, the same idea is repeated in the *Chasam Sofer*'s commentary to the Talmud (*Chasam Sofer Al Sugyos Ha-Shas*, Jerusalem, 1991, no. 27 p. 46d). The letter to the Kaliver Rebbe has since been found in a Sofer family archive. Rav Hamburger concludes that no evidence has proven that there are forgeries in the *Iggeros Soferim* collection.[69]

Rav Shmuel Wosner (note in the back of Rav Yitzchak Fuchs, *Tefillah Ke-Hilkhasah*, pp. 536-538, republished in *Responsa Shevet*

---

68. "In the end, all of the words in this responsum are mistaken; therefore it is clear that these are not the words of the *Chasam Sofer* and this responsum should be ignored."
69. "There has never been proof of a forgery."

Ha-Levi 4:11) quotes Rav Feinstein's objection and states that, with all due respect, the claim of forgery cannot be accepted. He says that "anyone who recognizes the style of the responsum will realize immediately that they are the words of the *Chasam Sofer*."

Rav Wosner explains that the best way to fulfill *tefillah be-tzibbur* is for the leader to pray and everyone listen to his prayer, fulfilling their obligation through the leader. Since it is unrealistic to expect everyone to listen carefully to such a long prayer, the Sages decreed that everyone who can should pray silently on their own. Ideally, they should pray with the leader, but the Sages moved it earlier so the leader can prepare his prayer. When everyone prays together silently, this is a fulfillment of *tefillah be-tzibbur*. But an even better fulfillment is praying together with the leader.[70]

More recently, Rav Simcha Rabinowitz (*Piskei Teshuvos*, vol. 1 90:14 n. 175) points out that while a few authorities agree with Rav Feinstein, the vast majority agree with the *Chasam Sofer*. Among those who agree with Rav Feinstein are Rav Yosef Chaim Sonnenfeld (*Responsa Salmas Chaim* 130) and the *Responsa Chavatzeles Ha-Sharon* (*Orach Chaim* 2). Among those who disagree are the *Mishnah Berurah* (109:14), Rav Ovadiah Yosef (*Yabi'a Omer* 2:7; *Yechavveh Da'as* 5:6), Rav Yitzchak Elchanan Spektor (*Responsa Be'er Yitzchak* no. 20), Rav Avraham Karelitz (*Chazon Ish, Orach Chaim* 19:7), and more. Additionally, biographies of the *Chafetz Chaim*, Satmar Rav, and Steipler Gaon report that they sometimes followed this practice of praying together with the leader, rather than waiting until after *Kedushah* to begin.

---

70. There is a separate view, based on the Rambam, that distinguishes between prayer with the community (*tefillah be-tzibbur*) and prayer of the community (*tefillas ha-tzibbur*). When everyone prays together silently, that is prayer with a community. When the leaders prays out loud, that is prayer of the community. See Rav Hershel Schachter, *Nefesh Ha-Rav*, pp. 124-127; Rav Moshe Sternbuch, *Mo'adim U-Zemanim* 1:7.

Rav Henkin on Carlebach *Minyanim*

Rav Yosef Eliyahu Henkin (d. 1973) was the leading halakhic decisor in America of his day. He was the address for the most difficult halakhic problems. Additionally, as the President of Ezras Torah, he made decisions for the famous Ezras Torah Luach, which set the rules for synagogues across America.

Rav Henkin had strong opinions on many topics, some of which never took hold. For example, he considered non-Orthodox weddings, even if performed completely non-halakhically, to be a form of common-law marriage that required a *get*, a religious divorce. Rav Moshe Feinstein famously dissented, allowing for the annulment of those marriages when necessary to allow children to marry halakhically. In another area, Rav Henkin insisted that the Lakewood Yeshiva stop its practice of making *kiddush* before *shofar* blowing on Rosh Hashanah. The yeshiva refused to listen, arguing that they were following the practice of the Slabodka yeshiva.

Regarding cantors, *chazzanim*, Rav Henkin followed a long and illustrious history of rabbinic critics. Throughout the generations, rabbis have denounced various practices of *chazzanim*. Rav Henkin was particularly concerned with the practice of *chazzanim* repeating words or singing tunes without words. The former issue has largely, but not entirely, subsided. However, the latter is common practice in Modern Orthodox, Yeshivish, and Chassidic synagogues. The *chazzan* will fit the words to a tune by including "nai nai nai." Rav Henkin explicitly forbids this for the following reason, based on a contradiction in the *Magen Avraham*.

I. The *Kohanim*'s Song

At the end of each of the three blessings of *Birkas Kohanim*, the *chazzan* says the final word and then the *kohanim* sing a tune without words while the congregants quietly recite the *Ribbon* prayer, after which the *kohanim* say the concluding word of the blessing. In other words, there is a lengthy pause in the *kohanim*'s recitation for a song and prayer, during which the *kohanim* sing a wordless tune. This is the current common practice.

The Rema (*Shulchan Arukh, Orach Chaim* 128:45) describes the practice slightly differently. The way he has it, the *kohanim* sing the last word as the congregation recites the prayer. The *Magen Avraham* (ad loc., 73) objects that the congregation must listen to the blessing and may not recite a prayer while the *kohanim* sing the last word. Therefore, he suggests singing after the last word, at least for the first two blessings.

The *Magen Avraham* then asks a question that is important for contemporary practice: The *Ribbon* prayer has to be recited during the *kohanim*'s blessing. If the singing and prayer happen after the final word, how is that considered during the blessing? He answers that the singing of a wordless tune is an extension of the blessing.

II. Singing *Kaddish*

However, the *Magen Avraham* seems to contradict this ruling earlier in his commentary. The Rema (ibid., 124:8) writes that when a *chazzan* says the concluding phrase "*ve-imru amen*," the congregation should not answer "*amen*" after him but together with him. The *Magen Avraham* (ad loc., 14) goes even further. He says that when the *chazzan* sings the phrase at length, the congregation should not wait for him and should just shout out "*amen*" while he is singing. He explains that the tune is an interruption (*hefsek*) to the blessing.

This seems to be a clear contradiction between the two rulings of the *Magen Avraham*. Is the tune an extension of the blessing or an interruption? He was well aware of this problem and explains his different conclusions. If the tune is too long, if the break within the blessing extends for a long period, then it is an interruption. If not, it is part of the blessing. This is not particularly clear guidance, leaving much up to the judgement of the rabbi and *chazzan*.

III. Rav Henkin's View
In 2013, forty years after Rav Henkin's death, the first volume of a new collection of his responsa was published as *Gevuros Eliyahu*. The book contains many previously unpublished rulings as well as excerpts from his rulings on the synagogue calendar. All of this is excellently footnoted. The book contains many fascinating and important rulings, such as about a woman saying *Kaddish*, prayer in public schools, and the use of electricity on Shabbos.

In responsum 15, Rav Henkin objects to singing "empty" (wordless) tunes during the blessings of *Shema*. He considers these tunes questionable interruptions (*chashash hefsek*). While he does not explain, I believe he means that the *Magen Avraham*'s definition of an interruption is unclear and therefore wordless tunes might be too long and therefore constitute an interruption.

He says not to object that great rabbis have sung wordless tunes during prayer, apparently proving that the practice is permissible. They sang the tunes out of great spiritual arousal. Therefore, their songs were part of the prayer. We cannot reach those spiritual heights.

In responsum 21, Rav Henkin discusses singing during prayer. He approves it based on Chassidic and Sephardic practices. Broadly speaking, Chassidic men sing during prayer on Shabbos and holidays. Sephardim, who generally have more ancient customs, also sing. But they are careful not to repeat words, their tunes are brief and simple, and they all sing together—*chazzan* and congregation. Sephardim sing the words, not just "nai nai nai" in between words. Rav Henkin points out that Young Israel synagogues follow a similar practice. Rav Henkin adds that he objects to tunes that repeat words or have no words at all.

In responsum 149 (par. 9), Rav Henkin discusses *birkas kohanim*. He adopts a revised version of the *Magen Avraham*'s suggestion. The *Magen Avraham* advocated reciting the *Ribbon* prayer after the *kohanim* finish the blessing, while they sing, but only for the first two blessings. Rav Henkin suggested this be done for all three blessings, so there is no interruption in the blessing.

IV. Common Practice

Rav Henkin's objection to wordless tunes applies not only to Carlebach-style *minyanim* but also to many contemporary synagogues. However, it seems not to be common practice. The community seems to have never adopted his strict ruling on this subject. This is particularly evident regarding *birkas kohanim*. I am not aware of any synagogue in which the *kohanim* sing after finishing the blessings.

Additionally, I find his logic difficult to understand. The *Magen Avraham* justifies the *Ribbon* prayer after the blessings because the brief singing is not an interruption. Rav Henkin seems to have turned that around and ruled that the *Ribbon* prayers should be recited after the blessings because the singing is an interruption. If it is, then why sing at all? And why is it not too late for the prayer, as the *Magen Avraham* objected?

Perhaps Rav Henkin was concerned that our *birkas kohanim* tunes are longer than those in the time of the *Magen Avraham*. Indeed, I have seen some synagogues in which the extended tune for the third blessing is sung for the first two, as well. Therefore, he was concerned that these tunes may be an interruption. In other words, this is a case of doubt (*safek*).

The concern is sufficient to delay the tunes until after the blessing, which is a biblical commandment. However, the *Ribbon* prayer is merely a talmudic custom, and therefore allows for leniency in this doubt.

What to Do About a *Yarmulke* #Fail

Long-standing custom dictates that Jewish men cover their heads. Authorities debate whether it is an actual law or just a strong custom, with the consensus concluding it is a custom. But when we recite God's name, in either a blessing or prayer, the matter becomes more severe. Even people who do not wear a *yarmulke* at work put one on to pray or recite a blessing. But what do you do if the *yarmulke* accidentally falls off and you only notice after you are done praying?

In a book on the halakhic force of customs, *Imrei Barukh: Tokef Ha-Minhag Ba-Halakhah*,[71] Rav Baruch Simon addresses this question. One reason for various customs is the biblical prohibition against following the practices of other religions (*chukkos ha-goyim*). Following the Jews' emancipation, this prohibition became a dominant theme in the complex integration of Jews into Christian society—what are we allowed to do and what is off limits?

Prior to that, Rav Shlomo Luria (*Responsa Maharshal*, no. 72) concluded that wearing a *yarmulke* is only a custom, not a law. The Vilna Gaon (*Bi'ur Ha-Gra, Orach Chaim* 8:6) ruled that you are not even obligated to wear a *yarmulke* while you pray. However, the *Taz* (*Orach Chaim* 8:3) added the consideration of *chukos ha-goyim*. Since Christians would regularly remove their head coverings, particularly before praying, Jews may not follow this

---

71. New York, 2015.

practice. According to the *Taz*, sitting without a *yarmulke*—and certainly praying bareheaded—is biblically prohibited.

Rav Simon quotes Rav Moshe Feinstein (*Iggeros Moshe, Orach Chaim* 4:40:14) who distinguishes between sitting and praying bareheaded. Christians do the former merely out of convenience. However, they pray bareheaded as a religious conviction. Therefore, Rav Feinstein rules, praying without any head covering—even by accident—is forbidden and the prayer is invalid. If your *yarmulke* accidentally falls off during prayer, you have to pray again after you cover your head.

Rav Simon then quotes Rav Shlomo Zalman Auerbach (*Halikhos Shlomo, Hilkhos Tefillah* 2:16) who says that you do not have to pray again if your *yarmulke* accidentally falls off during prayer. A footnote explains that Rav Auerbach held that Christians today do not remove their head coverings before prayer as a matter of religious principle. They may have once done so out of conviction, but now they do so as a matter of social convention. Therefore, praying bareheaded is not a practice of another religion and, while it should be avoided, does not require repeating the prayer.

Rav Simon's overview is interesting but incidental to his overall purpose of surveying the literature about customs. Another book delves deeply into the subject of head coverings. Rav Ari Wasserman's *Otzar Ha-Kippah: Kippos, Kovi'im Ve-Atifas Ha-Rosh*[72] is an exhaustive, comprehensive two-volume study of head coverings in Jewish law. He leaves no stone unturned, no responsum unquoted. Section 4, chapter 9 discusses the case of prayer while accidentally bareheaded.

Rav Wasserman points out that Rav Feinstein ends his responsum with wording that might imply uncertainty about his conclusion. However, that specific question was asked by Rav Ephraim Greenblatt, who reported that Rav Feinstein ruled strictly on the matter (*Rivevos Ve-Yovelos* vol. 2 no. 483).

---

72. Jerusalem, 2014.

In addition to quoting Rav Auerbach, Rav Wasserman cites the *Yeshu'os Moshe* (3:15), Rav Moshe Stern (in the journal *Or Yahel*, issue 4 p. 109), *Lev Yehudah* (*Yoreh De'ah* no. 64), *Az Nidberu* (3:5), *Shemesh U-Magen* (*Orach Chaim* no. 16), and *Or Le-Tziyyon* (vol. 2, 7:13) as ruling leniently. Rav Ovadiah Yosef, in an approbation to *Netzach Yosef* (by Rav Yosef Bar Shalom), explicitly disagrees with Rav Feinstein. Rav Yosef says that since following a practice of another religion is only forbidden if you do it with the intent to imitate gentiles, if your *yarmulke* falls off by accident you lack that intent and therefore do not violate the prohibition.

In conclusion, authorities clearly differ whether to repeat a prayer if you accidentally prayed without a *yarmulke*. While the consensus seems to be lenient, it isn't clear to me whether the practice follows Rav Feinstein. In such a situation, ask your rabbi what to do. But remember to put your *yarmulke* on before asking.

The Short *Minchah*

Some yeshivas (and offices) have the practice of shortening the *minchah* prayers by utilizing the "short *minchah*" (or "*heikha kedushah*"). However, customs differ exactly how congregants should act during this shortened service.

The Rema (*Orach Chaim* 124:2; 232:1) cites the Maharil, who says that in an emergency, the prayer leader should not repeat the *Amidah*. Rather, the prayer leader immediately begins the prayer out loud, continues out loud through the *Kedushah* section until the blessing *Ha-Kel Ha-Kadosh*, and then proceeds silently. At the same time, the congregants recite every word in those first three blessings together with the leader and then continue silently on their own. In this way, *Kedushah* is recited quickly with the leader and the prayer is recited only once, without repetition.

The *Beis Yosef* (*Orach Chaim* 234) says that this was the common Sephardic practice for *minchah* every day, even without an emergency. However, the rabbis in Tzefas, where he lived, attempted to stamp out that practice, excommunicating anyone locally who observed it. Rav Ovadiah Yosef (*Yechavveh Da'as* 3:16) quotes other Sephardic authorities who similarly opposed this practice. However, as noted above, the Rema allows it in unusual circumstances.

Rav Yosef (ibid.) allows the practice when the repetition of the prayer is endangered. For example, if there are only ten men in the *minyan* and some will fail to respond "*amen*" to the blessings, the prayer is almost in vain (*Shulchan Arukh, Orach Chaim* 124:4). In such a case, it is better to have a *heikha kedushah* than a bad repetition.

The *Ba'er Heitev* (124:4) notes different practices regarding the *heikha kedushah*. Sephardim begin their silent prayer together with the leader. If they all stay at the same pace, they will end at the same time. However, Ashkenazim begin their silent prayer only after *Kedushah*. If they all keep the same pace, the leader will finish before everyone else because he will be done with three blessings as they begin their first. Rav Eliezer Melamed (*Peninei Halakhah, Tefillah* 19:5) suggests that an Ashkenazi who prays slowly should pray *Minchah* together with the leader so he can finish in time to answer *Kaddish*. In my experience, if you pray very slowly and try to pray together with the leader, you may have trouble reaching *Kedushah* in time.

Rav Hershel Schachter (*Nefesh Ha-Rav*, pp. 126-127) quotes Rav Joseph B. Soloveitchik as preferring the Sephardic practice. He believes that the *Kedushah* should be part of your *Amidah* prayer. When the leader is repeating the prayer, he is reciting a prayer as everyone's representative and the *Kedushah* is part of it. However, when the leader is merely saying the first three blessings out loud, the *Kedushah* will only be part of your prayer if you are saying the prayer together with the leader.

While the permission mentioned above only applies to emergencies, others have adopted it as standard practice. Offices are concerned that people must return to work quickly. The yeshivas reportedly argue that their students are losing time from learning—that constitutes an emergency situation. Rav Nathan Kamenetsky describes this as "the common assumption" (*Making of a Godol*, improved edition, p. 612). However, he adds that his father, Rav Yaakov Kamenetsky, "explained that since the Reader's repetition was instituted for the benefit of those individuals who were too unlearned to pray on their own (*einam beki'im*) and had to listen to a Reader, it was recited only in synagogues (*batei kenesses*), never in study halls (*batei midrash*) where only scholars congregated" (ibid.)

Pollard's Blessing

In 2015, Jonathan Pollard was released after spending thirty years in prison. He was sentenced to life in prison after pleading guilty to spying on the United States. There are two possible responses to release after such a long sentence. One is to become bitter over the time lost, the life that could have been lived. The other is to be grateful for the end of the ordeal, the new beginning. I cannot fathom the depth of his experience, but I hope he can find his way to seeing the opportunities in his future.

When he was released, he faced an interesting halakhic question: Should he *bentch gomel*, recite the traditional blessing thanking God for salvation? This is a response of hope, of seeing the end of the past and the beginning of the future. His ability to recite this blessing lies in the conditions of his imprisonment and release. As always, the details make all the difference.

I. Four Salvations

The Gemara (*Berakhos* 54b) says that four people need to *bentch gomel*: someone who travels by sea, journeys in the desert, becomes healed from illness, or is released from prison. These four categories are derived from Psalm 107:

1. travel by sea: "they that go down to the sea in ships" (v. 23)
2. journey in the desert: "they wandered in the wilderness in a desert way" (v. 4)

3. healed from illness: "He sent His word, and healed them, and delivered them from their graves" (v. 20)
4. released from prison: "such as sat in darkness and in the shadow of death, being bound in affliction and iron" (v. 10)

Tosafos (*Berakhos* 54b sv. *Arba'ah*) point out that the Gemara's list follows a different order than the Psalm's verses. Why does the Gemara skip back and forth? Tosafos answer that the Bible lists the cases in decreasing order of danger: first those traveling in the desert, then those sitting in prison, then those suffering illness, and finally those traveling by sea. In contrast, the Gemara lists the cases in order of frequency, those more common appearing earlier in the list. However, *Talmidei Rabbenu Yonah* (quoted in *Ma'adanei Yom Tov, Berakhos* 9:30) quote a responsum of Rav Hai Ga'on in which he explains it the opposite way. According to Rav Hai Ga'on, the Gemara lists the cases in the order of danger while the Bible lists them in order of frequency. It seems that according to Tosafos, both the imprisonment and illness on which this blessing is recited must be life threatening. According to Rav Hai Ga'on, this need not be true because they are less severe than traveling by sea and journeying through the desert.

II. Severities

Two general approaches emerge in the commentaries regarding this blessing. Ashkenazic authorities tend to see this blessing as reserved for those who emerge from life-threatening situations. For example, the Rosh (*Berakhos* 9:3) says that the custom in Germany and France is to refrain from reciting this blessing when traveling from city to city because there is no danger to life. He also quotes the Ri Migash, who rules that only someone who recovers from a serious illness should recite this blessing. The Ra'avad (quoted in *Birkei Yosef, Shiyurei Berakhah, Orach Chaim* 219:1) rules that the blessing only applies to a life-threatening illness.

However, the Rosh notes, the *Arukh* implies that even someone whose headache goes away should recite this blessing. Similarly, in a responsum, the Ri Migash (no. 90) rules that someone who is released from debtors' prison—i.e., who faced no threat to life—should recite the blessing. According to the Ri Migash, the blessing on release from prison is about regaining freedom, not salvation from death.

The *Shulchan Arukh* (*Orach Chaim* 219:8) rules that you recite this blessing after recovering from any serious illness, even if it was not life threatening. However, the Rema (ad loc.) says that the Ashkenazic practice is to only recite the blessing after a life threatening illness. Similarly, the *Magen Avraham* (ad loc., 1) writes that you only recite the blessing after exiting a life threatening imprisonment. The *Birkei Yosef* (ibid.) argues that release from any prison sentence merits recitation of the blessing, like the Ri Migash.

III. Recent Authorities

Based on all the above, it would seem that Sephardim—who generally follow the *Shulchan Arukh* and *Birkei Yosef*—would recite the *gomel* blessing on release from prison regardless of the sentence. Ashkenazim—who generally follow the Rema and *Magen Avraham*—would only recite the blessing on release from a potential death sentence.

The *Mishnah Berurah* (219, *Bi'ur Halakhah* s.v. *chavush*) explains that the *Magen Avraham*'s view is based on a threat to life . Regardless of the sentence, if the prisoner faced a threat to his life—such as being held in a highly dangerous prison—then he should recite the blessing. The *Mishnah Berurah* adds that the *Magen Avraham*'s ruling was intended even for Sephardim who follow a more lenient view on this blessing. Since the *Shulchan Arukh* rejects the view of the *Arukh* that even a minor illness merits this blessing, he requires a serious illness that could lead to a life threat. Similarly, the *Shulchan Arukh* requires an imprisonment that could lead to a life threat, not just a minimum security prison stay.

However, the *Kaf Ha-Chaim* (219:11)—an important Sephardic authority—rules that even someone imprisoned in a comfortable prison for a monetary matter should recite the blessing. Following the Ri Migash, he explains that the blessing here refers to a lack of freedom. Once that freedom is regained, you should saying the blessing.

The first Lubavitcher Rebbe, in his discussion of blessings in his prayerbook (*Seder Birkos Ha-Nehenin* 13:2), takes a middle position. He says that someone released from a death sentence or from prison on a monetary matter for which he was held in chains recites the blessing. The aspect of being held in chains is a reference to the language of the verse (Ps. 107:10), "being *bound* in affliction and *iron*."

The *Arukh Ha-Shulchan* (209:25) adds another consideration. On the one hand, he rules leniently that even someone released from prison on a monetary matter recites the blessing. However, he explains that this view—of Ri Migash—connects the blessing to renewed freedom. Someone released from a lengthy prison stay, for whatever reason, regains his freedom, for which he recites the *gomel* blessing. But this only applies if he is truly free without any conditions. If, for example, he is subject to home arrest, then he cannot recite the blessing because he is not truly free.

Rav Eliezer Melamed (*Peninei Halakhah, Berakhos* 16:11 and in his *Harchavos*, ad loc.) says that most authorities—Ashkenazic and Sephardic—rule that someone released from prison for a long stay recites the blessing. He offers two reasons: First, like the Ri Migash, many believe that this blessing applies to renewed freedom. Additionally, any extended imprisonment involves at least a little threat to life.

IV. Conclusion

Should Jonathan Pollard have bentched *gomel* on his release? On the one hand, he was never given a death sentence, so a simple reading of the *Magen Avraham* would imply that he should not recite the blessing. However, the *Mishnah Berurah* adds that any threat to life while in prison would merit a blessing on release. If his prison stay was at any time life-threatening, then he would recite the blessing. On his release, he became free from the position of possibly being in a life-threatening prison situation.

Other authorities are more open to the blessing because they see it as a response to regaining freedom. On his release, Pollard gained his freedom and therefore, presumably, should have recited the blessing.

However, the conditions of his release also make a difference. If he had been released to home arrest, then everyone agrees he should not have recited the blessing. Additionally, if his movement had been restricted within the country, he would not have recited the blessing because he would have lacked freedom. I suspect, but am not certain, that since he is not allowed to leave the country, then he should not have recited the blessing. But I leave that to his rabbi to decide.

Prayer and the Longest *Shiur*

In December 2015, my friend Rav Shlomo Einhorn accomplished the Herculean task of teaching Torah for eighteen hours straight, streaming online. He did this to raise funds for the yeshiva he heads. When I told my children about this before the event, they asked when he will pray. I responded, "who says he has to?" Rav Einhorn actually prayed online, adding commentary when he was allowed to speak. However, the question remains whether he was exempt from prayer.

I. Interrupting Learning Torah

The Mishnah (*Shabbos* 9b) says that you interrupt learning to recite *Shema* but not to pray (recite the *Amidah*). In the Gemara (11a), R. Yochanan says that this only refers to people like R. Shimon bar Yochai and his colleagues, who learned Torah full time. But people like us, says R. Yochanan, interrupt our learning for both *Shema* and prayer. Rashi explains that since we will interrupt our Torah for work, we must also interrupt it for prayer.

However, the Mishnah earlier discusses other cases—such as getting a haircut—which we do not interrupt even for prayer. Why would Torah be less important? The *Ba'al Ha-Ma'or* (on the Rif, *Shabbos* 3a) distinguishes between whether there is time to pray afterward. When getting a haircut or eating, you do not interrupt your activity if you will have time to pray afterward. If not, you interrupt. The discussion about Torah refers to the latter case, when there is no time to pray afterward because your learning will extend beyond the prescribed time for prayer. People like R. Shimon bar Yochai do not stop their learning even though they will completely miss this prayer.

The Ran (on the Rif, *Shabbos* 3b-4a) rules as follows:

- If you started learning after the time to pray or recite *Shema* begins:
  - For a rabbinic obligation like prayer, you do not interrupt your learning if there will be time to pray after
  - For a biblical obligation like *Shema*, you stop immediately even if there is time to recite it later.
- If you start learning before the time has begun, then when the time arrives you never have to interrupt your learning if there will be time afterward to pray or recite *Shema*.

II. Interrupting Teaching Torah

However, that is discussing your personal learning. Teaching Torah to others might be different. The Gemara (*Berakhos* 13b) says that R. Yehudah Ha-Nasi's *Shema* consisted of only the first verse. Since he was teaching Torah, when the time for *Shema* arrived he would say the first verse and continue teaching.

The Gemara (*Berakhos* 5b) says that prayer should come right after waking up (connected to your bed, so to speak). Presumably, this means that you should not do anything meaningful before praying, including learning Torah. *Talmidei Rabbenu Yonah* (on Rif, *Berakhos* 3a s.v. *Al Tefillasi*) says that Rashi forbids learning Torah before praying but other French rabbis permit it. However, that only refers to personal learning. When teaching Torah to the public, we have to be concerned that the class will not gather after prayers. Therefore, even Rashi would allow a Torah class before prayers. As proof, we see from above that R. Yehudah Ha-Nasi taught Torah before praying!

The *Shulchan Arukh* (*Orach Chaim* 89:6) rules like *Talmidei Rabbenu Yonah*. However, the Rema (ibid., 106:2) takes this even further. He equates someone teaching Torah to R. Shimon bar Yochai. Since R. Shimon bar Yochai did not interrupt his learning even if he would miss prayer entirely, similarly someone teaching Torah to others may miss prayer.

III. Conclusion

The *Chayei Adam* (16:3) implicitly rejects this extension of the Rema.[73] The *Ma'amar Mordekhai* and *Levush* (both cited in *Bi'ur Halakhah* (106:2 s.v. *ve-im*)) point out that the Rema went further than the *Talmidei Rabbenu Yonah*. The *Mishnah Berurah* (106:8) seems uncomfortable with the ruling of the Rema, quoting others who disagree.

During his marathon *shi'ur*, Rav Einhorn davened. I'm not sure whether technically he had to. There is room for a halakhic authority to rule either way.

---

73. See also *Kitzur Shulchan Arukh* 8:5 and *Shulchan Arukh Ha-Rav, Hilkhos Talmud Torah* 4:4.

Tzitzis at *Ma'ariv*

Should we be careful to wear *tzitzis* when praying the evening *ma'ariv* service? Rav Mordechai Eliyahu (*Responsa Ma'amar Mordekhai*, vol. 2 no. 3) explores this question. The argument in favor goes as follows: We are careful to wear *tefillin* and *tzitzis* while reciting *Shema* in the morning because the third paragraph includes the obligation to wear *tefillin* and *tzitzis*. If we fail to wear them while reciting the obligation, then it appears like we are testifying falsely, or rather to our own faults.

Rav Eliyahu gives a fairly brief answer, which I will expand further and add sources. The *Magen Avraham* (24:3) quotes the *Zohar* as saying that if you read *Shema* without wearing *tzitzis*, you are testifying falsely about yourself. The *Machatzis Ha-Shekel* (ad loc.), a supercommentary to the *Magen Avraham*, argues that this requirement can be traced even to the Gemara.

The Gemara (*Berakhos* 14b) says that someone who recites *Shema* without wearing *tefillin* testifies falsely. But that is just about *tefillin*. Rashi (ad loc., s.v. *ke'ilu*) explains that he testifies falsely about God, who said that we will wear *tefillin* but we do not. *Talmidei Rabbeinu Yonah* (ad loc., s.v. *kol*) explains that he testifies falsely about himself, for failing to fulfill the commandment he reads. This logic, the *Machatzis Ha-Shekel* argues, can also be applied to the commandment of *tzitzis*.

The *Pri Megadim* (ad loc., *Eshel Avraham* 3) agrees with the *Machatzis Ha-Shekel*. He also quotes Tosafos (*Menachos* 43b s.v.

chosam), who say that *tzitzis* testify that the Jews are servants of God—note the language of "testify."

From all this, you could conclude that you must also wear *tzitzis* while reciting *Shema* at night. Rav Eliyahu does not discuss this, but you could ask why we are not also discussing wearing *tefillin* at night while reciting *Shema*. Isn't that commandment also mentioned in the third paragraph of *Shema*? I would answer that the commandment of *tefillin* does not apply at night, therefore you are not testifying falsely by refraining from wearing them at night. While *tzitzis* also does not apply at night, authorities debate whether that means we are exempt from wearing *tzitzis* at night, or whether night-time clothes (e.g., pajamas) are exempt from *tzitzis*. According to this latter opinion, we would still be testifying falsely by reciting *Shema* at night without wearing *tzitzis*.

However, the *Shulchan Arukh* (*Orach Chaim* 24:1) only says that you *should* be careful to wear *tzitzis* while reciting *Shema*, not that you must. From this, Rav Eliyahu deduces that there is no concern about testifying falsely. This admonition is for a different reason, which Rav Eliyahu does not explain. While he does not quote it, the *Bi'ur Ha-Gra* (ad loc.) also says that this is not a solid rule (*de-mi-dina ein tzarikh*). Interestingly, the *Arukh Ha-Shulchan* does not quote any of this, implying he disagrees with even the stringency.

Additionally, while Rav Eliyahu does not discuss this, the Maharsha seemingly disagrees with the *Machatzis Ha-Shekel*. The Maharsha (*Chiddushei Aggados, Berakhos* 14b s.v. *kol*) connects the false testimony to *tefillin* because it is one of the three signs of God's covenant with Israel (together with circumcision and Shabbos). According to this explanation, you cannot extend the concept of false testimony from *tefillin* to *tzitzis* because the latter is not one of the three signs.

Therefore, while it is good to wear *tzitzis* while reciting Shema, and not remove your *tzitzis* before *ma'ariv*, this does not rise to the level of an obligation.

Answering a Priest's Blessing

It is not uncommon for a Christian neighbor or friend to offer a blessing to a Jew or to anyone else. Often, these blessings colorfully invoke biblical themes in meaningful ways. Freestyle blessings are part of Christian culture. How should a Jew respond to these blessings? Obviously, a blessing offered in the spirit of friendship should be received in the same spirit. Anything else would be rude. But words have meaning and the precise form of reception can make a difference. We don't want to make an inadvertent theological statement greater than intended.

I. Amen

The Talmud Yerushalmi (*Berakhos* 8:8) seems to answer this question. "A gentile who recites a blessing, answer 'Amen' after him. R. Tanchum said: If a gentile blesses you, answer 'Amen' after him. As it says, 'You shall be blessed from all the nations' (Deut. 7:14)." A gentile blessing a Jew is not just a personal expression of friendship; it is a fulfillment of a biblical prophecy. While the verse literally means that the Jewish people will be blessed more than other nations, it can also be translated as saying that other nations will bless the Jews. In offering a personal blessing, a Christian fulfills a biblical promise. To this, ostensibly we answer "Amen."

Amen is not a small word; its meaning runs deep. The word appears in two places in the Pentateuch (Num. 5:22 and throughout Deut. 27). It indicates approval and confirmation.

The Talmud (*Sanhedrin* 111a) adds a theological aspect to this confirmation. The three letters of *amen* (אמן) can serve as an acronym for "God, the faithful king" (Rashi, ad loc.). In other words, responding "Amen" to a statement indicates our belief that God confirms that statement. When you answer "Amen," you are attesting to a divine truth, you are stating your faith in the blessing and its divine source. The Talmud (*Sanhedrin* 110b) asks from what point in a child's development he merits a place in the afterlife. One answer is from birth. Among other answers, each of which deserves lengthy treatment, is that a child merits a place in the world-to-come when he begins answering "Amen." Elsewhere, the Talmud (*Berakhos* 54b) surprisingly says that someone who answers "Amen" is greater than the one who recites the blessing. Answering "Amen" is an act of faith, an act of joining together in prayer.

The Mishnah (*Berakhos* 51b) says that you must say "Amen" after you hear a Jew recite a blessing. However, you may only recite "Amen" after a Kusi's (Kuthite's) blessing if you hear the entire blessing. *Talmidei Rabbenu Yonah* (ad loc., p. 40a s.v. *kol zeman*) explain that with a Jew, as long as you hear God's name in a blessing, you must respond "Amen." You know what he is doing and what he is saying, so the response is honest and appropriate. However, the Kusim were idolators who were forced in biblical times to join the Jewish people but never completely gave up their idolatry (2 Kings 17:24-30). Instead, they combined worship of God with idol worship, in what is called syncretism. Even if they say part of the blessing properly, they could add to it or change it to include their idols. You cannot say "Amen" to that, because you might be attesting to their idols. However, if you hear the entire blessing without deviation, you can assume that they have God in mind and therefore respond affirmatively with "Amen."

II. Amen to a Classical Blessing

Talmidei Rabbenu Yonah then quote the authors' teacher, Rabbenu Yonah, who lived in thirteenth-century Christian Spain. Rabbeinu Yonah says that after a gentile's blessing, you may answer "Amen." Since his intent is to bless God and you hear the entire blessing from him, you may affirm the blessing. The Rosh (*Berakhos* 8:5) offers a slightly different reason for the same ruling. He says that if you hear the whole blessing and it refers only to God, you can assume that the gentile has God in mind. A gentile does not intend for another being if he mentions God. Note that the Rosh lived in late thirteenth-century Christian Germany and early fourteenth-century Christian Spain.

However, the Rambam (*Mishneh Torah, Hilkhos Berakhos* 1:13) rules that you may not say "Amen" after a gentile's blessing. The resolution of this ruling with talmudic texts remains a challenge. The Vilna Gaon (*Bi'ur Ha-Gra* 215:2) struggles and can only reconcile the ruling by positing a textual emendation in the Rambam's text.

In *Shulchan Arukh* (*Orach Chaim* 215:2), Rav Moshe Isserles (Rema) adds a gloss that you may say "Amen" after a gentile's blessing if you hear the entire blessing. The Vilna Gaon disagrees and allows saying "Amen" even if you hear only a part of the blessing. He reads the Rosh differently, as assuming that a gentile refers to God and therefore you do not need to hear the whole blessing. These two opinions reflect Ashkenazic practice. More recently, Rav Ovadiah Yosef (*Yalkut Yosef* 215:2) rules like the Rambam, that you may not answer Amen to a gentile's (Christian's) blessing, reflecting Sephardic practice.

III. Amen to a Freestyle Blessing

All of the above addresses a classical blessing, the kind we find in a prayerbook. These blessings praise God for His various great works and follow strict wordings that cannot be altered. That isn't quite what we are discussing, nor is it the subject of R. Tanchum's biblical inference. R. Tanchum was discussing a gentile blessing a Jew, not God.

Regarding such a blessing, the question seems to be whether we can assume that a gentile refers to God when offering a freestyle blessing. When he recites one of the standard Jewish formulas for blessing, we can make that assumption (according to Rabbenu Yonah and the Rosh). What about when he recites a freestyle blessing?

The *Sefer Chasidim* (13th century, Germany; no. 527) says that if a gentile says to you "may *my* god help you," you should not respond "Amen." But if he says "may *your* God help you," then you should answer "Amen." What if he simply says "may God help you"? *Sefer Chasidim* does not offer guidance in that case.

More recently, Rav Betzalel Stern (*Be-Tzel Ha-Chokhmah* 3:39:10, cited in *Piskei Teshuvos* 215:6) discusses this case. He deduces from the Rema's statement that we say "Amen" only if we hear the entire standard blessing; if we hear a freestyle blessing then it does not fit the Rema's condition. Therefore, we may not respond "Amen" unless the gentile specifically blesses you in the name of "the God of Israel." I am not aware of any authority who disagrees, although I see room here for a different conclusion. When a Christian offers a blessing in the name of God rather than Jesus, he might be intending the same thing as when I say a blessing in the name of God. However, without an established authority weighing in on the subject, I feel obligated to accept the only existing opinion. (I have written to some leading scholars for their opinions—see Addendum.)

IV. Conclusion

If we cannot affirm a gentile's blessing, how do we understand R. Tanchum's biblical inference? R. Tanchum means that the nations will bless the Jewish people in the name of the one true God. This sometimes happens today and will continue to occur in the future. As a nation devoted to God, we affirm blessings in His name and not in the name of any other deity or ambiguous reference.

But that leaves us in an awkward situation. If a Christian blesses a Jew in the spirit of friendship, even in the name of God but not in the name of "the God of Israel," how do you respond in the same spirit? You don't want to answer "Amen" to a blessing that might be directed to anything other than God. *Piskei Teshuvos* (215 n. 38) suggests answering "thank you." I suggest responding with a reciprocal blessing. If someone blesses you, bless him back. I think that fully expresses the spirit of friendship and avoids inadvertent acceptance of unclear references to God. By taking "Amen" out of the picture, we are able to respond honestly and respectfully.

Addendum

I sent this question to Rav Eliezer Melamed and he replied that if a Christian blesses you with the name Jesus, you should thank him in a way that is pleasant. If he blesses you with the name God, you should answer "Amen."

The Bencher App

What good is an app for bentching, reciting the blessings after a meal, when we cannot use it on Shabbos? That was the reaction I heard from many people when NCSY announced its new, free Bencher App. This attitude neglects a few things. First, people bentch during the week also, not just on Shabbos. Second, sometimes people new to observance want to practice saying prayers in order to become more fluent. This is especially true when those prayers are sung out loud. It can be embarrassing when you mispronounce a word out loud.

But more importantly, the wildly popular *NCSY Bencher* was never just about bentching. It is a cultural experience. The NCSY Bencher (made by the supremely talented David Olivestone) is designed to assist Jews in their religious growth. It is full of songs and prayers, translated into English and transliterated to allow for easy pronunciation of the Hebrew for those who do not read Hebrew as quickly as they sing.

These songs are commonly sung at Shabbos meals, mitzvah events (e.g., weddings) and the many NCSY gatherings. They come from Bible, prayers, and religious texts like Midrash and Talmud. Song is a method of uniting a group. When everyone sings together, they join in unison despite the many different backgrounds and temperaments. While people may disagree about many things, when they sing they are united. This is a powerful emotional experience. The *NCSY Bencher* allows newcomers to feel that unity, to join the group almost immediately and feel like they belong.

In this sense, the *NCSY Bencher* is less a tool for prayer as it it is for fitting in. Someone who has never kept kosher can join together religiously with the rabbi's son in a melodic praise of God. However, the drawback has always been that you have to know the tunes in order to join the singing. Those with a good ear can learn the songs quickly but many people (including me) were born without that talent. Technology changes that equation.

Just like GPS leveled the field between those with a good sense of direction and those directionally challenged, the NCSY Bencher App empowers those who are musically challenged. The app includes all the songs, translations, and transliterations from the classic *bencher*. It also contains recordings of musician Aryeh Kunstler singing the songs (sometimes in multiple tunes). You can listen to the songs over and over until you learn the tunes. Newcomers will be able to prepare for Shabbos and other occasions, avoiding potential embarrassment. You don't have to be a quick musical study to join the special unity of NCSY singing and Shabbos *zemiros*.

Even old-timers can benefit from the app. Some of us only know a few tunes and can expand our repertoires with the app, enhancing our Shabbos meals with variety. Some of us routinely butcher the songs and can use the private refresher course that the app offers.

Additionally, while it is strangely downplayed, many people do not have a tradition to sing *zemiros* at the Shabbos table. I say strangely downplayed because if your family is not blessed with musical ability, singing *zemiros* becomes torturous. There is an erroneous idea that if a prayer or song is published in a prayer book or blessing booklet, everyone must recite it. This is incorrect. Different communities have different traditions and a wise publisher will include as many traditions as possible to maximize the market for his product. You, the consumer, have to know your traditions or pick one. I am aware of reports that both Rav Joseph B. Soloveitchik and Rav Menachem Shach did not sing *zemiros*. I do not know whether this represented a widespread Lithuanian tradition or just their families' custom. Regardless, that tradition exists.

If you are someone who does not sing *zemiros* regularly, occasionally you might be put in a position where you have to sing *zemiros* or other songs. While you may remember the tunes more or less, the NCSY Bencher App provides a refresher course. This is a great tool for learning, reviewing, and learning to fit in. It is a Litvak's survival tool in an increasingly Chassidic world and a newcomer's survival tool in the religious world.

Turning a Lower East Side
Church into a Synagogue

I. Buying a Church

Judaism demands that its adherents separate from other religions, both physically and spiritually. Our study of other religions, and the attention to which we pay them, is highly limited by the verse, "Do not turn to the idols" (Lev. 19:4; *Mishneh Torah, Hilkhos Avodah Zarah* 2:2). In general, we are taught to stay away from their religions for our own spiritual health.

The question has arisen numerous times whether a community may buy a church building to be used as a synagogue. When neighborhood demographics change, this may prove the most financially viable option for all parties. However, there is something denigrating to a religion when it is treated as easily replaced by another. To true believers in their religion, their house of worship would decline in purpose if used for another religion. On the other hand, perhaps repurposing another religion's house of worship constitutes a minor victory, a sanctification of the impure. In the 1850's, such a question arose in a political battle over the oldest Eastern European synagogue in New York.

II. The Status of Christianity

You might think that Christianity's potentially unique status within Jewish thought would allow for additional leniency. While Rambam deemed Christianity a foreign worship of classical status, other important authorities consider it in an intermediate status—not polytheism but not a sufficiently pure monotheism either. According to this latter view, which by my accounting is the slight majority, perhaps there is no problem whatsoever with converting a church into a synagogue. Maybe since a church is good for gentiles, it can easily be transformed into a synagogue for Jews. Interestingly, the main authorities who discuss the issue of converting a church into a synagogue explicitly adopt (elsewhere) the latter view about Christianity but do not include it in their deliberations on this subject. I deduce from their silence that it is irrelevant. This is not a discussion of the inherent value of Christianity but of its relationship to Jews and Jewish worship.

Rav Yosef Shaul Nathanson (*Sho'el U-Meishiv*, second series, vol. 1 no. 51; third series, vol. 3 no. 29) argues that the type of religion under which Christianity is classified (*shituf*) is permissible for gentiles. Rav David Tzvi Hoffmann (*Melamed Le-Ho'il, Orach Chaim* 16) rules similarly. Rav Hoffmann's successor, the great Rav Avraham Elya Kaplan, began annotating Rav Hoffmann's responsa before their initial, posthumous publication. However, he passed away prematurely before getting far. In his fifth and final footnote (to responsum 20), he points out that the status of Christianity for gentiles is unconnected to the question of Jewish participation in it. Rav Ya'akov Ettlinger (*Arukh La-Ner, Sukkah* 45b s.v. *ve-ha*) rules similarly. The discussion below is based primarily on authorities who believe that Christianity does not constitute classical idolatry. Despite that, it is still a foreign religion for Jews and forbidden practice for Jews in which to partake.

III. Lower East Side Dispute

In 1852, the first Eastern European synagogue in New York City, and the first Russian synagogue in America, opened in the Lower East Side. It was called Beth HaMedrash, not to be confused with a later break-away named Beth HaMedrash HaGadol. The next year, Rav Avraham Asch was appointed rabbi. However, one of the congregants, Rav Yehudah Mittleman, was also an ordained rabbi. These two clashed about the appointment of a specific individual as *shochet*, the ritual slaughterer. Rav Mittleman left the synagogue and started his own. In 1856, the Beth HaMedrash bought a Welsh church and converted it into a synagogue, dedicating the new home on Shavuos eve with Rav Avraham Rice of Baltimore in attendance. This was neither the first nor the last time that a synagogue used the premises of a former church, but it seems to have generated the most halakhic discussion. Apparently, Rav Mittleman attempted to obtain rabbinic disapproval from Europe for the use of a former church as a synagogue. In response, Rav Asch looked to Europe for rabbinic approval.[74]

Rav Mittleman inquired of the great rabbinic authority, Rav Yosef Shaul Nathanson—of Rav Mittleman's hometown Lvov— whether a congregation may purchase a Protestant church and convert it into a synagogue. In his question, which is repeated in the response, Rav Mittleman describes in detail the nature of worship in what he seems to call a Welsh-Scotch Lutheran church. The detail is surprising to find in rabbinic literature. At one point, he seems to call it a Lutheran Church. At another, he says it is a Methodist church, although maybe I am misunderstanding the use of language. It seems clear from the language that Rav Mittleman was asking for a prohibitive ruling. The responsum was issued in 1858 while the synagogue moved into the converted church in 1856. It is not clear whether the delay was due to limitations in communications or some other reason.

---

74. On the basic history, see J.D. Eisenstein, "The History of the First Russian-American Jewish Congregation" in *Publications of the American Jewish Historical Society*, vol. 9 (Baltimore, 1901), pp. 63-67. Rav Asch left the synagogue and in 1859 founded Beth HaMedrash HaGadol.

Rav Nathanson (*Responsa Sho'el U-Meishiv*, first recension, vol. 3 nos. 72-73) quotes the *Magen Avraham* (154:17), who cites a responsum of Rav Eliyahu Mizrachi (1:79) that a house used for idolatry may be used for prayer. Even though items used for idolatry may not be used for prayer because they are disgraceful, a building is different. The *Magen Avraham* suggests that the difference lies in a house being connected, more or less, to the ground. And the ground can never be forbidden due to idolatry.

Some, such as the *Dagul Me-Revavah* (ad loc.) and *Chasam Sofer* (glosses, ad loc.; Responsa, *Orach Chaim* 42) bring proof from a comment of Tosafos (*Megillah* 6a s.v. *tiratra'os*) that a building is also forbidden. The Gemara (*Megillah* 6a) says that the biblical promise that "And he shall be as a chief in Judah, and Ekron as a Jebusite" (Zech. 9:6) means that in the future, the princes of Yehudah will teach Torah in Roman theaters and circuses. Tosafos quote an opinion that this refers to houses of pagan worship, which are derogatorily called theaters and circuses. However, Tosafos reject the possibility that Torah will be taught in such disgraceful places. This seems to imply that Torah study, and presumably prayer, should not take place in buildings previously used for foreign religions.

Rav Nathanson rejects this proof because Tosafos do not use the word forbidden. Tosafos say that it is difficult to interpret the Talmud that way, meaning that it is difficult to say that this biblical prophecy refers to pagan houses of worship. It doesn't seem like the prophet would promise something relatively unseemly as such a good sign. But it is not forbidden. Rav Nathanson then disagrees with Tosafos and suggests that the conversion of a pagan house of worship to a house devoted to the worship of God is actually a great praise of God. Idolatry will be wiped off the face of earth so that even the central places of idolatry will be dedicated to God.

In 1858, Rav Ya'akov Ettlinger of Altona, Germany, sent a responsum on the same issue to Rav Avraham Asch (*Binyan*

Tziyon 1:63). Rav Ettlinger sides with Tosafos against the *Magen Avraham*. He advances the consideration that gentiles are permitted to embrace Christianity but counters that Jews are not, therefore this does not point to leniency. He concludes that he rules strictly but allows for reliance on the *Magen Avraham* in a time of great need. Additionally, since the church purchased for Rav Asch's synagogue was originally built as a private house, this offers another reason for leniency.

IV. Later Authorities

In a responsum dated 1900, Rav David Tzvi Hoffmann (*Melamed Le-Ho'il, Orach Chaim* 20) addresses the same issue. He accepts Tosafos as forbidding the use of a house of foreign worship for prayer. After pursuing and rejecting a number of possible ways to reconcile Tosafos with the *Magen Avraham*, Rav Hoffmann concludes that they disagree. However, in the specific case he was considering, he ruled leniently because the building had ceased serving as a church decades earlier.

Rav Yisrael Meir Kagan, the author of *Mishnah Berurah* (154:45), says that common practice follows the *Magen Avraham*'s lenient ruling. The famous mid-twentieth century halakhic authority of the Lower East Side, Rav Moshe Feinstein (*Iggeros Moshe, Orach Chaim* 1:49), disagrees with this statement of the *Mishnah Berurah* and concludes that common practice in the United States is to be stricter. He was not willing to forbid prayer in synagogues that were converted churches but he also would not permit the practice of buying a church for synagogue use.

PART 6: THE POWER OF SPEECH

Is Careful Language Possible?

The eightieth *yahrtzeit* today of Rav Yisrael Meir Kagan, author of the important works *Chafetz Chaim* and *Mishnah Berurah* (among others), offers us the opportunity to consider whether his rules for careful speech are realistic.[75] While forbidden speech comes in many forms, I would like to focus on the cases where *lashon hara*—true but disparaging information—is permissible. The *Chafetz Chaim* (1:10:2) lists seven conditions that must be fulfilled before saying negative information. Many learn this list and conclude that they cannot abide by the overly strict regulations. However, I contend that the rules that are not nearly as strict as commonly thought. They are realistic when applied properly.

Here are the seven conditions one of my children brought home from school on a refrigerator magnet:

1. You must be certain that the information is 100% accurate.
2. You must be sure that the wrong has been committed.
3. You must speak to the wrongdoer first and try to persuade him to rectify his behavior.
4. You cannot exaggerate the matter in any way.
5. Your intention must be only to help the person who is being victimized (the person you are telling the Loshon Hora to).

75. Originally published August 30, 2013, 24 Elul 5773. Rav Yisrael Meir Kagan passed away on September 15, 1933, 24 Elul 5693.

6. If you can achieve the same result without speaking Loshon Hora you must use that option.
7. Your words cannot cause the person to suffer a greater loss than *halakhah* would impose.

These correspond to the list of seven conditions in the *Chafetz Chaim* (1:10:2):

1. **Certainty:** You must personally witness the events you are considering describing. If you heard it from someone else, you may not repeat it unless you know with certainty that it occurred as described.

    However, later (2:9:2), the *Chafetz Chaim* omits this condition. In a footnote (9), he explains that when someone else may be saved from damage by this information, you must reveal it even if you are uncertain. In a further note to this footnote, the *Chafetz Chaim* adds that if you are certain about the information, your failure to reveal it to prevent further damage violates the prohibition against "standing by your fellow's blood." If you are not certain, then it is a mitzvah (positive act) but not obligation to reveal the information. However, you must add proper disclaimers that clearly delineate the limitations of your information. (See similarly in 1:4:10:43.)

    Going back to our list, in a footnote (5), the *Chafetz Chaim* implies that you may repeat information you heard (without certainty) about someone in a specific case that will prevent damage to a third party. But in our case (in the list), preventing damage is so remote that it is insufficient to permit revealing the negative information.

2. **Consideration:** You may not reach your judgment hastily but must carefully consider whether the person's actions can be

explained in a positive way. You must look at the context to understand what has occurred and why.

3. **Rebuke**: Before repeating damaging information about someone, you must approooach him and gently rebuke him and try to convince him to change his ways. Only after (and if) you fail may you then tell others about his misdeeds.

   The *Chafetz Chaim* adds later (par. 7) that if you know he will not listen to you, then you can skip this step. However, when you tell others, you must do so in front of at least three people. This leniency is very surprising because the Rema (*Orach Chaim* 608:2) rules that even if you know someone will not listen to your rebuke, you must still confront him once. Why does the *Chafetz Chaim* exempt people from that initial rebuke? The *Chafetz Chaim* (Introduction:Imperatives:5) clearly disagrees with this Rema. See also *Mishnah Berurah* (*Sha'ar Ha-Tziyun* 608:13), where Rav Kagan quotes views consistent with his position here and relies on them slightly to take a middle position.

4. **Precision**: You must tell the story precisely, without any exaggeration. If you exaggerate, you lie and inflict additional damage. Additionally, you may not omit any information that sheds a slightly better light on the information. The *Chafetz Chaim* writes similarly, regarding a potential partnership (2:9:2) and marriage prospect (2:9:6), that you may not exaggerate the information.

   However, he writes (1:4:10:43) about warning your children or students to stay away from someone who is a bad influence, that you may exaggerate if necessary. Rav Binyamin Cohen (*Chelkas Binyamin* 1:10:2; *Chelkas Binyamin*, ad loc., 10) struggles with this contradiction and suggests that you are allowed to exaggerate if it is really necessary. It all depends on the circumstances, the potential damage that might occur to the innocent if you do not exaggerate.

5. **Intent:** When telling the negative information, you must intend to help others and not damage the person who is the subject of the information.

   Later, the *Chafetz Chaim* (2:9:11, n. 28, asterisk) writes that this condition is subject to a debate between the *Sema* (*Choshen Mishpat* 461:28), who requires it and the *Taz* (ibid., s.v. *kedei*), who does not. According to the *Taz*, by protecting others you are doing a mitzvah, regardless of your intent. However, the *Chafetz Chaim* argues that, according to the *Taz*, if you have the wrong intent then you will inevitably fail one of the other conditions. Rav Binyamin Cohen (ad loc., *Bi'urim* 15) suggests that the debate between the *Sema* and the *Taz* do not apply to *lashon ha-ra* and that both would agree that intent is irrelevant. However, he is explicitly disagreeing with the *Chafetz Chaim* on this.

6. **Last Resort:** You may only tell damaging information if you cannot accomplish your goal in another way. *Lashon ha-ra* must be your last resort.

7. **Appropriate Results:** You may only tell damaging information if the subject will suffer consequences that are consonant with *halakhah*. If he will be overly punished, you may not reveal the information.

   However, the *Chafetz Chaim* points out in a footnote (12) that this can cause an impossible situation. A thief in an area where the government punishes thieves beyond halakhic requirements will have free reign over Jews, who may not reveal his crimes. Therefore, the *Chafetz Chaim* writes, we may set aside this condition to prevent harm in the future. In the next section, I note places where the *Chafetz Chaim* seems to contradict this leniency. Instead, he suggests that you may only reveal the information indirectly if the criminal will not suffer undue consequences.

My point in this exercise is not that readers should conclude that these rules can be dismissed. Rather, these rules are nuanced. Like all areas of *halakhah*, this subject requires detailed study and inquiry of halakhic authorities. The more we study these laws, the more we are able to apply them properly and internalize them.

Preventing Damage

I. Disproportionate Punishment

Understanding the laws of improper speech (*lashon ha-ra*) requires also knowing when they do not apply. The Sages tell us that the "leprosy" of the *metzora* was caused by *lashon ha-ra*.[76] Later, the Torah (Lev. 19:16) commands "You shall not go about as a talebearer among your people; nor shall you stand idly by your neighbor's blood." This latter verse prohibiting talebearing is immediately followed by a prohibition against watching your friend suffer, which the Sages interpreted to mean that you must intervene to prevent someone from being physically or financially damaged.[77] This juxtaposition is no coincidence.

Without specifically citing this latter mandate but clearly influenced by it, the *Chafetz Chaim* rules that you may speak what would otherwise be forbidden as *lashon ha-ra* to save someone from harm.[78] Normally, permitted talebearing requires seven conditions.[79] Among them is that the repercussions to the subject be commensurate with Torah law. However, if someone will be overly punished, then you may not tell the story. For example, you presumably may not tell a member of an organized crime family the name of someone who stole his wallet (absent other

---

76. Rashi, Lev. 14:4 from *Arakhin* 16b.
77. *Sanhedrin* 73a
78. *Chafetz Chaim*, part 1 ch. 10 par. 1; see also part 2 ch. 9 n. 1.
79. Ibid., part 1 ch. 10 par. 2, which is explored in depth in the previous section.

considerations). While the thief, if caught, may be able to return what he stole, which is otherwise sufficient cause for informing on him, the physical injury he may suffer, perhaps even death, is well beyond the Torah's punishment.

This limitation severely hampers our ability to report crimes. If someone convicted would be subject to serious prison violence, as some claim, then reporting him would be forbidden as *lashon ha-ra* (regardless of *mesirah* issues).

II. Preventing Damage

However, the *Chafetz Chaim* explicitly acknowledges the impossible situation that would generate.[80] Indeed, he uses that result as an argument that this ruling cannot be true. "If not so, no one will ever save his friend from a beating." Instead, he differentiates between past crimes and future threats. You may not tell about a past crime if the perpetrator will be overly punished. However, if your intention is to warn potential future victims, then the extent of possible punishment is irrelevant if there is no other way to save them. While he does not state it explicitly, I believe he is concerned for the mandate not to stand idly by someone's blood.

This explicit discussion is complicated by contradictions. Later, in that very chapter, the *Chafetz Chaim* rules that you may only denounce a liar to prevent him from spreading future untruths if you fulfill all seven conditions, including that of exaggerated punishment.[81] We see a similar ruling in the same chapter about someone who will publicly denounce another in the future.[82] All conditions still apply. The same is repeated later in the book.[83]

---

80. Ibid., n. 12.
81. Ibid., par. 6; see n. 22.
82. Ibid., pars. 13-14.
83. Ibid., part 2 ch. 9 par. 2. See all this in Rav Binyamin Cohen, *Chelkas Binyamin* on *Chafetz Chaim*, part 1. ch. 10 CB n. 17.

Given the clear statement and convincing rationale to permit *lashon ha-ra* in order to prevent damage, regardless of the possible extent of punishment, why does the *Chafetz Chaim* contradict this position? I have no conclusive answer but offer the following suggestion and welcome other possible resolutions.

III. Naming Names

Forbidden speech does not need to be direct or name the subject. As long as his identity is revealed, as long as the speech is damaging, it qualifies as *lashon ha-ra*.[84] However, the *Chafetz Chaim* slightly amends this position. Among the seven conditions mentioned above to permit saying *lashon ha-ra* is that there is no other way to prevent the harm. If another remedy exists, you must pursue it.[85] The *Chafetz Chaim* rules that if you can reveal the information and identity indirectly, you must do so rather than state it explicitly.[86] While this type of speech is still forbidden, it is apparently a lesser offense than direct *lashon ha-ra* and must be preferred.

I tentatively suggest that this might explain the above contradiction in the *Chafetz Chaim*'s rulings about preventing damage. You must save other people if you can. The Torah requires vigilance in protecting the innocent. If we fail to stop criminals because they will be overly punished, we allow them free reign to victimize us and destroy our communities. However, if the perpetrator will be overly punished, we should bring about his capture indirectly.

If this interpretation is correct, the *Chafetz Chaim* is saying that in such a situation you may—you must!—cause the perpetrator's identity and actions to be revealed, but you may not do so directly.

---

84. Ibid., part 1 ch. 1 par. 8.
85. Ibid., part 1 ch. 10 par. 2.
86. Ibid., part 2 ch. 9 n. 35.

While normally you must choose the lesser offense if it is an option, in a case of exaggerated punishment you may only act indirectly. Or perhaps said differently, you must create a situation in which an indirect revelation will protect the community.

Too Busy to Tell the Truth

Sometimes lying is allowed, even in such mundane ways as how we answer the phone. Clearly, lying should be avoided whenever possible. The Torah emphasizes: "*Mi-dvar sheker tirchak* – Keep far from a false matter" (Ex. 23:7). Truth is a prime value in Judaism, described as God's signature (*Shabbos* 55a).

Yet, other values sometimes take precedence. Peace famously overrides truth. Hillel ruled that you may praise a bride as beautiful even if she really is not (*Kesubos* 16b). Another value that apparently takes precedence over truth is privacy.

I. Unavailable

In a startling ruling, Rav Yitzchak Fuchs (*Halikhos Bein Adam Le-Chaveiro*, p. 374) quotes Rav Shlomo Zalman Auerbach and Rav Shalom Yosef Elyashiv as permitting you to say that you are not there if you cannot take a visitor or telephone call. Of course, you should preferably tell them the truth, that you are busy. However, if this will anger or offend them, you may lie or have someone else lie for you.

Rav Auerbach added that this permits you to leave a voice mail message saying that you cannot answer the phone. Really, you might be able to answer but choose not to for whatever reason. However, you are not required to divulge that information so you may simply say that you cannot answer (ibid., n. 51). Rav Auerbach also quoted Rav David Tzvi Hoffmann as instructing his wife to tell people who asked for him during his nap that he cannot be disturbed because he is preparing his lecture. Presumably this was during his later years, when he was a weak, old man. That sleep afforded him the strength to teach and therefore could be considered preparation (ibid., n. 52).

Ostensibly, this is an example of peace overriding truth, for which we have a talmudic precedent. However, there is more to this equation. These great sages added that you are not obligated to interrupt your activity, whatever it may be, to greet visitors or engage in their business. Additionally, you are not required to divulge your reasons. Just because someone calls you or knocks on your door, you do not lose your right to privacy. Therefore, as a last resort, you may lie to get rid of them.

II. Other Options

However, this permission has limits. First, you may not do so in front of children. They are impressionable and may see this as a primary response rather than a last resort (ibid.). Additionally, you may not do this regularly. Even when lying is permitted, you may not become a habitual liar. The prophet denounces those who "have taught their tongue to speak lies" (Jer. 9:4), implying a regularity that in itself forbids non-truths, even if otherwise acceptable.

Yet I find this permission bewildering. Is it really so hard to simply say that you are "unavailable"? This is a catch-all term that is vague but accurate. Why lie when you can firmly but pleasantly assert the truth? Perhaps there is no such word in Hebrew (or German, for Rav Hoffmann). Personally, I prefer vague truth over polite lie. I suspect these sages would agree and were speaking about circumstances in which this is impossible.

I am likewise puzzled by the permission to maintain an occasionally false voice mail message. Why say that you cannot answer the phone when you can simply identify the home and ask the caller to leave his information? "Hello, you have reached the Schwartzes. Please leave your name, number and reason for calling after the tone. Thank you." Why be imprecise and possibly incorrect?

Hilkhos "Bli Neder"

I. No Vow

A common feature of Orthodox speech is the phrase "*bli neder*," a disclaimer that the speaker does not intend to vow. We are careful not to invoke a biblical oath in our promises because if we fail to fulfill the promise completely, we may violate a prohibition. While we certainly intend to keep our word, we wish to limit the cost of failure.

However, we would be wrong to utilize this halakhic phrase improperly. There are cases when it is necessary and cases when it is superfluous. The pedantic among us, in whose number I occasionally count myself, want to use the phrase appropriately. Therefore, we should explore when saying "*bli neder*" is warranted.

II. Plain Vow

A typical vow (*neder*) or oath (*shevu'ah*) invokes God's name. However, the concept of *yados nedarim* (extensions of vows) means that even a partial language, such as that excluding God's name, is also considered a vow or oath.

Additionally, the concept of *kinuyei nedarim* (idioms of vows) includes language other than the explicit word "vow." Even if you promise or commit to do something, or use any similar language, you are accepting a vow.

With all this in mind, it seems that if you promise to do something, you are effectively obligating yourself. Therefore, it is appropriate to include a *"bli neder"* whenever promising, swearing, or committing about anything. The *Kitzur Shulchan Arukh* (67:4) states:

> It is good to become used to [saying *"bli neder"*] even when you say you will do something religiously neutral [*devar reshus*], so you do not stumble on the sin of *nedarim*."

Note that you must still fulfill your promises even if you say *"bli neder."* The Torah commands: "He shall do according to all that proceeds out of his mouth" (Num. 30:3). Saying *"bli neder"* only removes the additional prohibition against violating a vow.

III. Mitzvah Vow

The *Shulchan Arukh* uses ambiguous language about committing to do a mitzvah. In one place (*Yoreh De'ah* 203:6), it says that someone who says he will do a specific mitzvah, such as learn a specific chapter of Torah, may take a vow to encourage himself. The implication is that merely stating that he will do the mitzvah is not a vow in itself. Elsewhere (ibid., 213:2), it states that someone who says he will learn a chapter of Torah (Rema adds: or any other mitzvah) is as if he vowed to do it. Is it a vow or not?

Shakh (203:4) notes this apparent contradiction and dismisses the earlier language. He quotes multiple sources that rule that saying you will do a mitzvah is binding as a vow. You can take an explicit vow in order to strengthen your implicit vow, as a form of personal encouragement. But even without that addition, you still effectively have vowed to perform that mitzvah.

The *Chida* (*Birkei Yosef, Yoreh De'ah* 213:2) leans in the other direction. Saying you will do a mitzvah is "as if" you take a vow but is not quite it. You are not technically bound by a vow.

However, the consensus seems to follow the *Shakh*. See, for example, *Kitzur Shulchan Arukh* (67:4) and *Ben Ish Chai* (*Re'eh*, year 2, no. 4), cited approvingly by Rav Mordechai Eliyahu (*Responsa Ma'amar Mordekhai*, vol. 2 *Yoreh De'ah* no. 17). Therefore, whenever you say you will do a mitzvah, you should add "*bli neder.*" Otherwise, the penalty for failure is even greater.

IV. Mitzvah Act

Customs are binding as vows. While this subject is broad and requires greater elaboration, a relevant manifestation of this phenomenon is the acceptance of a new practice. If you begin a new mitzvah practice or custom, and you know it is not required but are doing it anyway, you are accepting it as a vow. Therefore, the *Shulchan Arukh* (*Yoreh De'ah* 214:1) recommends that anytime you begin a new stringency or custom, you say that you are doing it "*bli neder*" so it does not become binding as a vow.

V. Charity

The *Shulchan Arukh* states twice (*Yoreh De'ah* 203:4, 257:4) that when you pledge to charity, you should add "*bli neder.*" This addition, which is directly from the Rosh (*Nedarim* 1:8), applies to a *Mi She-Beirakh* pledge made in many synagogues after being called to the Torah. When asked how much you are donating, you should say the amount "*bli neder.*" However, this requirement for charity vows goes further than for other vows.

The *Shulchan Arukh* (*Choshen Mishpat* 212:8) quotes two opinions regarding thinking about giving to *tzedakah*. According to some, if you decide in your mind to give to *tzedakah*, that is a binding vow even though you did not verbalize the commitment. According to others, it is only binding if you say it. The *Shulchan Arukh* concludes that all opinions would agree that nowadays, when donations cannot be made to the Temple in Jerusalem, a charitable vow must be verbalized.

However, the Rema (ad loc.) disagrees with that conclusion and rules that if you decide conclusively that you will give a specific amount to charity, you are bound by a vow to give it, even if you do not verbalize it. If you wish to change your pledge, you must try to get the vow annulled. The Rema similarly quotes both opinions in *Yoreh De'ah* (258:13) and sides with the second view. Therefore, you even need to add the *"bli neder"* about charity pledges.

VI. Precedence

Rav Mordechai Eliyahu, in his *Darkhei Eliyahu*, adds a footnote to *Kitzur Shulchan Arukh* (67:2), which argues that order counts when saying *"bli neder."* Tosafos (*Beitzah* 20a s.v. *Nazir*) say that when making a vow, once the words come out of your mouth, you cannot revoke them. Therefore, Rav Eliyahu states, you must say *"bli neder"* before the language that would otherwise imply a vow. If you say *"bli neder"* after, it's too late.

Based on this, during a *Mi She-Beirakh* after being called to the Torah, when asked how much you pledge, you should say (for example), *"bli neder* 18 dollars" rather than "18 dollars *bli neder."*

Swear to G-d

I. Swearing

Jews are averse to swearing—taking oaths—for two reasons. One, as we discussed previously, is the severity of the prohibition against violating an oath. Another is the prohibition, listed among the (so-called) Ten Commandments, against using God's name in vain. If you swear to God falsely, you not only violate an oath but also use the divine name improperly.

That raises the question what constitutes God's name. The Holy Language is Biblical Hebrew. What if you use God's name in another language in vain? What if you swear to Gott or to God? The answer to this question can potentially affect a number of related laws.

1. **Cursing:** We are biblically prohibited from cursing someone with God's name. What if we curse someone in English? Does that fall under the prohibition?
2. **Prayer:** We are allowed to pray in any language. If we pray in English and use God's name translated into English, do we fulfill our obligation for prayer?
3. **Erasure:** We may not erase God's name. What if we write it in English? Can we erase it? Or do we have to write G-d to avoid the potential problem?
4. **Blessings:** We are obligated to recite a blessing before and after eating food. If, for any number of reasons, we are unsure

whether we need to recite a blessing, we generally do not recite it out of doubt because doing so might constitute a forbidden unnecessary blessing. Can we recite the blessing in another language?

II. Writing

An important source in this discussion is the *Shakh* (*Yoreh De'ah* 179:11) in the laws of forbidden pagan practices. The Rema (ad loc., 8) writes that the prohibition against chanting a verse to heal a wound is only in Hebrew. The *Shakh* quotes the *Bach*, who disagrees, since we may not recite a verse in another language while in a bathroom. The *Shakh* argues that the bathroom is different because you may not study any Torah there. But God's name in other languages is not holy and may even be erased. Others note that Rashbatz (Responsa 1:2) had already also ruled that you may erase God's name in another language.

The *Gilyon Maharsha* (ad loc.) quotes the *Chavos Yair* (no. 106), who rules that if you transliterate God's name in another language into Hebrew letters, then you may not erase it. Presumably, he would also be careful about saying God's name in another language.

III. In Vain

Rav Akiva Eiger (Responsa, no. 5) rules that God's name in other languages is a *kinnui*, a nickname or idiomatic reference. Therefore, it may be erased and said in vain without any prohibition. However, he adds that reciting a blessing is a stricter issue and forbidden. Elsewhere (Commentary to *Megillah* 17), he points out the difficulty in translating God's name. Rav Akiva Eiger quotes Moses Mendelssohn, who translated it as "Der Evigger, the Eternal." While this captures the time element of God's four-letter name, it lacks the implication of mastery, *adnus*. Therefore, translations of God's name are not really the name.

Rav Ya'akov Ettlinger (*Binyan Tziyon*, no. 68) differentiates between erasing a name and saying it. While the *Shakh* is correct that we may erase God's name in other languages, that does not mean we may say the name in vain. We can pray in other languages and we may not curse someone with God's name in a different language. Therefore it must also be prohibited to say it in vain. The *Chayei Adam* (5:1) rules likewise.

However, others disagree. For example, *Arukh Ha-Shulchan* (*Orach Chaim* 202:3) rules that there is no prohibition in saying God's name in other languages. Therefore when you have a doubt whether to recite a blessing, you may do it in other languages. He says that he personally does it frequently.

IV. G-d

Rav Chaim Ozer Grodzinski (*Achiezer*, vol. 3 no. 32) follows Rav Akiva Eiger but adds, based on *Rosh Hashanah* (18b), that one should prevent God's name in any language from being treated disrespectfully, even when no other formal prohibition is violated. Therefore, he recommends writing "G-d" (really "ג-ט") so that God's name in another language is not mistreated. He also quotes Rav Yonasan Eybeschutz (*Tumim* 25) who rails against people who write "*adieu*" in letters, which are thrown in the garbage, since "*adieu*" literally means "to God." That is disrespectful treatment of God's name (although Rav Grodzinski adds that "*adieu*" has evolved into an independent, mundane word).

Rav Joseph B. Soloveitchik (quoted in *Nefesh Ha-Rav*, pp. 160-161) follows Rav Akiva Eiger's view. He used to say that writing "G-d" is *am haratzus*, "ignorant," because "G-d" is also an idiomatic reference to God. Similarly, the *Mishnah Berurah* (85:10) writes that you may erase God's name in any other language. Rav Soloveitchik added that the Geonim (quoted in commentaries to *Nedarim* 7) have a *chumra* (stringency) to refrain from even saying a divine nickname in vain. However, the position of the Geonim is not normative.

V. Conclusion

Authorities debate whether you may say God's name in languages other than Hebrew in vain. According to the *Binyan Tziyon* and *Chayei Adam*, it is a problem. According to Rav Akiva Eiger, *Mishnah Berurah*, Rav Chaim Ozer Grodzinski, and Rav Soloveitchik, it is not. All of those quoted above (except the *Bach*) agree that you may erase God's name in other languages. However, Rav Eybeschutz and Rav Grodzinski rule that you should prevent these names in other languages from being treated disrespectfully by writing, for example, "G-d." Of course, if you are writing a book that you do not expect will be treated disrespectfully, there is no reason to write "G-d" according to any of these authorities.

Rav Moshe Feinstein (*Iggeros Moshe, Orach Chaim*, vol. 4, no. 40 par. 27) writes in a responsum to Rav Ephraim Greenblatt that if you can say a blessing with a name in another language, there must be a problem of saying that name in vain. However, he seems to rule differently in *Iggeros Moshe, Yoreh De'ah*, vol. 1 no. 172; *Orach Chaim*, vol. 2 no. 49. I don't know how to reconcile these different responsa.

How to Undo a *Minhag*

The term *minhag*, literally, "custom," actually refers to multiple types of practices with different kinds of obligations. By better understanding these differences, we can explore which *minhagim* are subject to removal and how to accomplish that, if you so wish.

Generally speaking, a *minhag* is a type of *neder*, an explicit or implicit vow to observe a practice. Some *nedarim* are subject to annulment through *hattaras nedarim*, annulling vows, which is a fairly common practice. When can we do *hataras nedarim* on a *minhag* we no longer wish to observe? When can we stop observing it even without *hattaras nedarim*?

I. Types of *Minhagim*
There are four types of customs, four scopes of customs and three sources of customs.

Types:
1. **Legal:** You mistakenly thought that a practice is forbidden and therefore refrained from it. It isn't an actual law, so it is a *minhag*.
2. **Ruling:** You had a question and asked your rabbi. While the question is a matter of debate, he ruled for you. This ruling is your *minhag*. Others might follow another view and have a different *minhag*.
3. **Pious Practice:** You adopt extra practices and stringencies out of religious fervor, a desire to do extra.

4. **Fence:** Out of concern that you might sin, you erect a safeguard, an extra stringency to protect you from sinning. This is your personal fence and not a rabbinic enactment. It is your *minhag*.

Scopes:

1. **Personal:** A *minhag* can be your own personal practice, self-tailored to match your personality and inclinations.
2. **Family:** Many families have unique practices that are handed down for generations.
3. **Local:** While we do not see this much today, in past generations there were unique regional and city *minhagim*.
4. **Universal:** Some *minhagim* are observed by the entire Jewish people (more or less).

Sources:

1. **Self:** A *minhag* can be something that you adopt. You find a specific practice meaningful so you start doing it yourself.
2. **Inherited:** As is often the case, we are taught *minhagim* by our parents.
3. **Mandated:** A third source of *minhag* is a practice an ancestor adopted specifically that his descendants should follow. This has halakhic significance.

With all this in mind, let's address when you can remove a *minhag*. Two debates are crucial for understanding this topic. Rav Baruch Simon's *Imrei Barukh: Tokef Ha-Minhag Ba-Halakhah* contains three chapters (chs. 3-5) that are very useful in understanding this subject.

II. Permit Us

The (Babylonian) Talmud (*Pesachim* 50b) tells the story of Bnei Beishan who had the *minhag* of refraining from going to the marketplace on Friday, in order to ensure proper preparation for Shabbos and avoid any potential Shabbos violations. They wished to annul this *minhag* that they had inherited. Rabbi Yochanan told them that they could not because Proverbs (1:8) says: "Listen, son, to the rebuke of your father and do not abandon the teaching of your mother."

The Talmud Yerushalmi (*Pesachim* 4:1) says that if people observed a *minhag* because they thought it was the actual law, then if they ask, you can permit it for them. If they knew it was not required by the technical law and still observed as an extra measure, then even if they ask, you cannot permit it for them.

The Talmudim take *minhagim* seriously. You cannot simply drop a custom that you don't like. However, there may be ways of removing them.

III. Fences

The Ramban and many others (e.g., Rashba, Ra'avad, and Rivash) understand the story of Bnei Beishan as teaching that a custom adopted as a fence cannot be removed. However, *minhagim* that are not intended as fences may follow different rules. A pious practice, as described above, can be annulled through *hattaras nedarim*. The Rosh disagrees, arguing that even a *minhag* adopted as a fence may be annulled. According to the Rosh, Bnei Beishan could have asked for their *minhag* to be annulled with *hattaras nedarim*. Rabbi Yochanan merely told them that, as things stood at the time, they were bound by the *minhag*. But they could have gotten out of it with *hattaras nedarim*.

Significantly, the *Shulchan Arukh* (*Yoreh De'ah* 214:1) follows the Rosh, as do all subsequent standard authorities. However, the

Pri Chadash (*Orach Chaim* 497, par. 5; followed by *Chayei Adam* 127:9) writes that, even according to the Rosh, all or most of the people subject to the *minhag* have to annul it. If an individual receives his own (mistaken) annulment, it is ineffective and he is still bound by the *minhag*.

Rav Shlomo Luria (*Responsa Maharshal*, no. 6) adds that a custom can only be annulled by someone not bound by it. Therefore, a custom universally practiced by Jews cannot be removed. The *Shakh* (*Yoreh De'ah* 214:4) follows this ruling, as does the *Pri Chadash* (ibid., par. 6), who say that "this is clear." Therefore, universal Jewish customs can never be annulled.

III. Mistaken Practice

All agree that a practice adopted due to a mistaken understanding is not binding. For example, if you thought a specific food is forbidden and therefore refrained from eating it, and later discovered that there is no basis to consider the food forbidden, you may freely eat that food. The *minhag* is not binding. You do not even need to do *hattaras nedarim*.

The *Pri Chadash* (ibid., par. 2) uses this to explain a rabbi's halakhic ruling on a controversial subject. If there is a long-standing debate about a practice and a community follows one specific view, can they switch to another opinion? Quoting the Maharshdam (Responsa, *Yoreh De'ah* 40), the *Pri Chadash* explains when and why this is allowed. If a contemporary rabbi proves to his satisfaction that the view the community follows is incorrect, he has rendered their practice a *minhag* based on a mistake that does not even require *hattaras nedarim*.

In other words, if there is a debate between Rashi and Rambam, and the community's former rabbi had ruled like Rashi, the new rabbi has to prove that Rambam was right and Rashi wrong in order to uproot the established ruling. The *Pri Chadash* adds that few are qualified to resolve such debates conclusively. He says that in his times, in the seventeenth century, only one or two in a generation are capable. (He invokes the concept of a *gadol ha-dor* without using the term.) The *Chayei Adam* (127:10) follows this *Pri Chadash* but only mentions one per generation, presumably for stylistic and not substantive reasons.[87]

One of the proofs for this ruling is *Chullin* 111a. Rav bar Shva went to eat at his teacher Rav Nachman's home. Rav Nachman served liver, which some forbid because of the difficulty in removing blood from the meat. When house servants or other guests informed Rav Nachman that his student was refusing to eat the liver, clearly following the strict view, Rav Nachman instructed them to force the liver down his throat. Rather than show respect for this alternate view, Rav Nachman took a stand for leniency because he had decisively ruled that eating liver is permissible (when prepared properly).

IV. Received Customs

The rules about annulling customs we have discussed so far have generally referred to the people who initially adopted the customs. If you decide to fast on every Monday to enhance your spirituality (i.e., a pious *minhag*) or as a way to avoid forbidden foods that are more common in your weekly routine on Monday (i.e., a fence), can you change this practice? Most *minhagim* we observe today are received from previous generations.

The Maharshdam (ibid.) argues that you may not annul a received custom. Only the people who accept a custom may annul it because only they know the full reason the custom was adopted.

---

87. Note that the *Chayei Adam* includes this ruling in his chapter on *kitniyos*, which he did not consider a mistaken custom but a fence. As we discussed elsewhere, even Rav Ya'akov Emden, the most authoritative view against *kitniyos*, believes it is a binding custom. See my essay, "Kitniyos II," *Torah Musings*, April 6, 2009.

Subsequent generations, who inherit the practice, must follow it. He proves it from Bnei Beishan, who were not allowed to annul the custom (according to the Ramban, et al).

The *Pri Chadash* (ibid., par. 8) disagrees. He argues that the heir has the same power as the originator. If the person who accepts a custom can annul it, so can his descendants. In this, he follows the Rosh (as above) that Bnei Beishan could have annulled their custom but their question was whether they must follow it absent annulment.

The *Pri To'ar* (39:32) takes a middle position. When someone accepts a practice with the intent that his descendants must follow in his footsteps, that custom is binding on them. Otherwise, absent that explicit intent, the custom is a personal stringency that his children need not follow.

V. Local and Family Customs

Who or what is Beishan? The *Pri Chadash* (ibid., par. 7) explains that Beishan is a contraction of Beis She'an (or Beit She'an or Beth She'an), a city in Israel that still exists. The people of that city, the members of Beis She'an, approached Rabbi Yochanan about discarding a local custom. The *Pri To'ar* (ibid.) disagrees and assumes that Beishan was a family name. Members of that family asked Rabbi Yochanan about their family custom.

According to the *Pri Chadash* a local custom is binding. As long as you associate with that place, you must follow its customs. The Mishnah (*Pesachim* 50a) states that someone who comes from a place with a specific custom must observe it even if he is spending time elsewhere. The Gemara (ad loc., 51a) adds that if you move to a new place, then you become a member of that city and adopt its customs.

Therefore, if you live in a city with a custom you wish to discard, you can move to a city with a contrary custom. However, this only works if the new place has a custom that contradicts the custom of the old place; the new custom overrides the old one. If you move to a city that has no standard custom, in which many people with different customs coexist within one community, then there is no new custom to override the old custom. You must continue practicing your old custom.

Rav Moshe Feinstein (*Iggeros Moshe, Even Ha-Ezer* 1:59) writes that there is no such thing as a local custom in America. Everyone who moves to America must keep their prior customs. Similarly, Rav Shlomo Zalman Auerbach (quoted in Rav Yerachmiel Fried, *Yom Tov Sheini Ke-Hilkhaso* 19:5) rules that Jerusalem has no single custom and no one who moves there may change his customs, except for a few unique customs accepted by all the communities there.

However, according to the *Pri To'ar*, there is also a concept of a family custom. Even if you move to a place with an established custom, you still have to follow your family customs. Rav Yosef Shalom Elyashiv also rules this way.[88] Rav Hershel Schachter ("*Hashbei'a Hishbi'a*" in *Beis Yitzchak* 39 [2007]) explains that some customs are family-based and some locale-based, although they are not always easy to differentiate. You must follow a family custom even if you move to a place that has a different custom. He adds that if you change families, you change family customs. One example is a woman who marries and, generally speaking, adopts the customs of her husband's family. However, sometimes a man with little knowledge of his lineage (e.g., a *ba'al teshuvah*) marries a woman of prominent lineage and adopts her family's customs.

---

88. As quoted in Rav Moshe Fried, *Responsa Va-Yishma Moshe*, pp. 267-268; *Sefer He'aros Al Masekhes Pesachim*, p. 293, both cited by Rav Baruch Simon, ibid., p. 71.

VI. Undoing a Custom

In summary, you can discontinue a custom if:

1. It falls into the category of a mistaken custom;
2. It is based on a prior halakhic ruling and one of the unique Torah scholars of the generation rules against this practice;
3. All (or most) of the people subject to the custom formally annul it (which is not possible with a universal custom);
4. You move to a place with a contrary custom, except for family customs;
5. You change families.

Lincoln's Angry Letters in Jewish Law

When Abraham Lincoln was angry, he would write a "hot letter" full of his emotions and then file it away, labeled "never sent, never signed." This seems like an important method of venting, expressing your anger, without damaging any individuals or relationships. What does *halakhah* say about writing an unsent angry letter? Since your letter contains *lashon ha-ra*, gossip, are you allowed to write it? Keeping a diary achieves a similar purpose, allowing you to express your anger privately. Is it permissible?[89]

Three possible questions arise. First, are you allowed to say *lashon ha-ra* if no one hears it? Second, are you allowed to say *lashon ha-ra* in order to vent? And third, is writing the letter considered bearing a grudge?

---

89. A reader pointed out the following advice in Rav Kalonymus Shapira's *Chovas HaTalmidim, A Student's Obligation: Advice From the Rebbe of the Warsaw Ghetto* (Aronson, 1995, ch. 9, p. 205): "You want to clear that hatred from your heart but aren't managing to do so. So try the following exercise: Write him a letter. Don't send it— just hide it away somewhere. In that letter, disparage him as much as the angry snake you have inside wants to. For a few days, take out the letter and read it aloud. Imagine that you are standing opposite the person you hate, and are throwing all the slurs and insults in that letter straight in his face. After a few days of this, the anger will surely leave your heart. And if you have a minimal degree of sensitivity, you will run to make up with him, too."

I. To Yourself

It seems that the prohibition of saying *lashon ha-ra* only applies in front of other people. *Chafetz Chaim* (1:2:1) states: "It is forbidden to say *lashon ha-ra* against your friend, even if it is true, even in front of one individual, and even more so in front of many." It sounds like you may say it if there is no one who can hear it. However, if you write it and then someone reads it, you have transferred the information. Would the prohibition then apply when the other person reads it? If the author left the paper and then someone later found it, would the author violate the prohibition retroactively? The Dirshu edition of *Chafetz Chaim* (published 2015; 1:1:8 n. 35) quotes from the *Nesivos Chaim* (ad loc., no. 10) that, indeed, an author only violates the prohibition when someone reads the gossip. It further quotes the *Shi'urei Iyun* that if the writer has since deceased, he still receives the sin. Lincoln kept his letters, which were later found after his death. Had he burned them, or deleted the draft e-mail, he would not face any potential *lashon ha-ra* problem.

II. Venting

However, venting is a valid reason to say *lashon ha-ra*. *Chafetz Chaim* (1:10:14) lists the conditions that permit saying *lashon ha-ra*. The fifth condition is that you must have a constructive purpose, which is the primary condition of them all. In an unnumbered footnote, he adds that if your intention is to calm worry in your heart, that also constitutes a constructive purpose. However, he points out that all the other conditions must also be fulfilled.

Rav Binyamin Cohen (*Chelkas Binyamin*, ad loc., n. 39) cites *Sefer Chasidim* (64) as the source for this ruling. *Sefer Chasidim* says that if someone comes to you to unload his heavy heart, it is a mitzvah for you to listen. Implicit in this mitzvah is that the other person is allowed to unload.

Rav Daniel Z. Feldman (*False Facts and True Rumors*, Maggid, 2015, p. 104) writes:

> The very act of talking is productive as an emotional support. Accordingly, such unburdening of the mind should be permitted even if the listener is not likely to offer concrete advice. It seems that this justification is grounded not only in the productive benefit but also in that there is no intent to disparage the individual being discussed, but rather to provide therapeutic relief to the speaker.[90]

However, Rav Feldman points out (p. 105 n. 36) that "some studies indicate that 'venting' either keeps initial anger running longer..." This brings us to the next issue, bearing a grudge.

III. Bearing a Grudge

The Torah (Lev. 19:18) forbids taking revenge and bearing a grudge. The Dirshu edition of *Chafetz Chaim* (Prohibitions, n. 51) quotes an article in the journal *Marpei Lashon* (vol. 2, p. 64) that distinguishes between writing in a diary with anger and with introspection. If you write with anger, as if you are still pained by the injury, then you are bearing a forbidden grudge. However, if you write introspectively, reflecting on how you feel and how you can change, then you are not bearing a grudge but contemplating your attitudes. The latter is permissible. The article's author states that Rav Shlomo Zalman Auerbach reviewed and agreed with the article.

Intent is crucial in this matter. Somewhat similarly, Rav Ya'akov Kamenetsky (*Emes Le-Ya'akov, Orach Chaim* 156 n. 182, cited by

---

90. Rav Feldman later adds: "A 'venting license' should not be taken as a free pass to widely disparage the source of one's anger. Emotional unburdening should be accomplished with a very limited number of people (preferably, one person) and should not involve the widespread dissemination of negativity."

Rav Feldman above) distinguishes between two types of venting. You are allowed to vent if you are upset that someone wronged you and was never adequately punished. However, you are not allowed to vent in order to publicize the wrongdoing as a punishment. If your goal is to spread the *lashon ha-ra*, then the venting is forbidden. Your intent must be constructive in some way.

IV. Conclusion

If you write an angry letter and then destroy it, and you write to unburden yourself and/or look for ways to improve, then you are not violating the prohibitions of bearing a grudge and *lashon ha-ra*. Even if your intent is proper, you must try to minimize the damage. You may want to keep the letter for your own reference but you should be careful what happens to it.

Denigrating the Dead

I. Identifying the Gatherer

Traditionally, people see the *mekoshesh,* the man in the desert who gathered wood on Shabbos (Num. 15:32-36), as a story about the laws of Shabbos. However, it also teaches us about the proper attitudes to history.

The Gemara (*Shabbos* 96b) records R. Akiva's attempt to identify the *mekoshesh* as Tzelophechad (Num. 27:1-7), who died in the desert and whose daughters inherited his portion in the land of Israel. His daughters said that "he died from his sin" (ibid. 27:3), implying that it is a sin with which we should be familiar. R. Akiva suggests that this sin was the previously mentioned gathering of wood on Shabbos.

R. Yehudah ben Beseirah responds to R. Akiva with apparent horror. Whether he is correct or not, R. Akiva spoke improperly. If Tzelophechad was the *mekoshesh,* the Torah did not mention it for a reason. If the Torah covered up this unflattering fact, by what right does R. Akiva reveal it? And if R. Akiva is wrong, then he has slandered Tzelophechad.

Rav Binyamin Yehoshua Zilber (*Responsa Az Nidberu* 14:68) sees this passage as proof that the laws of *lashon ha-ra* apply to the deceased. Otherwise, what is R. Yehudah ben Beseirah's criticism of R. Akiva?

II. Dead Men Don't Care

However, this view faces a challenge, as well. The *Mordekhai* (*Bava Kama* 8:106) cites an ancient enactment forbidding slander of the deceased. If Torah law forbids slander of the deceased, why do we need a post-talmudic enactment reiterating a biblical prohibition?

Indeed, Rav Yaakov Kamenetsky (*Emes Le-Ya'akov Al Ha-Torah*, Gen. 37:18) answers the following question in two ways. Why, a student asked him, does the Torah tell the story of the nastiness between Yosef and his brothers? Isn't this one big tale of *lashon ha-ra*? Family politics can be ugly, and we are prohibited from telling those stories. Rav Kamenetsky responds that there is no prohibition to speak ill of the deceased. The above-mentioned enactment forbids telling false stories about the dead, but true stories are permitted. Perhaps more importantly, the story of Yosef and his brothers does not entail nastiness and politics when understood correctly, which he proceeds to explain at length.[91]

Rav Kamenetsky has strong talmudic support for his position. The Gemara (*Berakhos* 18b-19a) discusses whether dead people know what transpires in this world. Within this discussion, the following passage appears (19a):

> R. Yitzchak said: Anyone who speaks after the dead is as if he speaks after a stone. Some say because they do not know and some say they know but do not care. Is this true? Did not Rav Papa say: Someone said words against Mar Shmuel [after his death] and a reed fell from the ceiling, cracking his skull? A Torah scholar is different because God demands his respect.

According to the opinion that the dead do not know what we say, we do not hurt them with *lashon ha-ra*. But there is another

---

91. See also *Arukh Ha-Shulchan, Orach Chaim* 606:4

opinion, that the dead know but don't care. We say that "sticks and stones may break my bones but words will never hurt me," but we do not mean it. We are hurt by unkind words, even if true, because we care what other people think about us. However, the dead have different priorities. In both this world and the next, people's opinions aren't important. In this world, we have trouble accepting this but in the next world, when people have properly ordered priorities, they are able to accept this unimportance. In the afterlife, not only don't sticks and stones hurt people, words don't hurt either.

According to this, we can understand why the post-talmudic sages enacted a prohibition against slandering the deceased. The dead either don't know or don't care what we say, so we can say anything about them, even if untrue. However, to protect the deceased's legacy, the sages forbade spreading lies about the dead.

Yet, according to Rav Kamenetsky, what was R. Yehudah ben Beseirah's challenge to R. Akiva about the *mekoshesh*? Dead people either don't know or don't care what we say. If so, why should R. Akiva refrain from identifying the *mekoshesh* as Tzelophechad?

III. Dead Rabbis

Perhaps this can be explained based on the end of the above passage from *Berakhos*. While the dead allow us to speak badly about them, God forbids us to denigrate Torah scholars. The Targum Pseudo-Yonasan (Num. 15:32) says that the *mekoshesh* sinned for a good purpose. He realized that the punishments for violating Shabbos had not been fully explained. He sinned so that Moshe would have to ask God about the punishment process, thereby clarifying this difficult Torah subject.[92]

From this, it seems that the *mekoshesh* was a Torah scholar. Even though one may normally speak improperly about the deceased,

---

92. See also Tosafos, *Bava Basra* 119b sv. *afilu.*

even lying about them (until the post-Talmud enactment forbade it) since the dead do not know or do not care, a Torah scholar is different. An insult of a Torah scholar is an insult to the Torah. While the scholar himself may not care about the insult, God does. Therefore, the *mekoshesh* identification does not challenge Rav Kamenetsky's view that the rules of *lashon ha-ra* do not ordinarily apply to the deceased.

There Is No Mitzvah to Be a *Freier*

Nice guys do not have to finish last. Nor must they suffer from people who refuse to play by the rules. Jewish law allows for self-defense in many different ways, including financially.

Judaism does not require someone who is hit to turn the other cheek but allows you to hit back. According to some, this isonly if there is danger of you being hit again. The Gemara (*Yoma* 23a) says that the prohibition against taking revenge does not apply to physical violence. This would allow you to hit back. However, the Rambam (*Mishneh Torah, Hilkhos Dei'os* 7:7) omits this limitation on the prohibition, apparently forbidding physical revenge, as well. (He either interpreted the Gemara differently or had a variant text.)

The Rosh (*Bava Kamma*, ch. 3 no. 13) rules that if someone is hitting you, you may hit back and are completely exempt from damages. He started it, so you may defend yourself. While you must use minimal force to end the situation, you may physically defend yourself or others against an attack.

Similarly, if someone tricks you into agreeing to an unusually low price, you do not have to be the "*freier*" (Israeli slang for "sucker") and pay for it. The Gemara (*Bava Metzi'a* 49a) says that your "yes" and "no" should be righteous, meaning you must fulfill your words—when you say "yes" or "no," follow up on those agreements. The Gemara continues that if you agreed to buy something and then change your mind, you have not violated a technical prohibition (since there was no formal acquisition), but you are still subject to a curse: "He who exacted payment for the generations of the Flood and the Dispersion will eventually exact payment from someone who fails to keep his word." Seemingly, even if you are tricked, once you agree to a price you must pay it or suffer the curse.

Rav Osher Weiss (*Responsa Minchas Asher*, vol. 2 no. 112) addresses this question in contemporary Israel. "Shimon" offered to buy the residence he had been renting from "Reuven." Shimon offered a lowball price and Reuven, who remembered the prices from before recent rises in real estate values, agreed. Before proceeding, Reuven learned that the real value of the residence was much higher and realized that Shimon had intentionally tricked him. Is he required to sell at the lower price?

Aside from other details that relate to this specific case, Rav Weiss argues that Reuven is not required to honor the earlier price. There is no mitzvah to be taken advantage of by dishonest people. Rav Weiss quotes the *Chinukh* (338), who says that the prohibition to insult someone does not apply when someone insults you first. While it is praiseworthy to hear your own insults and refrain from responding, this practice is not obligatory.

The Rema (*Shulchan Arukh, Choshen Mishpat* 228:1) writes that if someone is insulting himself, you may insult him also. Later authorities struggle to understand this ruling. Most follow the *Sema* (ad loc., no. 4), who explains that this person is acting so improperly that the prohibition no longer applies to him. The *Be'er Ha-Golah* (ad loc., no. 5) reads the Rema as referring to "him," meaning the second party who is now allowed to insult the first. In other words, the Rema follows the *Chinukh*, who allows responding to an insult with another insult.

Rav Weiss then takes a big step, applying this principle broadly. The Torah does not require you to suffer someone's insults. Similarly, you do not have to be someone's sucker in a financial deal: "The rules of justice and morality do not require someone affronted to quietly accept someone else's trickery."

He briefly quotes the Gemara (*Megillah* 13b) that asks why Ya'akov, on meeting Rachel, said that he was her father Lavan's brother (Gen. 29:12). Ya'akov was Rachel's cousin, not her uncle. The Gemara explains that the following conversation ensued between the two. Ya'akov asked Rachel to marry him. She replied that he cannot marry her because her father is a master of trickery. Ya'akov replied that he is Lavan's brother, i.e., peer, in trickery.

Is it proper for Ya'akov to (try to) trick someone who is going to trick him? The Gemara defends this practice with the following citation:

> With the merciful you show yourself merciful, with the upright you show yourself upright, with the pure you show yourself pure; and with the crooked you show yourself shrewd (2 Sam. 22:26-27; Ps. 18:27-28).

While Rav Weiss does not quote this, the Meiri (*Bava Kamma* 123a) offers a succinct application of this principle:

> It is forbidden for the righteous to walk in a path that has any aspect of trickery.... However, if they have business dealings with tricky people and are concerned that if they [the righteous] proceed simply, the tricky people will prevail, they [the righteous] may [use trickery] in order to protect themselves from the others.

No one is permitting dishonesty. They are permitting leveling the playing field, realistic behavior that does not automatically disadvantage those who are honest. The Torah does not require you to be a *freier*.

PART 7: INTERNET & SOCIAL MEDIA

Instagram and Jewish Law

New media and technology still fall under the classical rules of ethics. Their usage can and must be examined with an open mind but also with a keen eye for propriety. Instagram is an image- and video-sharing service that allows users to post their own pictures and videos, view those of others, follow members, indicate appreciation of pictures, and leave comments. I'd like to explore a few halakhic issues regarding Instagram use.

As a form of communication, Instagram use is subject to interpersonal *halakhah* with all its nuances. How you communicate—the language you use and the interactions in which you engage—must conform to Jewish ethical standards. Before we go into detail, two basic rules of behavior must be mentioned:

1. You may not post or view pictures of people inadequately clothed or in any way sexually suggestive.
2. Additionally, you must follow all relevant laws regarding permitted use of images.

I'd like to discuss some issues that impact the core nature of Instagram—posting pictures and videos online. This feature is certainly not unique to Instagram; most forms of social media allow it. Be that as it may, this discussion is particularly relevant to Instagram and similar services (like Flickr and YouTube).

I. Hurtful Pictures

Posting pictures and videos can embarrass others in a variety of ways. The most obvious are images of someone else from an embarrassing incident. Whether someone was drunk or otherwise incapacitated, or was young and particularly foolish, you need to know the line between playful teasing and embarrassing. You are allowed to have fun with your friends and family by posting funny pictures online. But you may not embarrass anyone else. The Gemara (*Bava Metzi'a* 58b) compares embarrassing another to murdering him.

Hurtful pictures go one step farther. Posting a picture that hurts someone's feelings or damages someone's reputation is a form of attack. Hurting someone's feelings is biblically prohibited as *ona'as devarim* (*Bava Metzi'a*, ibid.). You may think that this only applies to a verbal insult or attack—after all, "*devarim*" means words. However, the Torah (Lev. 25:17) merely says "*lo sonu*" and does not differentiate between methods of delivering this harm.[93]

Similarly, *lashon ha-ra* is not limited to words. The *Chafetz Chaim* (1:1:8 n. 13) quotes Onkelos (Lev. 19:16), who translates "Do not be a talebearer" as "*lo seichol kurtzin*." Rashi (ad loc.) explains that this refers to the way gossippers motion with their eyes. Even indirect gossip, even mere motioning without any words, qualifies as forbidden *lashon ha-ra*. As it says in *Mishlei* (Prov. 6:12-13), "A base person... winks with his eyes, scrapes with his feet, points with his fingers." *Lashon ha-ra* does not have to be actual words.

Therefore, you may only post a damaging picture or video if you fulfill the conditions that permit *lashon ha-ra*.

---

93. See Rav Daniel Z. Feldman, *The Right and the Good: Halakhah and Human Relations* (Yashar, 2004), pp. 20-21.

II. Unauthorized Pictures

Somewhat related but a bit broader is the question of posting someone's picture without permission. If you capture an image of a friend in a compromising position, can you post it to Instagram without the friend's permission? Even non-malicious circumstances raise the question. If I take a picture of my wife at a restaurant and people at another table are in the shot, can I post that picture with only my wife's permission and not that of the other people?

A remote possibility exists that I could be doing great harm to others. Perhaps those people were secretly negotiating an important deal, conducting a job interview while the candidate is still employed elsewhere, or nurturing a romance that they were not yet ready to reveal to the world. If someone they know stumbles on the picture through the interlocking world of social media, the secret will be revealed. Proverbs (11:13) denounces those who reveal secrets as gossipers.[94]

Setting the issue of publicizing aside, halakhic authorities debate whether you may take someone's picture without his permission. Some Jews, at least a century ago, objected—for mystical reasons—to having their picture taken under any circumstances. Presumably, we should honor their concerns. However, Rav Yosef Chaim Sonnenfeld (*Salmas Chaim* 2:19) rules that we are not required to be concerned. If we follow the view that allows taking pictures, we may take pictures of anyone, even against their open objections.[95]

Rav Menashe Klein (*Mishneh Halakhos* 7:117) disagrees. He rules that if a person considers a picture to be damaging in any way, others may not subject him to it. Even if he will take his own picture, he can choose to permit metaphysical injury to himself

---

94. See also *Sha'arei Teshuvah* 3:225
95. See also *Be-Tzel Ha-Chokhmah* 4:85

but forbid others from hurting him. Rav Klein adds that since you can sell pictures of yourself, someone who takes your picture without permission is stealing something of value from you.

Rav Shlomo Aviner (*Piskei Shlomo*, vol. 3 pp 146-147), who quotes the above sources, questions this last point of Rav Klein. The photographer is only "stealing" potential future profit, which is indirect theft for which he is not liable. Regardless, Rav Aviner adds another reason to forbid taking someone else's picture against his protests. The Torah (Lev. 19:18) commands you to love others as yourself. You may not treat others in a way you would not want to be treated yourself (*Shabbos* 31a). Since you would not want your picture taken without your permission, you may not take someone else's.

This applies with even greater force to posting someone else's picture online. Do not do to others what you would not want them to do to you. And if you have a uniquely free spirit and want every unguarded moment of yours memorialized in eternal online images, you must still act considerately to others.[96]

---

96. We have only touched some of the many issues that arise in using social media. See my article, "The Ten Tenets of Social Media" in *Jewish Action* (Fall 2012).

Skype and Jewish Law

Skype is one of a number of applications that allow for online video chatting. Essentially, it enables your computer or other internet device to serve as a video phone, with which you can talk and see your correspondent while he sees you. This raises a number of halakhic issues, some of which we will discuss.

Rav Dovid Lichtenstein, in his *Headlines: Halachic Debates of Current Events*,[97] explores topics "ripped from the headlines" through the lens of Jewish law with great clarity and expertise. Chapter 30, titled "The Webcam in Halacha," focuses mainly on issues of testimony and supervision, that are not particularly relevant to regular use of Skype. Two topics he raises are answering "*amen*" to a blessing heard via a webcam and reciting a blessing over seeing kings and scholars via a webcam. This is a direction I would like to follow.

I. Fulfilling *Mitzvos* on Skype

Can you fulfill a mitzvah to hear or see something by using Skype? For example, we end Shabbos with *havdalah*, even though you may technically perform work after praying. Can you hear *havdalah* via Skype? What about the Torah or Megillah reading?

Rav Lichtenstein (p. 403) quotes a debate between Rav Moshe Feinstein and Rav Shlomo Zalman Auerbach. According to Rav Feinstein (*Iggeros Moshe, Orach Chaim* 2:108, 4:91:4), a person can

---

97. OU Press, 2014

fulfill at least rabbinic obligations such as *havdalah* and *megillah* through a microphone or telephone. Rav Auerbach (*Minchas Shlomo* 1:9) considers an electronic reproduction of sound to be an entirely different creation through which one can never fulfill a mitzvah. As Rav Lichtenstein notes, many other authorities—such as Rav Tzvi Pesach Frank and the *Chazon Ish*—agreed with Rav Feinstein's position.

It would seem, then, that according to the majority of authorities, you can fulfill *mitzvos* via Skype, while according to Rav Auerbach, you cannot. However, the tide has changed among *posekim* as understanding of electricity has increased. Rav Chaim Jachter (*Gray Matter*, vol. 2, p. 239) writes:

The majority of authorities believe that one does not fulfill any *mitzvot* by hearing a sound through a microphone. In particular, most mid- and late-twentieth century authorities, who benefited from a greater understanding than their predecessors of how microphones operate, reject the use of microphones for the performance of *mitzvot*,[6] with the possible exception of Torah reading. They argue that one hears an electronically reproduced sound over these devices, whereas the Halachah requires one to hear the actual sound of a *shofar*, or voice of the reader.

[6] Besides Rav Shlomo Zalman Auerbach, these authorities include Rav Yosef Eliyahu Henkin (*Kitvei Hagaon Rav Y.E. Henkin* 1:122), Rav Moshe Shternbuch (*Teshuvot Vehanhagot* 1:155 and *Mo'adim Uzmanim* 6:105), Rav Eliezer Waldenberg (*Teshuvot Tzitz Eliezer* 8:11), Rav Ovadia Yosef (*Teshuvot Yechavveh Daat* 3:54), Rav Levi Yitzchak Halperin (*Teshuvot Ma'aseih Chosheiv* 1:1), and Rav Yitzchak Weisz (*Teshuvot Minchat Yitzchak* 3:38:16).

If that is the case, the majority of authorities would not allow you to fulfill a mitzvah via Skype. However, Rav Jachter (ibid., p. 240 n. 7) adds that the Torah reading may be different. Rav Moshe Sternbuch (*Teshuvos Ve-Hanhagos* 1:149,155) argues that you need to hear the Torah reading, not necessarily the reader's voice. Therefore, you may fulfill the mitzvah by hearing a microphone amplify the Torah reading. Rav Ovadiah Yosef (*Yalkut Yosef*, vol. 2, pp. 107-108 n. 14) rules likewise. Rav Mark Dratch, in his booklet *The Use of Microphones on Shabbat* (pp. 31, 36 n. 51), quotes from Rav Haskel Lookstein that Rav Joseph B. Soloveitchik permitted reading *megillah* with a microphone. Perhaps in unusual circumstances, you may use Skype to fulfill these *mitzvos*.

II. Answering "*Amen*" on Skype

What if you hear someone reciting a blessing on Skype? Normally, you are required to respond "*amen*" to a blessing and forbidden to otherwise respond "*amen*" (*Shulchan Arukh, Orach Chaim* 215:2; 124:8). What should you do if your Skype correspondent says a blessing?

Rav Lichtenstein (p. 404) quotes Rav Avraham Yitzchak Kook's responsum (*Orach Mishpat, Orach Chaim* 48) regarding hearing *kedushah* on a telephone or live radio broadcast.[98] Rav Kook ruled that only a *shofar* may not be heard electronically. While not ideal, all other *mitzvos* may, if necessary, be fulfilled over the phone or radio. Rav Lichtenstein builds on Rav Kook's ruling regarding answering "*amen*" and suggests that: "This ruling would likely apply to a live webcast or Skype session, as well, and thus one who hears a *beracha, Kaddish, Kedusha,* or *Borchu* over a webcam should respond."

Especially regarding "*amen*," it would seem that you should follow the practice of the Great Synagogue of Alexandria. The

---

98. All references here to radio mean a live radio broadcast.

Gemara (*Sukkah* 51b) says that the synagogue was so large that people in the back could not hear. Instead, the synagogue had someone wave a flag whenever it was time to say "*amen*." Tosafos (*Sukkah* 52a sv. *ve-keivan*) explain that as long as you know what blessing is recited, you may answer "*amen*" to it even if you do not hear it. The Rema (*Shulchan Arukh, Orach Chaim* 124:8) rules accordingly.

Based on this, you might think that you should answer "*amen*" to a blessing heard via Skype. However, Rav Jachter (p. 242) quotes Rav Auerbach as ruling that you should only answer "*amen*" if you are in the place where the blessing is recited. If you hear it on the radio, you should not respond. He quotes Rav Yosef Shalom Elyashiv (cited in *Avnei Yashfeh* 1:9) as equating hearing a blessing on a telephone or radio as similar to receiving a telegram informing you that a blessing will be recited at a specific time. Rav Jachter quotes Rav Moshe Sternbuch (*Teshuvos Ve-Hanhagos* 1:155) as ruling similarly. However, he notes that Rav Moshe Feinstein (*Iggeros Moshe, Orach Chaim* 4:91) rules that you should answer "*amen*" to a blessing heard via telephone or radio.

It seems that most authorities rule that you should not answer "*amen*" to a blessing you hear on a telephone or radio. Therefore, you should also not answer "*amen*" to a blessing on Skype. However, if you are in a situation in which you must rely on the lenient opinions that allow you to fulfill *havdalah* remotely, you presumably should respond "*amen*" to the blessings.

III. Seeing Kings and Scholars

When you see certain honored people, you recite a blessing on the sighting, praising God for making such people (*Berakhos* 58a). These people include leading Torah scholars, expert scientists, and kings. Do you recite the blessing if you Skype with them? If, for example, you have occasion to Skype with a leading scientist, should you recite the blessing?

Rav Lichtenstein (pp. 409-410) quotes the *Birkei Yosef* (*Orach Chaim* 224:1) who distinguishes between seeing a king and other people. The blessing on seeing a king is due to the awe and reverence one feels in his presence. Even a blind person experiences this and should recite the blessing. However, Rav Lichtenstein suggests, you do not feel this way when viewing a king on a screen. Therefore, you should not recite the blessing on seeing a king via Skype. Rav Lichtenstein leaves open the question of the other blessings. *Piskei Teshuvos* (224:12) seems to say that you should never recite a blessing on seeing something on a live broadcast, which would presumably include Skype.

IV. A Good Friend

The Gemara (*Berakhos* 58b) says that if you see a friend whom you have not seen in 30 days, you recite a *Shehecheyanu* blessing. If you haven't seen him in twelve months, you instead recite a *Mechayeih Meisim* blessing. The *Shulchan Arukh* (*Orach Chaim* 225:2) discusses a case that has renewed relevance in an age of social media. What if you have a friend whom you have never met? You are what used to be called "pen pals" and have only exchanged letters. Do you recite a blessing at your first meeting? The *Shulchan Arukh* rules that you do not.

Nowadays, with e-mail lists and social media, it is increasingly common to make friends without ever actually meeting. Do you recite a blessing at the first get-together, such as a "Tweetup"?[99] If you have even Skyped, does that count as meeting prior? Additionally, if you haven't seen a friend—someone you know in person—in 30 days but have Skyped with him, do you still recite the blessing when you meet in person?

99. "A tweetup is the actual face-to-face meeting of Twitter users for a specific objective." Source: https://www.hashtags.org/featured/what-is-a-tweetup-and-how-do-i-start-one/ (retrieved August 11, 2017)

To this last question, there is good reason to say that you should not. The *Birkei Yosef* (*Orach Chaim* 225:3) quotes authorities who rule that you do not recite the *Mechayeih Meisim* if you have even heard news about your friend within the past twelve months. According to this view, which seems to be normative, the blessing is only about seeing a friend after not seeing or hearing anything about him. The *Mishnah Berurah* (225:2) applies this to the *Shehecheyanu* on seeing a friend after 30 days as well, saying that since there are different opinions, you should refrain. If so, seeing a friend on Skype would prevent you from reciting *Shehecheyanu*.

However, later authorities question the *Mishnah Berurah*'s application of this condition to *Shehecheyanu*. Rav Shlomo Aviner (*She'eilas Shlomo* 3:83-84) writes that the *Mishnah Berurah*'s words are puzzling. Rav Ovadiah Yosef (*Yechavveh Da'as* 4:17) writes that, with all due respect, the *Mishnah Berurah* is wrong. I saw in a *sefer* I can no longer remember the suggestion that this comment was placed incorrectly and should really be on the text about *Mechayeih Meisim*. Therefore, this consideration does not answer our question about Skyping.

V. Seeing From Afar

Rav Ovadiah Yosef (*Yechavveh Da'as* 4:17 p. 86f.) discusses whether you should recite this blessing if you see your friend for the first time in 30 days on a live television broadcast. He quotes the *Yam Ha-Gadol* (24) who rules that you recite *Shehecheyanu* on receiving a phone call from a friend you haven't seen in 30 days because hearing your friend's voice induces joy. So too, it would seem, regarding seeing your friend on television or via Skype. However, Rav Yosef disagrees, saying that the blessing only applies to seeing someone in person, what the Sages meant by "seeing." Presumably this would also apply to a friend you have never seen before, even if you have exchanged e-mails, pictures or Skyped.

Seeing in person is a higher form of personal connection than any kind of social media or electronic meeting.

Rav Chaim Elazar Shapira, in his *Nimukei Chaim* (225:1), writes that people generally do not recite the *Shehecheyanu* on seeing a friend. He explains that saying the blessing for only some people and not others would hurt feelings. Therefore, it is best to refrain entirely from reciting the blessing. The *Ben Ish Chai* (Eikev, 14) similarly writes that the custom is to refrain from this blessing. *Piskei Teshuvos* (225:2) quotes others who say not to recite the blessing for various reasons. However, he adds that in exceptional circumstances where there is unquestionable joy, such as seeing a sibling or child after a long time, you should still recite the blessing.

If you Skype with your child who is studying in yeshiva in Israel and then go visit him, do you recite *Shehecheyanu*? Speaking from personal experience, there is a real joy in that visit even though you have frequently spoken and Skyped. I suspect that halakhic authorities will rule that you should still recite the *Shehecheyanu* blessing despite having communicated via phone and Skype. In the end, this is about expressing your joy to God. When that joy is unquestionable, I suspect the blessing still applies.

After writing this, I asked Rav Shlomo Aviner whether a parent whose son is studying in yeshiva in Israel and communicates via Skype should recite the *Shehecheyanu* blessing on seeing him. He replied that he should.

SoundCloud and Jewish Law

SoundCloud is one of many online services that allow users to upload audio recordings for others to hear. This raises a number of potential halakhic issues. The halakhic literature contains a good deal of discussion of copyrights, which I do not want to address here. Instead, I would like to explore the halakhic issues surrounding recording and posting a Torah lecture online without permission. Assuming that the speaker has no intent to sell recordings, so he is not losing money by your uploading a recording, can you circulate his teachings without his permission, perhaps even against his explicit instruction not to?

I. Keeping Secrets

The book of Leviticus begins with a redundancy: "And the Lord called to Moshe, and spoke to him from the tent of meeting saying" (Lev. 1:1). The Gemara (*Yoma* 4b) asks what the word "saying" adds, and explains that it teaches that Moshe needed permission to repeat what God had told him. More generally, you may not repeat what someone tells you until you receive explicit permission. The word "saying" was God's permission to Moshe.

The Gemara (*Sanhedrin* 31a) tells a story about a student who told a secret from the yeshiva study hall twenty-five years after the fact. Rav Ami expelled him and denounced him as someone who reveals secrets. Rashi explains that revealing a secret falls under the category of *lashon ha-ra*. Presumably, Rashi's source is Prov.

11:13: "A gossiper is one who reveals secrets." This seems to equate revealing a secret with forbidden gossip.

Rabbenu Yonah of Gerona (*Sha'arei Teshuvah* 3:225) offers two reasons why a person is obligated to maintain a secret:

1. The revelation may cause damage to the subject of the secret.
2. Doing so contravenes the will of the subject. It is the opposite of *tzeni'us* (more on this below).

Rav Ya'akov Ariel (*Be-Ohalah Shel Torah*, vol 1. no. 79) searches for the technical source of this prohibition. After a number of possibilities, he settles on the requirement to mirror God's attributes, to walk in His ways. Surprisingly, he does not entertain the possibility that it derives from the obligation to love others as ourselves. Just like we don't want our confidences breached, we should not reveal others' secrets.

Rav Hershel Schachter quotes Rav Joseph B. Soloveitchik as arguing that the theological source for modesty is the obligation to walk in God's ways. Just as God is called a "hidden God," we, too, must strive to cover ourselves in clothing and, perhaps more importantly, in deed (*TorahWeb*, "On the Matter of Masorah"). Rav Norman Lamm ("Privacy in Law and Theology" in *Faith & Doubt*, pp. 297-298) extends this to privacy. Part of our God-like hiding is maintaining our own privacy and that of others. Revealing secrets is a violation of *tzeni'us*, modesty.

II. Breaching Confidentiality

The Gemara (*Avodah Zarah* 28a) tells a relevant story. R. Yochanan was sick and asked a local healer for instructions to make a home remedy. She made him swear to the God of Israel that he would not reveal the secret. After he recovered, he publicly taught the remedy so others could benefit. He further explained that this was not a *chillul Hashem* because the wording of his oath was that he would not reveal the secret to the God of Israel, while he revealed it to the people of Israel. Technically, he kept his word. Additionally, he informed the woman before he taught the remedy in public.

This story teaches a few lessons. First, a public health concern overrides confidentiality. You may reveal a secret to protect other people's health. R. Yochanan was only allowed to reveal the secret because of the public need (*Responsa Chavos Ya'ir* 69, quoted in *She'arim Metzuyanim Ba-Halakhah, Avodah Zarah* 28a). However, R. Yochanan faced another barrier—his explicit promise. He still had to be concerned that violating his oath was a *chillul Hashem*. Rav Moshe Isserles (*Darkhei Moshe, Yoreh De'ah* 232) writes that, in such a case, you can avoid *chillul Hashem* if, before divulging the secret, you inform the individual that you are forced to compromise your oath. The *Shakh* (*Yoreh De'ah* 232:37) disagrees, because that only helped in the case where the original promise could be interpreted differently. Therefore, R. Yochanan's case cannot be generalized to other cases in which an explicit oath protects the confidentiality.

As an interesting postscript, the Talmud Yerushalmi (*Shabbos* 14:4) offers two versions of what the healer did after R. Yochanan revealed her secret. One version is that she committed suicide. The other is that she converted to Judaism. *Korban Ha-Edah* (ad loc., s.v. *is de-amrin*) explains that she was impressed that R. Yochanan gave away the medical advice for free rather than charging for it.

Rav Ya'akov Weil, of fifteenth-century Germany, issued two responsa that relate to this issue. In one, he points out that a witness with testimony in a hotly contested court case who was sworn to secrecy must request permission from the litigants before testifying (*Responsa Mahari Weil* 42). This is surprising because testifying in court is a mitzvah. Despite this obligation, the witness may not divulge a secret without permission (see *Shakh, Sema,* and *Tumim, Choshen Mishpat* 28:1).

In another case, a man was forced by gentiles to pay a bribe and sworn to secrecy. Rav Weil (*Responsa Mahari Weil* 53) rules that since the man was threatened with death, he certainly intended to keep his oath. Therefore, he is bound to secrecy despite the circumstances of his oath. If he gave his word and meant it at the time, he may not violate his promise even when there is a public need. However, Rav Moshe Isserles (*Yoreh De'ah* 232:14) says that it all depends on the circumstances. While the *Shakh* (quoted above) disagrees with the proof from R. Yochanan, this sensible balance seems normative. Rav Ya'akov Ariel (ibid.), in discussing whether a social worker is required to reveal confidential information, similarly concludes that it all depends on the specific needs of the case.

III. Mid-Conclusion

It seems that you may not release a recording of someone without his permission. Doing so violates his privacy. Significantly, Rav Moshe of Coucy, in his *Semag* (prohibition 9; quoted in *Hagahos Maimoniyos*, *Hilkhos Dei'os* 7:7) rules that if someone tells you that something is a secret, you must keep the secret even if he tells it to you in public. Therefore, you may not even release a public statement without permission from the speaker.

Note that there is no issue of theft. Bootleg recordings of a concert is not theft because you cannot steal sound. However, it is still forbidden if you cause the singer to lose money. But recording and releasing a non-commercial song or speech, for which the singer or speaker did not lose financially, is not theft but a violation of privacy (see Rav Zalman Nechemiah Goldberg in *Techumin*, vol. 6 p. 197; Rav Menachem Weisfish, *Copyright in Jewish Law* 13:6).

However, if there is a public need, then you may violate the person's privacy and release the recording. This is the first lesson from R. Yochanan's recovery. Shortly, we will turn our attention to what exactly constitutes a public need.

If you verbally promise (even without an oath) not to release the recording, then you are further bound to maintain the confidentiality, even if there is a public need, because of the *chillul Hashem*. According to some, you may tell the person in advance, thereby removing the *chillul Hashem*, and then release the recording. But if the need becomes great, there may be more room for leniency.

IV. Teaching Torah

Teaching and learning Torah are obligations. There is room to say that teaching a unique Torah insight, especially a practical conclusion, constitutes a public need. If so, we may be allowed to record and release a Torah lecture without permission of the speaker.

A related incident occurred 35 years ago. When the Israeli army invaded Lebanon the first time in 1982, with God's help it proceeded quickly through the country and laid siege on Beirut. Rav Shlomo Goren argued in an article that the Israeli army was halakhically obligated to leave one side of the city open so residents can flee (see *Mishneh Torah, Hilkhos Melakhim* 6:7). Rav Shaul Yisraeli sent a private letter disagreeing. He distinguished between a mandatory war (*milkhemes mitzvah*) and an optional war (*milkhemes reshus*). We are only limited to a partial siege in the latter type of war, while the war in Lebanon was of the former type.

To Rav Yisraeli's surprise, his private letter was soon published in the newspaper. Rav Goren wrote to Rav Yisraeli an apology for the confusion but added that he did not really need permission to publish Rav Yisraeli's Torah insights (note that Rav Goren published a critique of his views by Rav Yisraeli; this entire letter and Rav Yisraeli's response are published in *Techumin*, vol. 4). Rav Goren points out that the Tosefta (*Bava Kamma* 7:3) states that someone who overhears ("steals") another's Torah insights may repeat them to others (giving proper attribution to the source, of course). Based on this, the *Shakh* (*Choshen Mishpat* 292:35) rules that you may copy a Torah text from someone else's scroll even if he does not allow it. According to Rav Goren, teaching Torah is sufficient reason to set aside the prohibition against revealing confidential information (i.e., private teachings).

V. A Teacher's Responsibility

Rav Yisraeli counters that the Gemara (*Yoma* 4b), with which we started, forbids publicizing Torah without permission. This is because teaching Torah requires preparation. A teacher needs to think through his thoughts, challenge his ideas, word his lessons carefully. If someone thinks Torah out loud—testing ideas on an audience—he does not necessarily think his ideas are sufficiently developed for publication. He may still want to tweak the ideas or phrasing.

According to Rav Yisraeli, the Tosefta that permits stealing, i.e., publicizing without permission, a Torah insight refers to a public teaching. When someone teaches others, a member of the audience has the right to repeat the teaching even without the teacher's permission. But that is because the teaching was already offered in public. The teacher must have prepared and therefore the Gemara's insistence on permission no longer applies. According to Rav Yisraeli, teaching Torah only permits revealing a confidence if the original confidence was made in (some sort of) public.

Rav Moshe Feinstein (*Iggeros Moshe, Orach Chaim* vol. 4 no. 40 par. 19) goes even further. Different audiences call for different styles and even different content. You teach different material to experts, you offer greater nuance, than you teach beginners. Therefore, you may not repeat an insight without permission even if it was taught in public. In doing so, you violate the rights of the teacher.

VI. Conclusion

Based on all we have covered, it would seem that you may not post to SoundCloud (or publicize in any other way) a conversation without the permission of all involved. However, leeway exists in extenuating circumstances.

If I understand correctly, according to Rav Goren, you may record a Torah lecture and post it online without permission. According to Rav Yisraeli, you may only do this with a public lecture. And according to Rav Feinstein, you are never allowed to upload a Torah lecture without the speaker's permission. However, according to everyone, if you explicitly agree to maintain the confidentiality of the Torah teaching, then you may not violate that agreement because doing so constitutes a *chillul Hashem*, allowing for the exceptions discussed above.

Lashon Ha-Ra in the Internet Age

The classic work *Chafetz Chaim* on the laws of *lashon ha-ra*, damaging language, was written well over a century ago.[100] In the intervening years, the world has changed dramatically. Cell phones, e-mail, and social media were not even in the realm of science fiction; they were beyond the imagination. Today they are part of the fabric of our life. In this age of hyper-communication, how do the laws of *lashon ha-ra* apply? Answering this question requires profound knowledge and wisdom.

Rav Daniel Z. Feldman uses his vast store of talents to apply these laws to the contemporary environment in his book *False Facts and True Rumors: Lashon Hara in Contemporary Culture*.[101] Enhanced communication demands enhanced responsibility. The greater freedom of expression that individuals enjoy today generates a greater obligation for careful speech. Rabbi Feldman, my long-time friend and classmate, brings together three distinct literatures to create a compelling case that people must rein in their speech today more than ever.

Rabbi Feldman presents a conceptual view of *lashon ha-ra*. He wants to explain not just what is allowed and what is forbidden, but why. What is the point, the underlying rationale, of all these rules? Is *lashon ha-ra* forbidden because it damages the victim or

---

100. This essay was originally published in the *Jewish Link of New Jersey*, November 12, 2015.
101. Maggid, 2015

because it represents a malicious abuse of information? Before the publication of *Chafetz Chaim*, the laws of *lashon ha-ra* were generally discussed in ethical literature, Mussar works. Following this example, Rabbi Feldman masterfully mines the Mussar literature for psychological and sociological explanations of the rules of *lashon ha-ra*.

Halakhic literature, the legal codes and responsa, often intimidate students when laws are not easily identifiable. There is no section of *Shulchan Arukh* called "The Laws of *Lashon Ha-Ra*." Only an industrious scholar can find the stray rulings in unrelated sections, the decisions of later scholars in volumes of responsa, and the articles in rabbinic journals across the decades. Rabbi Feldman's encyclopedic sweep of halakhic literature, with his masterful footnotes, sheds an authoritative light on these complex but crucial rules.

Yet with all the changes in society, how do we properly apply these rulings from across the centuries? This is the biggest surprise in the book. Rabbi Feldman wields an impressive command of the sociological literature on communication, particularly but not exclusively in the internet era. Studies show a bias in how people interpret information, what is known as the "fundamental attribution error." If I hear about someone else's negative action, I assume it is representative of his character. However, when I commit the same act, I interpret it as out of character, not reflective of my nature. Facts are never just facts; they require interpretation. The laws of *lashon hara* guard against the bias of interpretation.

Unlike any other book on *lashon ha-ra*, Rav Feldman's impressive work surveys the sociological literature for information about the unexpected biases and impacts fostered by *lashon ha-ra*. Section headings include: the fallibility of memory, the illusion of confidence, confidence biases and disproportionate influence, confirmation bias, the online disinhibition effect, and more.

Combining Jewish law and an understanding of contemporary social interaction, this is the most important book on Jewish speech available today.

However, despite the severity of sinful *lashon ha-ra*, a modern society cannot function without free-flowing information. How can we vote without knowing about the candidate? How can we conduct business without knowing who are crooks? In a chapter titled "Contemporary Culture: Journalism, the Internet and Politics," Rav Feldman explores the implications of his opening remarks that, on the one hand, "to become informed and to inform others regarding these areas, especially in a democratic society, seems to be well within the bounds of purposeful and necessary speech." But on the other hand, "this justification does not detract from the vigilance and sensitivity required by the precepts involving *lashon ha-ra*." The greater power of communication in the Internet age requires even greater care with the laws of *lashon ha-ra*.

Journalists and bloggers perform an important service to society. However, if they fail to be fair and accurate, they abuse their power. Additionally, consumers of media have to be careful readers, maintaining a balance between a healthy skepticism about the reports and caution about potential danger. Accuracy is important in journalism, yet often elusive in contemporary media. The idea that the Internet corrects errors through global fact-checking masks the flaws in this process. If truth arrives at all on the Internet, it usually comes late and amid competing claims. True to form, Rav Feldman surveys contemporary sociological literature about Internet behavior, evaluating the halakhic implications.

Everyone slips, particularly regarding *lashon ha-ra*. However, when you spread disparaging information, how do you correct your mistake? Some suggest asking forgiveness from the victim of your verbal assault, whether specifically or generally. Rav Feldman quotes an intriguing suggestion from Rav Ahron Soloveichik, who recommends spreading positive information about your victim to counteract the effects of your *lashon ha-ra*. It is better to undo the offense than to merely ask for forgiveness.

This remarkable book teaches not only the laws of *lashon ha-ra* but the nature of communication today. More words, more texts, pings, and pokes do not necessarily mean better communication. By better understanding how we interact—how information affects us and others—we can enhance our own clarity of expression and comprehension. Rav Feldman teaches us not only how to communicate more responsibly but also more effectively.

Social Media for Shabbos

An interesting article raised the question of whether you may schedule e-mails or social media updates to occur on Shabbos. For example, I can post to my website and schedule the essay to appear on Friday night. Within an hour of that essay's publication, a third-party application Tweets the essays's title, first few words and link to my personal Twitter account. And if I could ever get the technology to work properly, it would also post a link to my Facebook account. The next morning, at 5 a.m. on Shabbos, the application sends an e-mail of the full text of that essay to my website's distribution list. Am I allowed to schedule all of this to happen on Shabbos?

The following are my tentative thoughts to begin discussion. As always, ask your rabbi. In all this discussion, we must keep in mind that at nearly all hours of the day, it is not Shabbos somewhere in the world. Someone reading the essay or Tweet need not be violating Shabbos. For that matter, a gentile, who is not obligated to observe Shabbos, may also read it.

I. Scheduling

In the above example, some of the computer functions happen on Friday and some on Shabbos. The essay is actually filed on Friday with an exact date and time of publication. If someone accesses the website before the publication time, the computer holds back the post. After the publication time, it shows the post. Nothing really changes on Shabbos.

However, the social media functions happen on Shabbos. The third-party application learns about the post on Shabbos, grabs the information, submits it to Twitter and Facebook, compiles it into an e-mail, and sends it out. Similarly, if I use an e-mail application that allows me to schedule an e-mail for Shabbos, it waits until the right time and then sends the e-mail out on Shabbos.

Truthfully, though, when an essay appears on Shabbos it is captured by other third-party applications and registered in search engines. However, I do not control any of those applications and suggest that I am not liable for their activity.

II. Server Activity

Therefore, I suggest that scheduling an essay for Shabbos does not cause any problem of computer activity. However, the social media actions may. As we discussed elsewhere,[102] sending an e-mail on Shabbos, which becomes permanently stored on a server, may be biblically forbidden (under the labor of *boneh*). Rav Shlomo Zalman Auerbach forbade it regarding a floppy disk and others debate whether this ruling also applies to archives on servers.

The third-party application's action is, in theory, indirect (*gerama*). I am just posting to my website. The application then, on its own, grabs that information and submits it to social media platforms. However, I arranged these functions and want it to perform them. This is the normal way of doing things. Perhaps, then, this is not *gerama* but the normal course of business.

If Tweeting or sending an e-mail is biblically forbidden, then the case we are discussing would be comparable to setting a fax machine on a timer so it sends a fax on Shabbos. *Piskei Teshuvos* (Shabbos vol. 1, 242:7; vol. 2, 263:46) forbids such an action. However, the widespread custom is certainly to allow setting timers before Shabbos to schedule forbidden activities to occur

---

102. "Texting on Shabbos," *Torah Musings*, July 21, 2011, section V.

on Shabbos, provided they do not generate noise or otherwise interfere with the Shabbos atmosphere. I suggest that the above activities qualify

III. Appearances

The final issue is one of *maris ayin*. While all observers are required to judge favorably and assume you did not violate any prohibitions, you are still obligated to avoid situations in which you appear to transgress Torah laws. The definition of precisely what this entails remains fuzzy. I was taught that it depends on what the average onlooker will initially think.

In the case of blogging or Tweeting on Shabbos, I suspect that we are still at the point where observers will suspect you of violating Shabbos. When people turn on their computers after Shabbos and see your updates that appeared on Shabbos, they will think you posted them on Shabbos. Scheduling is still a trick of the trade and insufficiently well known. However, disclaimers explaining the situation suffice.

IV. Business

All of the above refers to personal usage. If you are scheduling business updates for Shabbos, you run into the potential problem of *shabbason*. *Piskei Teshuvos* (Shabbos vol. 2, 222:1) quotes the *Chelkas Ya'akov*, who rules that allowing your business to run on Shabbos, even if you are not personally involved, entails a lack of resting. Your work needs to stop on Shabbos (see Rashi on Ex. 20:9 and Ramban on Lev. 23:24).

What is business? Blogs with advertisements are paid every time the blog is accessed. Is a Tweet directing readers to my website (if it has ads) considered business? Quite possibly.

V. Tentative Conclusion

Therefore, my initial reaction is that scheduling blog posts, Tweets, e-mails, etc. should only be done if it is for personal rather than business use and should include a disclaimer stating that it was scheduled before Shabbos.

Is the Fake Excuse App Kosher?

We've all been in uncomfortable situations in which a well-intentioned but socially awkward person will not leave us alone. Sometimes we have other pressing business. Other times we simply have given enough time to this needy person and need to move on with our day. Extracting ourselves from those situations can be tricky. A new app helps.

I. Excuses and Ethics

A new app called Gotta Go allows you to program excuses in advance. With the press of a button, you can active time-delayed texts and/or phone calls that will interrupt your conversation and enable you to leave immediately. You can claim any type of emergency, whether saving someone else's life, picking up a waiting relative, or helping a friend with a computer problem.

However, before using this app, we need to consider its ethical component. This is an app to help you lie. Purists will claim that any lie is wrong and that this app is inherently unethical. I'm not sure that is correct.

II. Lying for Peace

The Sages of the Talmud (*Avos* 1:18) state that there are three pillars in the world: truth, peace, and justice. In support of the first pillar, the Torah commands: "Stay far away from falsehood" (Ex. 23:7). However, at times, God seems to deviate from complete truthfulness. Sarah said that she considered her giving birth unlikely because her husband Avraham was old. When God told that to Avraham, He changed it to Sarah being skeptical because of her advanced age (Gen. 18:12-13). The Talmud (*Yevamos* 65b) explains that you are allowed to lie for the sake of peace, in this case to prevent Avraham from getting angry at his wife Sarah. Similarly, Beis Hillel would famously praise all brides as beautiful, even if they weren't (*Kesubos* 17a). R. Ilai says that it is permitted to lie (literally: "alter") for the sake of peace while R. Nosson says that it is a mitzvah (*Yevamos*, ibid.).

III. Peace and Truth

Rav Daniel Z. Feldman (*The Right and the Good*, 2004 edition, p. 75ff.) offers two possible explanations of the permission to lie for the sake of peace. According to one approach, peace is more important than truth: "in order to uphold peace, truth at times must be jettisoned" (ibid., p. 75). In such a situation, the lie is the lesser of the two evils. Or, perhaps, only damaging lies are forbidden, but lies that preserve harmony are allowed.

With this, he explains the disagreement between R. Ilai and R. Nosson whether lying for the sake of peace is merely permitted or obligatory. If the prohibition of lying is in effect in the context of peace, then lying must be optional. You are not required to violate this prohibition for the sake of peace, just allowed to do so. But if there is no prohibition in saying a lie that promotes harmony, then of course you must lie.

Rav Ya'akov Ariel (*Be-Ohalah Shel Torah*, vol. 1 79:4) follows this second approach. He addresses the question whether a social worker is obligated to testify in a divorce hearing that a woman confessed to committing adultery. Violating that confidentiality would compromise the ability of social workers in general to function. He suggests that the requirement for truth has limits, with specific exceptions. Primary among them is peace. He suggests that facilitating social workers is also an exception, but leaves that unresolved and instead pursues another line of reasoning in answering this specific question.

IV. Truth and Politeness

Hurting someone's feelings constitutes a lack of peace. Just like Beis Hillel could praise an ugly bride as beautiful to avoid hurting her feelings, we may do likewise in similar situations. Rav Yitzchak Fuchs (*Halikhos Bein Adam Le-Chaveiro* 20:19-47) provides a number of examples. If someone offers you cake that looks burned or otherwise unappetizing, you may say that you are not hungry. In order to avoid embarrassment, a woman who miscarries and then gives birth to a boy, when asked by friends when the *pidyon ha-ben* celebration for the first-born son, can lie and say that she is the daughter of a *kohen* or Levi so she does not have to make the celebration.

More to our point, if a visitor appears at your office or home and you do not have time to speak with him, Rav Fuchs (20:26) quotes Rav Shlomo Zalman Auerbach as permitting you to say that you are not there. You may do this to avoid offending the visitor by saying that you do not have time. Some people will respect that you are busy and others will not. Some will respect your busy schedule but take a long time in telling you how much they understand your lack of time. While it is best to be honest or to deflect with ambiguous responses, when you have no other choice, you may lie to avoid offending the visitor because peace takes priority. This seems to conflict with Rav Aaron Levine's conclusion that lying for the sake of peace "is permissible only if the objective is to end discord or prevent an actual rift... [not] merely to mollify or prevent the occurrence of a ruffled feeling" (*Moral Issues of the Marketplace in Jewish Law*, p. 18, quoting

Meiri, *Yevamos* 63a and Rav Yosef Epstein, *Mitzvas Ha-Shalom*, p. 547). Rav Fuchs and Rav Levine seem to disagree on the nature of the offense that permits a lie. According to Rav Fuchs, you can lie to avoid hurting someone's feelings. According to Rav Levine, you may do so only to avoid an argument.[103]

However, three caveats must be mentioned. First, you may not lie for the sake of peace in front of children (R. Levine, ibid.). This would be setting a terrible example for people who cannot yet understand the complexities of social interaction. Second, you may not habitually lie, even in a permissible way. Both of these are learned from the verse: "They have taught their tongues to speak lies" (Jer. 9:4). We should not teach children to lie and we may not teach ourselves to become liars.

Finally, we should avoid lies whenever possible. Lying for the sake of peace is a last resort. It is better to minimize the lie, if not avoid it altogether.

V. The Excuse App

Therefore, when it comes to the Gotta Go app that allows you to lie for the sake of peace, you may only use it in appropriate circumstances. If the app is the best way to avoid offending someone or getting into a fight (depending on the disagreement between Rav Fuchs and Rav Levine), then you may use it. For example, if someone pressures you into a meeting for which you have limited time, and you are concerned about insulting him, you may set the app to interrupt the meeting.

However, you should only use appropriate excuses. You do not want to wish harm on anyone, unduly worry your interlocutor, or malign anyone falsely. You do not want to say, "I have to leave because my mother-in-law was in an accident," because that would

---

103. Although in *Case Studies in Jewish Business Ethics* (Ktav, 1999), p. 19, Rav Levine seems to agree with Rav Fuchs.

constitute wishing harm on your mother-in-law and may cause the other person to worry. You also do not want to say, "I have to go because my father-in-law was caught selling meth amphetamine" because that would malign your father-in-law. It seems to me that the best way to use the app is to receive a text and say, "I'm sorry but I have to go," or receive a phone call and say, "I'm sorry but I need to take this."

Additionally, you should only use the app occasionally. If you rely on it too much, you will use it as a first resort and not a last resort. You risk becoming a habitual liar.

PART 8: FOOD & DRINK

Wine in All Its Halakhic Glory

At the Passover *seder*, we drink four cups of wine. Stereotypically, American Jews drink very sweet, low alcohol wine. However, the kosher wine industry has grown enormously over the past few decades so that consumers can choose from many different kinds of award-winning fine wines. I still drink the cheap sweet wine, but others have become connoisseurs.

Rav Daniel Ya'akov Travis, in his *Wine & Wisdom: A Halachic Overview of Fine Wines and Their Brachos*,[104] wants these connoisseurs "to take their expertise one step further and to add the *halachos* of wine drinking to their repertoire of knowledge" (p. 14). In a beautiful volume, with glossy pages replete with stunning wine-related pictures, Rav Travis takes readers through a wide array of halakhic topics about wine. He writes that he consulted extensively with halakhic authorities—the final chapter contains English responsa from Rav Ezriel Auerbach—as well as the CEO of an Israeli winery for technical expertise. The result is a readable guide of Jewish law that is neither particularly strict nor lenient, and which contains explanations of the wine-making process.

The Talmud and commentators discuss different kinds of wines and different potential problems with wines. Because these rabbis were so much closer to the wine-making process, they easily understood these terms and concepts. What are the implications of modern changes in the wine-making process, such as the addition

104. Jerusalem, 2015

of sulfites or cooking of the wine at key points? How much water can we add to wine before it becomes halakhically diluted? These are some of the issues Rav Travis addresses.

Rav Travis' neighbor once had to travel to a remote place in China for business. He could not bring wine with him and was concerned how he would make *kiddush*. The answer: Raisin wine. Crush raisins and soak them in water for three full days (Ashkenazim can have a ratio of 1:6 raisins to water; Sephardim should have a 1:1 ratio). Then remove the raisins and squeeze them into the water-turned-wine. You may make *kiddush* on this wine (ch. 7).

Can you leave wine uncovered? In the times of the Talmud and *Shulchan Arukh*, it was dangerous to leave drinks uncovered because poisonous snakes could leave their venom in the drinks. Nowadays, at least in most parts of the world, this is not a concern. Can we now make *kiddush* on wine that was left uncovered? Preferably not, because "leaving wine open to the elements weakens the wine's taste and aroma (*Magen Avraham* 273:1). It also allows dust and other particles to fall into the wine (*Divrei Malkiel* 4:1)" (p. 25). However, Rav Ezriel Auerbach rules that if you left the wine uncovered, you may recite *kiddush* on it as long as you are certain its taste has not been compromised (p. 187).

Why do Jews say "*le-chaim*" before drinking wine? The Zohar explains the fruit of the tree of knowledge with which Adam sinned was grapes, which he made into wine (*Tikkunei Zohar* 68a). Adam's punishment was death. When misused, wine brings death to the world. On the other hand, the Gemara quotes R. Akiva's toast at his son's wedding: "May wine and life be placed in the mouths of the rabbis; may life and wine be placed in the mouths of the rabbis and their students" (*Shabbos* 67b). When used properly, wine offers wisdom and insight.

Traditionally, wine is offered to mourners to comfort them (*Sanhedrin* 70a). Wine is also given to a man prior to his execution (Prov. 31:6). Because of wine's association with death, and its possibility of enhancing life, we traditionally say "*le-chaim*," meaning this wine should be for life and not for death.

Should you say *le-chaim* before reciting *kiddush*? The custom in Spain was to say it, and Sephardim tend to follow this (*Birkei Yosef* 174:11; *Kaf Ha-Chaim* 187:108-109). However, some Ashkenazic authorities object that the mitzvah itself will protect people from harm, so there is no need to say "*le-chaim*" during *kiddush* or *havdalah*.

Wine & Wisdom serves as a practical guide to Judaism's approach to wine drinking. With accessible explanations and conclusive rulings, it is a unique, esthetically pleasing halakhic guide.

Is Chinese Food on Xmas Kosher?

Supreme Court Justice Elena Kagan amused the nation when, during her 2010 Senate confirmation hearings, she responded to the question "where were you on Christmas day" that "like all Jews, I was probably at a Chinese restaurant." However, my *minyan* experience challenges the propriety of this practice.

Rav Yitzchak Hutner ruled that we may not observe days that are determined by the secular calendar.[105] This comes into play most famously on Thanksgiving, but also many other times during the year. While you may eat turkey any time you want, he holds that you may not specifically eat it on Thanksgiving. Most halakhic authorities disagree, but Rav Hutner's students follow his approach.

Every year, on the morning of December 25, I attend a late *minyan* along with many people who do not have work that day. However, not every shul adjusts their schedule for the day off. I used to live a block from Yeshiva Chaim Berlin, where Rav Hutner had served as *rosh yeshiva* and where his influence is still strong long after his passing. I remember that on any legal holiday, the shuls where his students were rabbi did not adjust their *minyan* schedules. The early commuter *minyanim* continued as if everyone

---

105. *Pachad Yitzchak, Iggeros U-Kesavim*, p. 109. On the use of the secular (or Christian, as some call it) date, see *Responsa Maharam Schick* (YD 171) and *She'eilas Shlomo* 1:328 in the name of Rav Tzvi Yehuda Kook who oppose using it and *Yabia Omer* 3:YD:9 who permits.

was still going to work, so as not to mark the day in any fashion. (Of course, the local *minyan* factory, which always has a *minyan* every half hour, was even more packed than usual with people who wanted to sleep a little later than usual.)

According to Rav Hutner, I believe, you may have Chinese food on any day you wish. However, you may not have it specifically on December 25 because that recognizes a day on the secular calendar. According to most other authorities, you may choose to eat Chinese food specifically on December 25.

However, you must of course still make sure it is kosher.

Converts Immersing Utensils

I. Immersing Utensils

Jewish law requires immersing utensils used with food in a *mikveh*. This only applies if the utensils are made of certain materials (generally metal and glass) and if they were previously owned by gentiles. For example, when a Jew buys silverware that was made by a gentile, he has to immerse it in a *mikveh* before using it. This is common practice in observant Jewish homes, based on a biblical verse (Num. 31:23; *Shulchan Arukh*, *Yoreh De'ah* 120). A surprising omission from law codes raises the question of what to do when common practice eludes explanation.

The *Sefer Ha-Chinukh* (175) includes the law of immersing utensils with that of an adult immersing in a *mikveh* to become pure. In other words, immersing a utensil purifies it. Why is it impure? The utensil could be impure because of the non-kosher meat a gentile presumably cooked in it. However, even new, never-used utensils must be immersed in a *mikveh*. Perhaps this law assumes that a gentile, who is not commanded on matters of ritual purity, would not be careful to keep the utensils pure. Either way, we have to assume this is a general rule that applies even in exceptional cases, even if we know that the utensils have been kept pure.

II. Late Nineteenth-Century Discussions

The question arose in the late nineteenth century whether a convert must immerse his previously owned utensils after his conversion.[106] To my knowledge, the first halakhic authority to ask this was Rav Yosef Zundel Hutner of Eishishok, in his 1880 legal work *Chevel Yosef* (*Chadrei De'ah* 120:1).[107] A convert obviously must either *kasher* all his food utensils or buy new utensils. Once he completes his conversion, he must observe the kosher laws fully. However, the utensils he buys or kashers before his conversion are owned by a gentile. Once he converts, does he have to immerse all those utensils? Rav Hutner notes that this is not the practice but does not have a good explanation why that is the case. He suggests that perhaps a convert's case is dissimilar from the biblical case, but leaves it as an open question.

Rav Tzvi Hirsch Shapira, in his influential compendium of commentaries *Darkhei Teshuvah* (120:4; published in the 1890's), quotes Rav Hutner somewhat inaccurately (I'm not the first to notice this). He says that Rav Hutner held the view that a convert must immerse his utensils.

Rav Yitzchak Aharon Ettinger, in his 1893 *Responsa Mahari Ha-Levi* (no. 109), implies that a convert does not have to immerse his utensils. He says that he is not aware of any mention of it in the *Shulchan Arukh*. Its omission from the code of religious law implies that it is not an obligation.

III. Early Twentieth-Century Discussions

In a 1918 sermon, Rav Shmuel Borenstein (*Shem Mi-Shmuel*, *Mattos*, vol. 3 p. 430) quotes his famous father, Rav Avraham Borenstein, author of *Avnei Neizer*, as offering a surprising

---

106. The entire discussion here refers to utensils the convert owned before his conversion. Any new utensils he buys after his conversion follow standard rules of immersion.

107. Rav Moshe Sternbuch, in a responsum cited below, quotes Rav Yitzchak Bamberger, in his *Yad Ha-Levi*, as exempting a convert from immersing his utensils. Rav Bamberger died in 1878, so he would slightly precede Rav Hutner. However, I could not find such a responsum in either volume of *Yad Ha-Levi*.

explanation why a convert does not have to immerse his utensils. When a convert enters the Jewish people, he acquires the status or sanctity of a Jew. At that time, his utensils receive the same status. Effectively, the utensils convert with him. I have trouble understanding this approach. However, Rav Avraham Borenstein was a very important halakhic authority and his opinion carries significant weight.

In a 1919 responsum, Rav Shimon Greenfeld (*Responsa Maharshag* 2:48) similarly points out that authorities have not said that a convert must immerse his utensils. He suggests that the obligation only applies when the utensils change ownership. Since a convert continues his ownership, he is not obligated to immerse the utensils.

Of the above authorities, the two who cast the longest shadows are Rav Shapira and Rav Borenstein, the authors of *Darkhei Teshuvah* and *Avnei Neizer*, respectively. The former implies that a convert must immerse his utensils and the latter that a convert need not. We should keep in mind that, generally speaking, immersing utensils takes time and effort (maybe an afternoon of work) but does not cost money. Ruling strictly does not entail additional cost for the convert. This leaves more room to rule strictly, especially since most authorities consider this a biblical obligation. The attempts to explain a convert's exemption have not been particularly convincing. It is hard to maintain even a long-standing exemption from a biblical obligation if it cannot be explained.[108]

IV. More Recent Authorities

Rav Eliezer Waldenberg addresses this issue in two responsa dated 1963 (*Tzitz Eliezer*, vol. 8, 19:5, 20:2). Unconvinced by the

---

108. Two examples that come to mind are refraining from the daily *kohen*'s blessing except on holidays and failing to sleep in a *sukkah*. Many authorities have attempted to reinstate those practices, despite the long documentation for the exemptions.

arguments that a convert need not immerse his utensils, Rav Waldenberg takes a middle approach. He recommends immersing them without a blessing. Rav Moshe Sternbuch (*Teshuvos Ve-Hanhagos* 1:549) concludes similarly.

Rav Yosef Shalom Elyashiv (quoted in *Kovetz Beis Ha-Midrash*, *Tammuz* 5711, no. 27, cited in Rav Shlomo Aviner's commentary to *Kitzur Shulchan Arukh* 37:1) dismisses the arguments exempting a convert from the practice. He believes that, like any other Jews, a convert must immerse his utensils. I do not have access to the original source, but he seems to require immersing the utensils with a blessing. Rav Shmuel Wosner (*Shevet Ha-Levi*, vol. 4, 92:2; vol. 6, 245:2) explicitly rules that a convert must immerse his utensils with a blessing.

In a recently published responsum, Rav Osher Weiss (*Responsa Minchas Asher*, vol. 3 no. 66) rules that a convert does not need to immerse his utensils. Rav Weiss stresses how common conversions are. The fact that this question did not arise until the late nineteenth century argues strongly for an existing practice to exempt converts from immersing their utensils after conversion. This long-standing practice should remain in place. He attempts to explain this exemption in a way that seems to follow that of Rav Greenfeld, mentioned above.

I inquired a bit as to standard practice today for converts. The general response seems to vary between immersion with or without a blessing. The Manhattan Beth Din for conversion, under the guidance of Rav Hershel Schachter, follows the middle position of requiring immersion of utensils without a blessing.

Demographics, *Terumah,* and Ingathering of the Exiles

The status today of the *terumah* portion of produce allotted to *kohanim*, as well as other agricultural *mitzvos*, is a story of population growth as well as a perplexing Maimonidean statement. Most agricultural *mitzvos* today are of rabbinic nature. One wonders about the contemporary impact of the talmudic statement (*Sotah* 14a) that Moshe was desperate to enter the land of Israel so he could fulfill all the land-based *mitzvos*. If Moshe would enter today, he would be unable to fulfill many of them on a biblical level! Yet that will change, and may already have, although it depends to some degree on your eschatological vision.

I. When *Terumah*?

The Rambam (*Mishneh Torah, Hilkhos Terumos* 1:26) writes something that might seem innocuous at first but is actually startlingly wrong. He writes:

> *Terumah* today, even in the places acquired by those who returned from Babylonia, even during Ezra's time, is not biblical but rabbinic. For biblical *terumah* is only in Israel in a time when all Jews are there. As it says, "when you come," [when you] all come like you did in the original conquest and as they will come in the future in the third conquest. Not like the second conquest, in Ezra's time, in

which only some [Jews] came and therefore the Torah does not obligate them [in *terumah* on a biblical level]. And so it seems to me is also the law regarding *ma'aser*, that today you are only obligated in it rabbinically.

This is difficult for two reasons. First, he bases his statement on a verse, yet that verse does not exist. Nowhere regarding *terumah* does the Torah say anything about entering the land. Second, the Talmud (*Kesubos* 25a) explicitly states that the condition of entering the land does not apply to *terumah*, as opposed to *challah* to which the condition applies. This Rambam contradicts the Torah and the Gemara! It is so wrong that it must be right. A scholar of his caliber does not make such basic errors. The resolutions offered to explain this passage are varied and have practical contemporary impact.

II. Conflicting Texts

The Maharit (Responsa, vol. 1 no. 25) suggests that the Rambam quotes a verse regarding *challah* (Num. 15:18), although that verse says "*be-vo'akhem*" and not "*ki savo'u*," as the Rambam quotes. Rav Shaul Yisraeli (*Eretz Chemdah*, vol. 1 p. 80) quotes the *Tzelach* (*Berakhos* 26a) as explaining that the Rambam intentionally changed the language of the verse to teach that any phrasing of the word implies a requirement of all Jews to return. He also quotes the Netziv, who suggests it is a copyist's error.

Interestingly, the collection of textual variants in the back of the Frankel Rambam discusses the problem of the verse. Unlike the Netziv's suggestion above, it points out that the verse exists in all manuscripts and printed editions, even in the Rambam's responsa (*Pe'er Ha-Dor* 16). It also adds that many times the Rambam quotes verses incorrectly.

The Maharit argues that while the Gemara differentiates between *terumah* and *challah*, the Rambam follows the view of

R. Yoshiyah in the *Sifrei* that equates the two. This debate over whether to equate the *mitzvos* can also be found in *Menachos* (67a). The *Or Sameïach* (ad loc.) takes the same approach. According to them, the Rambam rules contrary to the Gemara because he sides with a conflicting text.

III. Dividing the Land

Rav Chaim Soloveitchik explained this Rambam in two different ways. His father (*Beis Ha-Levi*, vol. 3 no. 1 ch. 4) quotes the answer he offered in his youth. According to the Rambam, *challah* is only rabbinic today for an essential reason, while *terumah* is rabbinic for an ancillary reason. The Gemara differentiates between the two because it discussing on an essential level. On that level, *terumah* really should be a biblical obligation today. However, for a side reason it is not. *Terumah* requires dividing the land and allocating it to the different tribes, and that requires all of the people entering the land. Lacking the required population and the division of the land, *terumah* cannot be a biblical obligation.

In his posthumously published novellae on the Rambam (*Chiddushei R. Chaim Ha-Levi*, *Hilkhos Terumos* 1:10; *Hilkhos Shemittah* 12:16), Rav Chaim adopts a different approach. He suggests that the Rambam derives the rule about *terumah* from *shemittah* and quotes that verse (Lev. 25:10). Just like *shemittah* requires a majority of Jews to enter the land, so too *terumah* and *maʾaser*. A key difference between *challah* on the one hand and *terumah* and *shemittah* on the other is when Jews leave the land. According to Rav Chaim, *challah* only needs all Jews to enter the land together at the time of conquest. Afterward, it is irrelevant how many Jews remain in the land. But *terumah* and other *mitzvos* require most Jews to be in the land, both at the time of conquest and beyond. Any time less than a majority remain in the land, the mitzvah loses its biblical force.

IV. Conditional Obligation

The *Chazon Ish* (*Zera'im*, *Shevi'is* 3:6; 21:5) explains that the Rambam learned *terumah* from *challah*, but only partially. The Gemara denies a full comparison but can still allow for a partial comparison. *Challah* is a biblical obligation as long as all Jews enter the land together at a time of conquest. The entering of the land is what generates the sanctity in the land that obligates in the mitzvah.

However, we know that is not true regarding *terumah* because the mitzvah was not observed during the years that Israel was being conquered and divided. Therefore, the entering could not have generated the sanctity and the obligation. Rather, the people—with a king and prophet—generated that sanctity through their agreement. However, we learn from *challah* that we need a majority of Jews in the land for the mitzvah. Therefore, the *Chazon Ish* adds, even during the exile, if a majority of Jews dwell in the land, then there is a biblical obligation of *terumah*.

Rav Isser Zalman Meltzer (*Even Ha-Azel, Hilkhos Beis Ha-Bechirah* 6:16), a leading student of Rav Chaim Soloveitchik, quotes and disagrees with his esteemed mentor. He reaches a conclusion similar to that of the *Chazon Ish*.

V. Demographics

According to the *Chazon Ish* and Rav Meltzer, if the majority of Jews in the world move to Israel then the mitzvah of *terumah*, among others, would regain biblical status. This will have practical impact in a number of ways, including cases of doubt. Wikipedia claims that there are 14.4 million Jews in the world, of which 6.5 million live in Israel, slightly less than half.[109] However, the definition of a Jew is unclear. Between Russians and Ethiopians in Israel, many of whose halakhic status is questionable, and Reform patrilineal

---

109. Wikipedia entry for "Jews," retrieved September 2, 2017.

issues in America, the number of halakhic Jews is unknown. There may already be more than 50% of Jews in Israel.

According to Rav Chaim, the majority of Jews need to be part of the initial wave of immigration, the conquest. This raises an interesting theological question. The Rambam (above) mentions three conquests: the first was in the time of Yehoshua, and the second in the time of Ezra. The establishment of the State of Israel is the third in history. If it occurred without the majority of Jews coming at one time, how will *terumah* (etc.) ever become a biblical obligation again? Does the Rambam, as explained by Rav Chaim, require an expulsion from Israel and then another return en masse? There are *midrashim* describing a terrible battle at the end of days in which the Jews are forced to flee. Is that what Rav Chaim would have in mind if he were alive today?

Perhaps the issue is what to consider a single conquest/return. Clearly the return does not need to be on the same day; that many people cannot arrive all on one boat or airplane. Maybe a wave of immigration can last a few years, maybe a decade. Is it possible that the non-stop immigration over the past hundred or so years counts as a single wave?

In the end, our job is to learn Torah and observe *mitzvos*. When the time comes, we will understand exactly what is supposed to happen.

Rewashing After the Bathroom

I. Washing for Bread

The Sages decreed that we must ritually wash our hands before eating a meal, defined as bread. This washing is done by pouring water from a cup two (or three) times on each hand, reciting a blessing, and drying the hands. The Gemara (*Chullin* 106a) offers two reasons for this enactment: a preparation for eating *terumah* in the future and a mitzvah.

What is this cryptic mitzvah? Rashi (ad loc., s.v. mitzvah)[110] explains that originally people were washing on their own out of concern for *terumah* and then the Sages formalized an obligation. Tosafos (ad loc., s.v. mitzvah) see these as two separate reasons: *terumah* and cleanliness. According to both Rashi and Tosafos, this requirement is not just for a functional washing but also a redemptive washing, intending to prepare us for a time when the Temple in Jerusalem is rebuilt and we will have to remain ritually pure to eat sacred food.

II. Rewashing

However, even someone who washes his hands properly can effectively undo the washing by making his hands dirty or impure. For example, someone who touches his feet has made his hands dirty and must rewash. What happens if, during a meal for which

---

110. As explained by *Pri Megadim, Orach Chaim, Mishbetzos Zahav*, introduction to *Hilkhos Netilas Yadayim*.

you washed your hands ritually, you have to use the bathroom? You certainly have to wash ritually afterward, even if you only want to drink or eat food other than bread (Rema, *Orach Chaim* 170:1). But do you recite a blessing on this washing?

The *Pri Megadim* (ibid.) connects this to a disagreement between Rashi and Rambam. According to Rashi (*Shabbos* 14a s.v. *askaniyos*), the *terumah* concern is that your hands move around a lot and might touch something improper, which is disrespectful to *terumah*. However, according to Rambam (Mishnah, *Taharos* 7:8, *Zavim* 5:12), the concern is more technical—that you might render your hands impure. The former reason is more general, while the latter must follow the technical rules of purity. Since using the bathroom does not automatically render a person's hands impure, according to Rambam you would not recite a blessing on washing your hands after using the bathroom during a meal. According to Rashi, you would.

III. The Blessing on Rewashing

However, the *Mishnah Berurah* (164, *Bi'ur Halakhah* s.v. *lachazor*) points out that this dichotomy is not very smooth. Authorities such as Rabbenu Chananel seem to adopt both criteria, saying in one place that the washing is due to impurity (*Shabbos* 14a), but in another place that there is a concern your hands became dirty (*Pesachim* 115b). The *Mishnah Berurah* explains that Rashi's concern for dirt includes impurity, which allows for the seeming contradiction. Therefore, if you go to the bathroom, you have to wash again and recite the blessing.

The Maharshal (*Yam Shel Shlomo, Chullin* 7:10), who preceded both the *Pri Megadim* and *Mishnah Berurah*, rules that you never recite a blessing on washing in the middle of a meal. The Sages never instituted such a blessing. Therefore, if you use the bathroom during a meal, you must wash with a cup and pour multiple times on each hand,[111] but you may not recite a blessing over the washing.

IV. The Great Compromise

Even though the *Shulchan Arukh* (*Orach Chaim* 164:4) rules that you should recite the blessing, many later codes follow the Maharshal's leniency. These include *Shulchan Arukh Ha-Rav* (164:2), *Kitzur Shulchan Arukh* (40:16), *Ben Ish Chai* (*Kedoshim* 22) and *Kaf Ha-Chaim* (164:16). However, the *Chayei Adam* (40:14) rules that you should recite the blessing, and the *Mishnah Berurah* (ibid.), after much vacillating, concludes that you should recite the blessing.

More recently, Rav Simcha Rabinowitz, in *Piskei Teshuvos* (164:5), follows the codes mentioned above who rule not to recite the blessing, which he says is the common practice (ibid., n. 10). Rav Eliezer Melamed (*Peninei Halakhah, Berakhos* 2:16) offers a compromise to resolve the dilemma. Noting that the common practice is to recite the blessing and that most authorities rule to recite it, but that there still exists great debate, he suggests omitting the blessing after urinating or if you do not plan to eat at least an egg's worth of bread. However, if you will eat a significant amount of bread and you did more than just urinate, you should wash with a blessing.[112]

I find the different arguments from common practice quite interesting. Both Rav Melamed and Rav Rabinowitz live in Israel today. However, Rav Rabinowitz is Charedi and Rav

---

111. Some people always wash that way after using the bathroom, but many follow the *Magen Avraham* (7:1) who rules that this is unnecessary and any simple washing suffices.
112. Rav Chaim Kanievsky, *Shoneh Halakhos* 164:2, in his summary of the *Mishnah Berurah*, also says that after urinating you should wash without a blessing. He also quotes his uncle, the *Chazon Ish*, as saying that if you recite the blessing, you didn't do anything wrong, and if you omit the blessing, no one should object.

Melamed Religious Zionist (Chardal). Presumably, their different evaluations of common practice result from their different social circles. Perhaps the ruling should be different, depending on your social circle.

PART 9: RECREATION & HOBBY

Chess in Jewish Law

The cerebral game of chess has long captured rabbinic minds. References to the game can be found even in Rashi's writings (*Kesubos* 61b s.v. *de-mitalela*). However, its status within Jewish law is complex and debated. Four areas in particular have sparked discussion among halakhic authorities—Shabbos, testimony, vows, and idolatry.

I. Shabbos

You would be wrong to take for granted the permissibility of playing chess on Shabbos. The issues raised include: making sounds, conducting business, and non-Shabbos behavior.

Apparently, on old chess boards, metal pieces that knocked into each other made musical sounds which might be considered forbidden on Shabbos. However, *Shiltei Ha-Gibborim* (Rif, *Eruvin* 35b nos. 2-3) permits this because the players do not intend to make music with these sounds. The Rema (*Shulchan Arukh, Orach Chaim* 338:5) follows the *Shiltei Ha-Gibborim*. Note that the *Magen Avraham* (ad loc., no. 8) confirms that the Rema is discussing chess (but requires using a special Shabbos set).

The *Magen Avraham* quotes from a Rav A. Sasson who argues that playing chess is similar to conducting business. He seems to mean that because chess was often played for money, even when you omit the prize, the game is still forbidden because of its usual practice. However, the Rema rules that chess is only forbidden when you play for money.

333

Many argue that chess is simply not appropriate for Shabbos. For example, the *Shemiras Shabbos Ke-Hilkhasah* (16:34) dismisses all arguments to forbid chess. However, earlier in the chapter (16:1), he says that this only applies to children. Adults should spend the day in spiritual—religious—pleasure. Similarly, Rav Moshe Feinstein (*Iggeros Moshe, Yoreh De'ah* 3:15:2) rules that chess is not technically forbidden but should be avoided because of *ve-dabbeir davar* (Isa. 58:13), by which I think he means that the game is not in the spirit of Shabbos.[113]

Interestingly, the Chida (*Birkei Yosef, Orach Chaim* 338:1) suggests that the great rabbis who have played chess, even during the week, must have done so in order to recover from depression. It was their strategy to heal and return to their Torah study. Therefore, their precedents cannot support a general permissive ruling.

II. Vows

J.D. Eisenstein (*Otzar Dinim U-Minhagim*, s.v. *shach*) quotes literature surrounding a case of a man who vowed to stop playing chess but then regretted his vow. He asked for permission to annul his vow. The rabbi of Ancona replied that the questioner certainly took his vow to prevent wasting time. However, since chess is a game of skill and not chance, and it refreshes the spirit, he may annul his vow.

III. Testimony

Eisenstein also quotes a discussion about professional chess players. Professional gamblers are barred from testifying in a Jewish court (*Shulchan Arukh, Choshen Mishpat* 34:16). Do chess players constitute gamblers? He quotes Rav Yoel ben Nosson

---

113. See also Rav Eliezer Melamed, *Peninei Halakhah*, Shabbos 22:13, in the *harchavos*, ibid., par. 2.

Finkerly of Alexandria who says that since chess is a game of skill and wisdom, it is not considered gambling. Chess players are generally highly intelligent and sophisticated. Therefore, a professional chess player is an acceptable witness.

IV. Idolatry

A chess set often serves as both decoration and entertainment. However, the game's most important piece poses a dilemma to Jewish players. The king is generally adorned with a cross. A cross represents Christianity, reminding us of the religion's foundational claim and also the centuries of Christian persecution Jews have suffered. The latter is an emotional claim but the former is legal. Jewish law prohibits the ownership of a foreign religious object. Must a Jew, therefore, break the cross on his king?

While many say that Christianity is an acceptable religion for gentiles, all agree that it is forbidden for Jews. If crosses represent a foreign religion to which Jews may not submit, may a Jew ever own one? This question arose for Jewish merchants who sometimes traded in religious jewelery. May they sell decorative crosses? Rema (*Shulchan Arukh, Yoreh De'ah* 141:3) records a leniency. While you may not obtain even indirect benefit from an item used for a foreign religion, you may sell an item that serves only a decorative purpose. Since no one has worshiped with the object, it is not forbidden.

However, the *Chokhmas Adam* (85:2) points out that this leniency only allows you to derive benefit from the item. You still may not own it, because people might think that it is your religious object. The only exception is an item that is used disrespectfully, in a way that no one would treat a religious object. Similarly, *Nachal Eshkol* (*Hilkhos Avodah Zarah* n. 50, quoted in *She'arim Metzuyanim Ba-Halakhah* 167:2 *kuntres acharon*) permits owning an oven with a cross on it. Since no one uses it for religious purposes, it is considered "disrespectful" and allowed.

Based on this, we might suggest that since a chess piece is also never used for religious purposes, it is considered a "disrespectful" item that a Jew may own. No one will think that it is your religious object because it simply is not one. It is a game piece.

Rav Asher Bush (*Sho'el Bi-Shlomo*, no. 60) argues that since everyone knows that the chess piece is not connected to Christianity, there is no issue whatsoever and you may even display it in a place of honor in your home. He quotes Rav Moshe Feinstein's ruling (*Iggeros Moshe, Yoreh De'ah* 1:69) that you may sell stamps with a cross for two reasons: (1) they aren't made for religious purposes, and (2) people do not consider the stamps (religiously) important. Rav Bush argues that the same logic applies to chess sets, particularly when the king is only one of many pieces.

Even if this is correct, the Jewish aversion to crosses is a long-standing tradition. Rav Chaim Soloveitchik would even rearrange silverware that happened to be placed like a cross (*Nefesh Ha-Rav*, p. 230). There is certainly room for Jews to refuse to decorate their houses with a chess piece containing a cross and instead break it to remove reminders of a foreign religion and a very violent history.

Video Game Idolatry

I. Video Game *Avodah Zarah*

A recently released, ground-breaking video game raises important questions for Jews, who pride themselves on their devotion to monotheism. *The Legend of Zelda: Breath of the Wild* (2017) is an open-world game, which means that the characters can roam free throughout a vast, imaginary world while attempting to achieve their missions. Throughout the world are shrines, which a player can approach and request game-related benefits. In a review video, you can see a shrine asking the character what he wants and granting him an extra life. Effectively, the character is asking an idol for assistance. Is a Jew permitted to play this game and ask the idol to grant his wish, or does playing in this way violate the prohibition against idolatry? I discussed this with a few rabbis and offer here my tentative thoughts.

There appear to be four potential issues here. The first is appropriate use of time. Is playing a video game of this nature, which has no educational value whatsoever, an appropriate use of time? If done in moderation, perhaps it can serve as recreation that refreshes a person to learn Torah. From what I understand, these types of games draw the player in for large amounts of time, almost addictively. That is a very serious concern but unrelated to the idolatry.

II. Virtual Worship

The second issue is whether this constitutes idolatry. There are two ways to violate the prohibition against idolatry. The Torah forbids worshipping any idol in the way it is normally worshipped. For example, the idol Markulis was worshipped by throwing rocks at it (one interpretation is that it was a statue of Mercury situated at crossroads and people would leave stones at the statue as they passed by on their travels; see *Arukh Ha-Shalem*, s.v. *Markulis*, vol. 5 p. 262). Additionally, the Torah forbids performing the four main practices in the Temple for any idol. These four are bowing, sacrificing, offering incense, and bringing a libation (*Mishneh Torah, Hilkhos Avodah Zarah* 3:2-3). In this case, the video game character is not bowing nor offering any specific prayer. However, the interaction with the idol—the request and granting of the benefit—seem to be the normal way of worshipping the idol. Whatever task is performed before being granted the benefit is the worship of the idol. Therefore, the character is violating the prohibition against idolatry.

But we cannot get past the point that the fictional character is worshipping idolatry, not the player. The player is playing a game. If there is a religion in which the way the religion is observed is by playing a video game, then a player might violate this prohibition. Until that time, he is just playing a game and not violating any prohibition. I have not heard anyone suggest to the contrary.

III. Mythology and Fantasy

A further commandment prohibits looking at and thinking about idols. "Do not turn to the idols" (Lev. 19:4) is seen as a wide-ranging rule against studying idolatrous culture and literature (*Mishneh Torah, Hilkhos Avodah Zarah* 2:1-2). This rule against learning about idolatry should forbid virtually worshipping the idol, as well. In playing the game, you are watching the idolatrous service as it happens, even though you are not technically participating in it.

Authorities are divided whether this prohibition applies to all idolatries or only those that are no longer worshipped. In response to a question whether a teacher may cover Greek mythology in class, Rav Moshe Feinstein (*Iggeros Moshe, Yoreh De'ah* 2:53) rejects the suggestion that because no one currently worships the ancient religion, the prohibition no longer applies to it. Instead, he offers permission from another angle, that the education should be from the perspective of debunking the false stories. Otherwise, according to Rav Moshe, studying or watching ancient idolatrous religions remains forbidden.

I recall hearing in the name of Rav Joseph B. Soloveitchik that he permitted studying Greek mythology for the reason Rav Moshe rejected, although I never confirmed this. Even if he did not, we can find others who suggest it. Rav Yair Chaim Bacharach (*Chavos Yair*, no. 1 secs. 11-12 s.v. *ve-adayin tzl"a*) suggests that the prohibition to say the name of an idol only applies to an idol that is currently worshipped. We may freely say the names of ancient idols. *Darkhei Teshuvah* (147:4) quotes a responsum of the *Beis Yitzchak* (1:YD:152) that agrees in principle with the *Chavos Yair* but is concerned that maybe someone in the world still worships the Greek pantheon. Because of this possibility, he refuses to consider Greek mythology an abandoned religion.

Some contemporary rabbis in Israel seem to follow the *Chavos Yair*'s approach. Rav Shlomo Aviner (*She'eilas Shlomo* 4:167; *Piskei Shlomo*, vol. 2 p. 45) begrudgingly permits the study of Greek mythology. He cautions that it is full of nonsense and is a waste of time. However, he allows for leniency if necessary because the idolatry has been long abandoned. Similarly, Rav Yehuda Henkin (*Bnei Banim* 3:35:2) writes that if the religion is abandoned, the gods are no longer considered idols.

In this game, the idolatry is completely fictional. Not only does no one currently worship it, no one ever did worship it. I believe that even Rav Moshe would not apply the prohibition to this religion because it is not, and has never been, a religion. It is simply fantasy.

IV. Beyond Prohibition

A further non-halakhic consideration, suggested to me by another rabbi, is desensitization. Just like with violence in the media, every time we engage with idolatry, even fictional, we become more accustomed to the concept. Interacting with an idol becomes understandable, on some level even normal. Perhaps this, alone, should give us pause before playing the game.

While these are tentative thoughts, I currently don't see any reason to forbid playing this game to relax for short periods of time. If it becomes addictive and takes large amounts of time (which is quite common), you should probably rethink your gaming habits. You also might want to consider whether you want to get involved with any kind of idolatry, even fantasy idolatry, because of its desensitizing nature. I would not recommend it.

Is Stand-Up Comedy Kosher?

The question of stand-up comedy's propriety comes from the same source as its benefits. Humor, we are told, is the best medicine. It relieves stress, spreads joy, and serves as a break from our busy lives. At its best, it can also serve as social commentary and political criticism, sometimes sparking positive change. In theory, comedy can inspire *teshuvah*, repentance, by highlighting religious inconsistency.

Crude comedy, which encompasses most of it, is surely improper. The forbidden language and sexual innuendo are the most obvious points of criticism. However, mockery and satire can be equally improper—denigrating people, institutions, and beliefs. When everything is subject to mockery, nothing is sacred, not even that which is literally sacred. Faith falls to the side when mockery runs rampant. *Tanakh* repeatedly attests to this. But what about comedy that lacks all of these elements? What about stand-up comedy with completely clean language that pokes fun without mocking or denigrating?

In an article in the Winter 2014 issue of *Jewish Action*, Rav Daniel Z. Feldman notes the existence of jokes within the Talmud and the statement that Rabbah would begin his lectures with a joke (*Shabbos* 30b). He goes further, quoting Rav Joseph B. Soloveitchik as saying that humor reflects an appreciation of what is important in life and what is not. We must maintain perspective, laughing at the trivial and worrying about the serious.

On the other hand, too much of a good thing is bad. Life is serious. If we spend all our time in levity, if we immerse ourselves in leisure rather than dip our toes in it, we have deviated from the lifestyle required by the Torah. The Sages (*Avos* 6:5) teach that one of the paths to acquiring Torah is "a little joking." The Gemara (*Sotah* 25b) includes "a group of mockers" among those who do not receive the Divine Presence. On the citation of this passage in the *Kitzur Shulchan Arukh* (30:6), Rav Shlomo Aviner (commentary, ad loc., vol. 1 p. 324) states that a little comedy is acceptable but not too much. Earlier (29:2, p. 308), he wrote his brief guideline for comedy: "a little with kosher content." Here, he adds that a few (approximately 5 to 15) minutes of stand-up is fine. However, when people gather together for longer periods of stand-up comedy, they are engaging as a group in an extended waste of time. That is forbidden (see also 31:3, p. 328).

Some might argue that Rav Aviner's limit is arbitrary. Who defines how much is too much? I suspect he would agree. The key is the need for balance, the focus on a life devoted to God and man, enhanced with some lighthearted joy. Imbalance is the enemy of mental and religious health. Too much stand-up, no matter how pure, is still unkosher.

Is Powerball Kosher?

The recurrent frenzy over the massive Powerball prizes raises a serious question about the halakhic and moral viability of lotteries. There is more to discuss than just the greed. We must remember that until relatively recently, lotteries were illegal in most states and were instead run by organized crime as the "numbers racket." Lotteries are a form of gambling that particularly impact poor communities, the people who can least afford it. Powerball—and lottery in general—raises important issues that may bring into question common features of our community. Since, as we shall see shortly, Rav Ovadiah Yosef forbids buying lottery tickets, how can our schools and shuls hold raffles and Chinese auctions? What message are we sending when we elevate gambling into an acceptable pastime, when *yeshivos* even reportedly buy tickets for their faculty?

I. Gambling in the Talmud

The primary source in the Mishnah (*Sanhedrin* 24b) is a statement that dice players are invalid witnesses, leading to a debate in the Gemara over why this is the case. Rav Sheishes says that the problem is *asmakhta*, a failure to truly commit to paying a bet because of a reliance on winning. Rami bar Chama disagrees and says that the problem with a professional gambler is the lack of a job and a sense of the value of money.

According to Rav Sheishes, any time someone places a bet with an expectation of winning (even if unrealistic), he does not really expect to pay the bet. Therefore, if he loses the bet, anyone who takes his money is guilty of stealing. According to Rami bar Chama, this either is not theft at all or not sufficiently obvious theft to invalidate someone as a witness. Rami Bar Chama only invalidates as professional gamblers a witnesses.

Another talmudic passage (*Shabbos* 149b) gives a person special permission to divide food at a Shabbos meal to his children with a lottery (obviously without any money). You may not even do this during the week to those outside the family because it constitutes gambling. Tosafos (ad loc., s.v. *mai*) say that we do not follow this Gemara, but the codes quote it. Others suggest that the concern is with a potluck meal, in which everyone contributes. If they contribute expecting to win a big piece but receive a small piece, there may be a problem of *asmakhta*.

II. Lotteries and Winnings

Regarding dice playing and gambling in general, medieval authorities disagree whether we follow Rav Sheishes or Rami bar Chama. The *Shulchan Arukh* (*Choshen Mishpat* 370:3) follows the Rambam, who rules like Rav Sheishes, effectively forbidding gambling. The Rema (*Choshen Mishpat* 207:13, 370:3) follows Tosafos, who rule like Rami bar Chama, thereby permitting occasional gambling. It would seem, then, that Ashkenazim who follow the Rema may buy lottery tickets while Sephardim, who follow the *Shulchan Arukh*, may not. That is how Rav Ovadiah Yosef (*Yabi'a Omer*, vol. 7 *Choshen Mishpat* 6) rules, although he adds that Ashkenazim should also refrain. Many others disagree regarding lotteries.

Rav Gedaliah Schwartz (*Sha'arei Gedulah*, p. 312) approvingly quotes a responsum by Rav Ovadiah Hadaya (*Yaskil Avdi*, vol. 8

Yoreh De'ah 5:3) in which this Sephardic authority distinguishes between people betting against each other and a lottery. In a classic case of gambling, one person wins and the other loses. It is *asmakhta* if the person who pays had assumed that he will win. In a lottery, the payout will always happen. Therefore, whoever runs the lottery and pays the winnings does not have *asmakhta* and even a Sephardi can buy a ticket. Rav Hadaya explains that this is why Jews have historically held lotteries to raise funds for charities.

Rav Ovadiah Yosef (ibid., par. 5) quotes this responsum and counters that, in a lottery, the winnings come from the proceeds of tickets sold. If any purchaser of a ticket assumed he would win, then the money he contributed to the pot is stolen because of the purchaser's *asmakhta*. He adds that Rav Yosef Chaim of Baghdad (*Responsa Rav Pe'alim*, vol. 2 *Yoreh De'ah* no. 30) explains that with historical lotteries, the winning was an object (like in a Chinese auction) and not a portion of the proceeds from the tickets sold.

Rav Ya'akov Ariel (*Be-Ohalah Shel Torah*, vol. 1 no. 111) offers a similar approach as Rav Hadaya. Without quoting any of the recent literature, Rav Ariel suggests Rav Yosef's objection and counters that lottery is different because people pay in advance. When you make a bet and do not put money down in advance, you may be relying on your winning the bet. But if you pay in advance, you clearly recognize the possibility of losing. This seems to be the view of Rabbenu Tam, followed by the Rema (*Choshen Mishpat* 207:13). I'm not sure that it would help Sephardim.

III. Lotteries as Investments

Rav Moshe Sternbuch (*Teshuvos Ve-Hanhagos*, vol. 4 no. 311) offers a different explanation of the mechanics of a lottery. He sees buying a lottery ticket as he purchase of a good, not a wager. Before the drawing, you can even sell the ticket for its original purchase price. Therefore, you are effectively investing in a fund that will use some of the proceeds to cover expenses and pay the remainder as a dividend to specific, randomly chosen investors. Rav Menashe Klein (*Mishneh Halakhos*, vol. 15 no. 176) follows a similar approach, as does Rav Aharon Lichtenstein (*Daf Kesher* 1:83-85, cited in Rav Chaim Jachter, *Gray Matter*, vol. 1, pp. 129-130). This approach allows Sephardim to purchase lottery tickets as well.

Rav Sternbuch (ibid.) also suggests that the odds of winning a lottery are so low that no purchaser assumes he will win. Therefore, there is no *asmakhta*. Additionally, there is no competition between two (or multiple) players, like in a card or dice game. Rather, this is a completely random process. This seems to fit in with the view of Rashi (*Sanhedrin* 24b s.v. *kol*) that there is no *asmakhta* when the wager is on something random that involves no skill.

Rav Joseph B. Soloveitchik (cited by Rav Jachter, ibid., p. 129) points out that these concerns do not apply to charity fundraising. Because giving money to *tzedakah* is a mitzvah, there is an assumption that people give willingly. Therefore, *asmakhta* does not apply to charitable pledges and donations (*Shulchan Arukh*, *Yoreh De'ah* 258:10). This means that Sephardim may participate in raffles and Chinese auctions for shuls and schools.

IV. Moral Concerns

However, some authorities have gone beyond the technicalities of theft when it comes to lotteries and gambling. The Rivash (Responsa, no. 432) decries gambling as "disgusting, abominable, and repulsive." Rav Ovadiah Yosef (ibid.) points out that many poor people spend money they cannot afford to lose on lottery tickets. They think about the highly improbable dream of winning rather than the reality of supporting their families. Lotteries prey on the poor, deepening their poverty and often leading to addiction.

For many people, gambling is a serious addiction. Lotteries affect those with addictions and deepen the financial troubles of those already suffering. When millions of people lose a lottery, as regularly happens with Powerball, we can focus our attention on the dreams of many and the newfound fortune of the rare winners. Or we can use this as a teaching moment about the millions of people who threw away money at a statistically negligible dream, about the negative social effects of government-sponsored gambling, and the addictions facing many within our own communities.

I do not think that the Rivash would consider Powerball kosher.

Superheroes in Jewish Thought and Law

Superheroes represent the dreams of the oppressed. Those who are weak and insecure imagine what they would do if they were actually more powerful. Like the neglected orphan Harry Potter who discovers he is a powerful wizard, the nerdy Peter Parker who gains super powers expresses the deepest dreams of the bullied. The lesson of superheroes is to use those powers for good, selflessly and humbly. This message is crucial because awkward teenagers inevitably grow up and often shed their weaknesses. They become successful and sometimes wealthy. Superhero stories teach them to user those newfound powers for good, to help the needy and bring solace to the weak.

I. Super Powers?

Do super powers exist in Jewish thought? The Torah specifically prohibits using supernatural powers, such as those of witches (Ex. 22:17), mediums (Deut. 18:11), and necromancers (ibid., 12). The Egyptian magicians reportedly duplicated some divine miracles (Gen. 41; Ex. 7-9). Rambam (*Mishneh Torah, Hilkhos Avodah Zarah* 11:16) derides at length all these supernatural forces as nonsense. The ancient equivalents of today's illusionists and mentalists fooled people with these so-called powers into worshiping idols. The Torah forbids consulting these frauds.

However, Ramban (*Sefer Ha-Mitzvos*, addenda to positive commandments, no. 8) takes a less severe stand. He does not deride these witches and sorcerers as fakes. Rather, he merely states that the Jewish path consists of placing complete faith in God. Accessing these supernatural forces is a forbidden distraction from God, who ultimately retains the power to override any other force.

Rashba (Responsa 1:413) goes even further. He places supernatural forces on par with the laws of nature. To the Rashba, what we understand we call science and what we do not we call supernatural. But really these forces are part of the way God created this world to function. However, we are forbidden to access those forces used in idolatry. (See also *Derashos Ha-Ran*, no. 12, p. 219 in the Feldman edition.)

According to Rambam, superpowers do not exist. They are fantasy and illusions. According to Ramban and Rashba, they might. Rav Yaakov Kamenetsky (*Emes Le-Ya'akov Al Ha-Torah*, Ex. 7:22) takes a middle position. He asks why we do not see real magicians today like they had in Egypt. Harry Houdini was certainly impressive, but he was an athlete and illusionist, not a conjurer of supernatural forces.

Rav Kamenetsky explains that God ensures balance in the world. If only God's messengers perform miracles, then people will be forced to believe in God and follow His prophets. To allow for free choice, God enables evil people to have corresponding power. In biblical times, when prophets abounded, so did false prophets and magicians. In later talmudic times, when the sages had less impressive powers, the magicians had correspondingly weaker abilities. Today, neither good nor bad superpowers exist. We live in a world of weakness and confusion. But if superheroes ever arise, supervillains will have to join the fight to allow for free will.

II. Super Obligations

If you have super powers, are you obligated to use them to save others? Can you go on vacation or retire? In the animated movie

The Incredibles, Congress passed a law placing liability for collateral property damages on superheroes. With skyrocketing insurance premiums, superheroes were forced to retire. Are they allowed to do this?

The Torah (Lev. 19:16) forbids bystanding, watching someone die without helping. "Do not stand by idly on your fellow's blood" requires us to attempt to save someone in mortal danger. The *Shulchan Arukh* (*Choshen Mishpat* 426:1) states:

> One who sees his friend drowning in a sea or bandits approaching him or a dangerous animal approaching him, and one can save him by himself or by hiring others to save, and did not save... and similar circumstances, [such a person] violates "Do not stand idly by your fellow's blood."

Note that we are even required to spend our money to hire someone to save a person in danger. Money concerns should not stand in our way of saving someone's life. But another consideration is notably missing. Neither *Shulchan Arukh,* the Rosh, nor *Tur* say that we are obligated to endanger ourselves in order to rescue someone else. This is particularly interesting because the author of the *Shulchan Arukh*, in his earlier work *Beis Yosef* (ad loc.), quotes the *Hagahos Maimoniyos* who states that we must endure danger to save someone else.

The *Hagahos Maimoniyos* quotes the Talmud Yerushalmi (*Terumos* 8:4) as his source for this obligation. The Yerushalmi tells of a time in which Rabbi Immi was imprisoned and presumably in mortal danger. Reish Lakish said that he would charge the prison and either kill or be killed in his rescue attempt. (Note that Reish Lakish was a famous bandit before he underwent a religious transformation, so he was well trained for this attempt.)

However, since the *Shulchan Arukh* and others do not follow this Yerushalmi, they must have had a reason. Generally speaking, we follow the conclusions of the Talmud Yerushalmi unless the Talmud Bavli disagrees. Because the Talmud Bavli was compiled approximately 150 years after the Talmud Yerushalmi, we assume its editors were aware of the Yerushalmi and only disagreed intentionally and conclusively. Therefore, commentators searched far and wide for passages in the Talmud Bavli that could be read as disagreeing with the above Yerushalmi.

One of the passages quoted as indicating disagreement is about Rabbi Tarfon's refusal to hide fugitives from the law (*Niddah* 61a). Accused murderers came to him, asking for sanctuary. He declined, saying that if they were guilty then he would also become guilty. Tosafos (ad loc., s.v. *itmarinchu*) quote the *She'iltos* who explain Rabbi Tarfon's refusal as a protective measure. He would not risk his life to save their lives. Some deduce from here that you are not obligated to risk your own life to save others.

But to what extent? Any excursion into public entails some degree of risk. Driving a car is risky. Are you exempt from saving someone's life because driving on the highway constitutes risking your life? On the other hand, overly risky behavior is suicidal. Firemen are trained not to run into a building about to collapse to save someone's life because of the risk. What is the limit?

A recent halakhic guidebook for Hatzolah emergency volunteers, *Hatzalah Ke-Halakhah* by Rav Adi Cohen, surveys the opinions on this subject. For the author and readers of this book, this is a very relevant question whose answer has real implications for them and their families. When do Hatzolah volunteers refuse to enter a dangerous situation and when do they charge forward? Based on a responsum of the Radbaz (vol. 5, no. 218 [1,582]), contemporary authorities utilize a 50% threshold (e.g., *Shevet Ha-Levi* 8:87; *Tzitz Eliezer* 13:100:4). If the chance of survival is greater than 50%, then you are biblically obligated to try to save someone's life despite the risk. That seems like a low threshold to me. On a personal level, I prefer a greater chance of survival than just 50%.

III. Super Murder

As a thought experiment, I was wondering what Jewish law would say about specific super powers. For example, if a Jedi or Sith kills someone with a Force choke, is he liable for execution? On the one hand, he directly caused a death and should be punished. On the other, I assume that any hand motions of a Jedi are unnecessary and that really Darth Vader can perform a force choke with his hands tied behind his back. If so, he technically committed no action. Can someone be executed for merely thinking about murder?

There is precedent for this question in halakhic literature. Authorities have discussed whether someone who kills by invoking God's name is liable for murder. Tradition teaches that when Moshe saved an Israelite slave's life by murdering the Egyptian taskmaster, he did so by invoking God's name. If someone did that in a different situation that did not involve saving someone, would the murderer be held liable? The author of *Responsa Halakhos Ketanos* (vol. 2, no. 98) argues that he is liable.

The Chida (*Devash Le-Fi, mem*, no. 5) distinguishes between types of murders. The Gemara (*Shabbos* 33b) tells the story of Rabbi Shimon Bar Yochai's (Rashbi) exit from the cave in which he hid for many years. After all that time of constant Torah study, he was shocked to see a Jew work. In his disappointment, Rashbi looked at the man with a devastating stare, causing him to die. Not everyone reads that story literally, but the Chida does. He suggests that killing someone by looking at him—without saying anything—is different than invoking God's name for murder. Someone who does the former is exempt from human punishment, while someone who does the latter is liable.

Rav Chaim Palaggi (*Responsa Lev Chaim*, vol. 2 *Orach Chaim* no. 188) argues that no one who kills in a supernatural way is liable for punishment. In such cases, God kills, not the person. Murder is the cessation of a life within natural means. A miraculous murder is out of human hands.

If a Force choke is comparable to killing silently, then perhaps the *Halakhos Ketanos* would hold a Jedi liable for such a supernatural murder. The Chida would seem to exempt him, as would Rav Chaim Palaggi. They would let Darth Vader get away with murder, but that is not surprising because Jewish law has a very high bar for execution. Presumably, he would get punished by divine hands instead, in this world or the next.

IV. Super Stretch

Mr. Fantastic is remarkably elastic. What would happen if he stretched his hand outside of his domain on Shabbos while carrying something? If, in his Brooklyn home, Mr. Fantastic picks up an apple, stretches his hand across Manhattan and over the Hudson River into New Jersey, and places the apple down in Teaneck, does he violate the Shabbos rule against carrying across domains?

This question is directly answered in the first Mishnah of *Shabbos* (2a) but if we add one twist, the issue gets more complicated. The Mishnah describes transferring objects from one domain to another with an example from everyday life: A poor man comes to your door and you want to give him money. You are in your house, one domain. He is outside the house, another domain (assuming there is no *eruv* to combine the domains). There is no way in which you can permissibly transfer an object into the poor man's hands—whether him putting his hand into your house and you placing the object in his hand or his taking it, or you sticking your hand out the doorway, etc. This would effectively forbid Mr. Fantastic from moving anything from Brooklyn to New Jersey.

But what if Mr. Fantastic doesn't put anything down? Maybe he just wants to show his new toy to a friend in Teaneck and then pull it back. What if, while standing in Brooklyn, Mr. Fantastic holds an object in his hand, stretches the hand to New Jersey, and then returns the hand and places the object back down in Brooklyn.

The Gemara (*Shabbos* 3b) addresses a similar case. If your hand is full of fruits and you remove it from the domain, can you bring your hand back with the fruits or must you stand like that—body in one domain and hand outside it—until Shabbos is over? The Gemara quotes a disagreement about it but then tries to delineate exactly which case is debated. One suggestion is that the debate is only about movement within ten *tefachim* (roughly 35 inches) of the ground. Above that, which includes normal arm height, there are no domains.

Tosafos (ad loc., s.v. *kan*) ask how there can even be discussion, albeit agreement, of someone who sticks his hand outside the domain while holding fruit above ten *tefachim* and wants to return the hand. This is perfectly acceptable behavior. You are allowed to stand at the side of the *eruv* and carry things in and out all Shabbos long if you keep everything above ten *tefachim*! Tosafos offers an explanation of the Gemara that need not concern us now. According to Tosafos, Mr. Fantastic may carry fruit and toys across state lines as much as he wants, as long as he keeps his hand above ten *tefachim* from the ground.

However, the Rashba disagrees with Tosafos and argues that you may not intentionally carry things outside the domain, even without putting it down and above ten *tefachim* from the ground. Among recent codes, the *Arukh Ha-Shulchan* (*Orach Chaim* 348:1) rules like Tosafos, and the *Mishnah Berurah* (*Bi'ur Halakhah* 348 s.v. *be-sokh*) follows the Rashba. Therefore, Mr. Fantastic has to ask his rabbi whether he should follow the *Arukh Ha-Shulchan* or the *Mishnah Berurah*.

V. Shape-Changing

Some superheroes have the ability to alter their appearance, change their actual physical shape. Can someone with such power change his shape on Shabbos?

One concern is coloring. You are not allowed to change something's color on Shabbos, including that of a person. Putting on lipstick, generally speaking, is a violation of this prohibition. Similarly, changing the color of your hair, eyes, or skin by shape-shifting is also considered coloring on Shabbos.

If you maintain your body color, you still face another concern with shape-changing—the Play-Doh question. Halakhic authorities forbid using Play-Doh on Shabbos for multiple reasons. One concern is smoothing (*memareiʾach*) the dough, which is forbidden. Others cite the prohibition against writing. The *Chayei Adam* (92:3) rules that you may not bake *challah* into specific shapes on Yom Tov. Even though you may bake, if you give the dough a specific shape—such as a fish—you violate the prohibition against writing on Yom Tov.

Initially, I found this application puzzling. How is baking a shape considered writing? After some thought, I look at it this way. Writing is generally a two-dimensional activity—letters on paper. However, placing three-dimensional letters next to each other is also a form of writing (setting the stage for the Scrabble question). If so, making a three-dimensional shape should also be similar to drawing a shape on a paper. Both are writing and forbidden on Shabbos and Yom Tov. With the advent of the three-dimensional printer, this comparison gains contemporary resonance. Some authorities sensibly apply this ruling to Play-Doh, as well.

I suspect that sculpting through shape-shifting is equivalent to sculpting with clay or dough. I cannot prove it but, I believe that shape-shifting also constitutes writing on Shabbos. I encourage any superhero with the power to shape-shift to bring his questions to the highest halakhic authorities so we can have some heavy thinkers weigh in on the subject.

VI. Super Damage

The Hulk has anger management issues. He represents the rage that boils inside all of us. If we fail to control ourselves, we may end up destroying our lives and hurting others despite our best intentions. In his rage, the Hulk often inadvertently destroys private property. Is he liable to pay for his accidental damage?

The Torah (Ex. 21:24-25) tells us the concept of "an eye for an eye" in a long, repetitive fashion, also listing "a hand for a hand, a tooth for a tooth," and others, including "an injury [*petza*] for an injury." The Sages of the Talmud and Midrash inferred legal points from the repetition.

The Gemara (*Bava Kamma* 26b) learns from the phrase about "*petza*" that we are liable for even accidental damage. If we break something, even accidentally, we have to pay for it. However, the Mishnah on the very next page (27a) rules to the contrary. Someone who accidentally trips on a clay pitcher that was left in public, and breaks the pitcher, is exempt from paying damages. But isn't that accidental damage for which the Gemara teaches we are liable?

Tosafos (*Bava Kamma* 27b s.v. *lefi*) explain this apparent contradiction by distinguishing between a completely forced act (*oness gamur*) and an accident. Despite the biblical requirement to pay for accidental damages, you are exempt from an *oness gamur*. The Rambam (*Mishneh Torah, Hilkhos Choveil U-Mazzik* 6:1) makes no such distinction and rules that you are liable for all property damage, even accidents. Later commentators are left to speculate how he resolved the contradiction.

The *Shulchan Arukh* (*Choshen Mishpat* 378:1) rules like the Rambam while the Rema (ad loc.) follows Tosafos. Therefore, according to the Rema, the Hulk would be exempt from paying for accidental damage if it constitutes an *oness gamur*. But does it? Is the Hulk really incapable of controlling his anger? From afar, it seems that he needs counseling for anger management. I find it hard to accept that his rage constitutes an *oness gamur*. On some level, he can be more careful and avoid reaching the state where he causes damage. On the other hand, perhaps I overestimate his ability to control his anger. Maybe he really has no control.

VII. Super Empowered

Regardless, there is another reason the Hulk may be exempt from paying for accidental damages. The Gemara (*Sanhedrin* 74a) discusses the case of accidental damage caused by an attempted murder. Somewhat surprisingly, the would-be murderer is exempt from paying for damages caused in his pursuit because he is liable for execution. Since a court can only apply one punishment, it uses the most severe, in this case execution.

The would-be victim who is fleeing for his life has every right to damage someone else's property. If you are fleeing for your life and you see someone's car with the door open and keys in the ignition, by all means jump in and drive away. Saving a life takes precedence over property rights. However, once the danger subsides, you have to pay for the damages you caused. If you crash that car, you have to pay the owner for the damage. He was just an innocent bystander.

However, a would-be rescuer is exempt from paying any damages. The Sages enacted a special exemption for rescuers. If not, people would hesitate before saving someone else's life. Living in the litigious society of today, we can easily envision an emergency technician ripping open the shirt of someone writhing in pain in order to administer medicine. And then the patient, after having recovered, sues the emergency technician for damage to the shirt. In order to encourage the saving of lives, such heroes receive special exemption from paying damages. If you need to steal a car to pursue an assassin, you do not have to worry about paying for any damage to the car. Save the life.

This exemption applies to all superheroes. When superheroes fight supervillains, they cause super damage. Buildings are leveled. Cars are flattened. Businesses are destroyed. But as long as the superhero was fighting to save someone's life, he is exempt from paying any damages. Therefore, the liability applied by Congress to superheroes in *The Incredibles* is not an obligation the Torah would support. Of course, you still have to follow local laws.

On the other hand, the author of *Hatzalah Ke-Halakhah* (ch. 7) warns emergency technicians not to overestimate the exemption. He quotes Rav Moshe Feinstein (*Iggeros Moshe, Choshen Mishpat* 2:63), who states that the exemption only applies to activities that are part of the life-saving efforts. If a car is blocking your ambulance, you can bang it out of the way. But if you have a clear path, you can't bang another car just for fun. And if you are in someone's home on an emergency call, you can't steal from him and defend yourself with this exemption. It does not apply to theft.

Superheroes, and even regular heroes, are not above the law. If anything, they need the law more. They need to remember that despite their talents and achievements, they are mere servants of the Lord.

Surviving Self-Endangerment

Life consists of risk-taking in big and small ways. Those who are completely risk-averse never leave their homes out of fear. We consciously rate the risks involved in various activities and judge whether we want to accept those risks. Some people are even willing to take risks that are universally recognized as serious life threats, with substantial possibility of death. At times, doing so is even a mitzvah. Should we thank God if we survive those risks?

The Gemara (*Berakhos* 54b) lists four groups of people who recite the *Gomel* blessing thanking God for saving them. Sephardim recite the blessing after any illness for which they are bed-ridden (*Shulchan Arukh, Orach Chaim* 219:8); Ashkenazim only after an illness that is so serious we would violate Shabbos to treat it (*Mishnah Berurah*, ad loc. 48). Do we say the blessing if we emerge from a life-threat we willingly accepted? After someone engages in a foolhardy extreme sport, should he *bentch Gomel*?

In his *Machazik Berakhah* (219:1), Rav Chaim Yosef David Azulai (Chida) quotes a debate on this subject. His father, Rav Yosef Azulai, ruled that the blessing was only enacted for someone who survived an external life threat, not something willingly undertaken. However, Rav Eliezer Nachum (author of *Chazon Nachum*) ruled that the blessing applies to anyone who survives any threat to life. This debate has many practical implications. Rav Eliezer Melamed (*Peninei Halakhah, Berakhos, Harchavos* 16:4) lists three:

1. **Elective Surgery:** Whenever anyone is placed under full anesthesia, he undergoes a risk to life. Does someone who chooses to undergo surgery *bentch Gomel* when and if he recovers? Rav Eliezer Waldenberg (*Tzitz Eliezer* 10:25:23) rules that someone who donates a kidney does not *bentch Gomel* on his recovery because he chose to enter this dangerous situation. Rav Ovadiah Yosef (*Yechavveh Da'as* 4:14) follows the view that you should recite a blessing on surviving a willingly undertaken danger and therefore rules that a kidney donor should *bentch Gomel* after recovery.

2. **Suicide Attempt:** Someone who is rescued from a suicide attempt has been saved from a life-threatening situation. However, he was the threat! Does he still *bentch Gomel*? Rav Chaim Palaggi (*Responsa Lev Chaim* 3:53) rules that he should recite the blessing because he was saved, as does Rav Azriel Hildesheimer (*Responsa Rav Azriel*, vol. 1 no. 29). However, Rav Ovadiah Yosef (ibid.) disagrees. Even though he generally rules that you should *bentch Gomel* when saved from self-imposed danger, he considers a suicide attempt different. Attempting suicide is a sin. How can someone recite a blessing generated by the sin?

3. **Release From Prison:** Some people who are convicted of a crime can avoid prison by paying a fine or ransom. If they choose not to pay and instead suffer the prison sentence, do they *bentch Gomel* on release? The Ri Mi-Gash (no. 90) rules that they should recite the blessing. However, while other authorities quote the Ri Mi-Gash as ruling that way, the *Sha'arei Teshuvah* (219:2) quotes him as concluding that one should recite the blessing without God's name. Rav Melamed does not quote this but Rav Simcha Rabinowitz (*Piskei Teshuvos*, vol. 2 219:11) sees this *Sha'arei Teshuvah* as a companion to the general view (of Rav Yosef Azulai) that someone who puts himself in danger should not *bentch Gomel* if he is saved.

Additionally, Rav Chaim Elazar Shapira (*Minchas Elazar* 4:47) discusses whether you may place yourself in life-threatening danger in order to learn Torah or earn money. He concludes that it is forbidden, and that others may not quote a Torah insight in the name of someone who endangers his own life in order to learn Torah (based on *Bava Kamma* 61a). However, if someone did place his life in danger for pure purposes in order to learn Torah and was saved, he may *bentch Gomel*, but not someone who undertook the danger for monetary profit. When it comes to profit, no one's intention is ever completely pure.

Gun Ownership in Jewish Law

Laws about gun control serve as perpetual fuel for political debates. However, everyone agrees that some people should carry guns in some circumstances. Whether police officers or soldiers, on duty or prepared for duty, some people need to carry guns in order to protect the public. In Messianic times, weapons will be turned into ploughshares (Isa. 2:4). Until then, weapons serve a necessary purpose in this unredeemed world.

Anyone who owns a gun needs to understand proper gun training, safety, and usage in order to avoid tragedy. These issues are crucial but not our topic. Here I am interested in exploring other aspects of gun ownership.

I. Bringing a Gun into a Synagogue

Rav Meir of Rothenburg (Maharam) is quoted as saying that you may not bring a long sword into a synagogue because it contradicts the purpose of prayer: prayer increases a person's life (*Berakhos* 8a, 54b) while a weapon shortens life (*Orechos Chaim*, *Hilkhos Beis Ha-Knesses* 7; *Kol Bo* 17; *Tashbetz* 202). Similar ideas can be found in a number of rabbinic passages. The Gemara (*Sanhedrin* 82a) says that you may not enter a *beis midrash* (study hall) with a weapon. The *Mekhilta* (Ex. 20:22) explains that using tools to fashion the stones of the altar is prohibited because the altar is intended to extend people's lives while iron shortens lives.

However, numerous rabbinic passages mention a sword in a *beis midrash*, such as *Shabbos* 17a, 63a; *Mo'ed Katan* 18a; *Sanhedrin* 94b. Rav Reuven Margoliyos (*Margoliyos Ha-Yam* 82a:34) suggests that a sword was brought to the entrance but not inside. This is somewhat difficult. However, all these passages refer to a *beis midrash* and not a synagogue.

Rabbeinu Peretz added a gloss to Maharam's comment that the only concern is when it is uncovered. This can be interpreted in two ways. One possibility is that Rabbeinu Peretz was qualifying Maharam's statement, saying that only an uncovered knife is forbidden (*Eliyah Rabbah* 251:10). Alternatively, Rabbeinu Peretz disagrees with Maharam and permits someone to enter a synagogue with a long sword but forbids someone whose head is uncovered to enter (*Birkei Yosef* 251:9).

The *Taz* (*Orach Chaim* 151:2) compares this rule to a similar rule requiring covering any knives on the table while *bentching*, reciting grace after meals, except on Shabbos and holidays (*Shulchan Arukh, Orach Chaim* 180:5, from *Orechos Chaim, Hilkhos Birkas Ha-Mazon* 8). The *Taz* asks why we have the option to cover a knife for bentching but not for prayer. He answers that covering works for both. However, at the table, we have small knives that we can easily cover. For prayer, we are discussing long swords that are hard to cover. However, if we can cover the long sword, then everyone agrees you can bring it into a synagogue.

Mishnah Berurah (151:22) and *Arukh Ha-Shulchan* (151:11) agree that covering is sufficient to allow bringing a gun into a synagogue. Rav Ovadiah Yosef (*Yechavveh Da'as* 5:28) adds that if you cannot cover the gun or put it in a safe place, you may rely on the lenient opinion and bring the gun uncovered into a synagogue.

Rav Eliezer Waldenberg (*Tzitz Eliezer* 10:18:6) adds another factor. A gun without bullets is relatively harmless. While you can use it to hit someone hard, you can do the same with a book or a pen. Effectively, removing the bullets from the gun disables it as a weapon, thereby permitting you to bring it into a synagogue. (He does not say that turning the safety on disables it.)

Therefore, he provides the following order of behavior:

1. In a time of danger or military preparedness, carry your gun with you according to your orders.
2. Otherwise, if it is no extra bother, remove your guns before entering a synagogue and give them to someone to watch.
3. If that is not possible, remove the bullets from the guns (you can still keep the bullets in your pocket, just not in the weapon). If possible, cover the guns also.
4. If you cannot remove the bullets, keep your pistol in its holster and cover any large gun with something like a jacket or *tallis*.

Again, safety has to come first. This rule should never place anyone's life in danger. Be smart and safe.

II. Carrying a Gun on Shabbos

The Sages forbade carrying utensils on Shabbos without a reason. Certain utensils contain more restrictions. A utensil primarily used in forbidden work is called a *"keli she-melakhto le-issur,"* and may only be carried in order to use the space in which it currently rests or for a permitted activity. For example, you may only carry a hammer if you want to use it for a permitted purpose, like cracking a nut, or if you want to put something like a book in its place. Is a gun like a hammer, a utensil for a forbidden purpose that may only be carried for a specific, permitted purpose or for its place?

Rav Shlomo Goren (*Meishiv Milchamah*, vol. 1 no. 61) argues that a gun is used for a permitted purpose. Since the only time a gun is fired is for self-defense purposes, which are permitted on Shabbos, the gun is not classified as a utensil for a forbidden purpose.

Rav Yekusiel Halberstam (*Divrei Yatziv, Orach Chaim*, vol. 2 no. 148) argues that a gun is primarily carried as a deterrent to instill fear. Most police officers never fire their guns. Since the primary purpose of a gun is to be carried, which is otherwise permitted on Shabbos, the gun is classified as a utensil for a permitted purpose. *Shemiras Shabbos Ke-Hilkhasah* (ch. 20 n. 28) quotes Rav Shlomo Zalman Auerbach as saying that during peacetime, guns are mainly used for inducing fear. Rav Eliezer Melamed (*Peninei Halakhah* 27:17) quotes Rav Auerbach (*Shulchan Shlomo*, vol. 2 308:16) similarly.[114]

Rav Ya'akov Ariel (*Be-Ohalah Shel Torah*, vol. 2 no. 32) disagrees with Rav Goren's argument (without quoting him by name). Rav Ariel points out that *piku'ach nefesh*, defense, is not permitted within the laws of Shabbos but overrides them, taking precedence over Shabbos. Shooting a gun for self-defense isn't a permitted Shabbos action but an action that is allowed even though it is forbidden on Shabbos.

Rav Ariel argues against the claim that guns are mainly for deterrent purposes. A gun serves as a deterrent because you can shoot it. If not for that otherwise forbidden activity, the gun would be useless. Therefore, it should be classified as a utensil for a forbidden purpose. Rav Zechariah ben Shlomo (*Hilkhos Tzava* 22:1, n. 1) agrees with Rav Ariel. *Shalmei Yehudah* (4:15) quotes Rav Yosef Shalom Elyashiv as similarly ruling that a gun is a utensil for a forbidden purpose.

The rabbis debate whether you may carry a weapon on Shabbos where there is no *eruv* (*Shabbos* 63a). R. Eliezer believes that weapons that you wear are like jewelery. The Sages disagree, arguing that since weapons will be abolished in the Messianic Era (Isa. 2:4), they are a disgrace to wear even now. The *Shulchan*

---

114. Rav Ephraim Greenblatt (*Rivevos Ephraim*, vol. 4 no. 88) quotes a friend who is unsure about the matter.

Arukh (*Orach Chaim* 301:7) rules strictly. Rav Yechiel Mikhel Epstein (*Arukh Ha-Shulchan, Orach Chaim* 301:51) explains that this is discussing a layman, but everyone agrees that a soldier's normal clothing include weapons. Rav Yekusiel Halberstam (ibid.) is not entirely satisfied with this approach and quotes other considerations. He also points out that the rabbis in Israel ruled strictly on this. Rav Binyamin Zilber (*Az Nidberu*, vol. 1 no. 70) disputes the distinction between a layman and soldier, which no prior commentary had mentioned.

Rav Nachum Rabinovich (*Melumedei Milchamah*, no. 68) rules that unless there is some security purpose, it is best to act strictly, if possible. But even the leniency only applies to wearing a gun in a holster or wrapped around your body, not in your hand or pocket.

Of course, whenever there is any question of a threat, you may carry a gun.

III. Reciting a Blessing on a New Gun

When you buy new items that make you happy, such as a fancy new suit, you may recite the *Shehecheyanu* blessing thanking God (*Shulchan Arukh, Orach Chaim* 223:3). However, since this blessing is optional, many refrain from reciting it (Rema, ad loc., 1). Rav Osher Weiss (*Responsa Minchas Asher*, vol. 1 no. 9) says that his mentor, Rav Yekusiel Halberstam, following in the path of his ancestor Rav Chaim Halberstam, never recited *Shehecheyanu* on new fruits or clothing, presumably because they did not feel sufficient joy over them.

Rav Shlomo Aviner (*She'eilas Shlomo*, vol. 3 no. 87) discusses whether you may recite a *Shehecheyanu* on buying a new gun. If it brings you joy, you should thank God for it. However, an argument can be made that a gun really symbolizes trouble. Should you recite a blessing on buying a defensive weapon? For example, Rav

Zerachiah Halevy (*Ha-Ma'or*, end of *Pesachim*) writes that we do not say *Shehecheyanu* on the mitzvah of counting the *Omer* because it reminds us of the destruction of the Temple. Similarly, a gun reminds us of our present danger. Rav Aviner counters that the situation, not the gun, causes sadness over the danger. The gun provides protection, which brings joy.

Rav Moshe Stern (*Be'er Moshe*, vol. 5 no. 67) rules that you should recite a *Shehecheyanu* on false teeth. Even though you have lost your real teeth, you still have joy from the replacements. Similarly, Rav Aviner argues, despite the unfortunate situation of danger, you still have joy from the purchase of the gun.

PART 10: DEATH

The 9/11 Memorial and Jewish Law

As a New York resident who worked in Manhattan on September 11, 2001, I will forever be haunted by the tragic day and its aftermath. However, visitors and future generations, including my own children, need more than personal memories. The 9/11 memorial and museum are intended to provide that. A November 2014 article in *First Things* by Catesby Leigh, an architecture and art critic, excoriates the National September 11 Memorial & Museum. I am hardly an architecture or art critic and I have not even visited the memorial or museum. However, I would like to discuss the concepts involved and the light Jewish tradition can shed on them.[115]

I. Monuments

The Torah (Deut. 16:22) explicitly forbids erecting monuments. After the Holocaust, Jewish authorities grappled with the need to remember and the biblical prohibition forbidding monuments. Medieval authorities debate the nature of this prohibition. Rashi (ad loc.) states that the Torah forbids erecting (single stone) monuments for sacrifices to God similar to those used by idolators. We may only use altars (made of multiple stones) in our worship of God. Similarly, Rav Moshe of Coucy (*Semag*, prohibition 41) says this prohibition is violated if two conditions are met: the monument is made of a single stone and is used for sacrifices.

---

115. I am certain some people will expect a discussion here of whether *kohanim* may enter the memorial. I do not know and am not willing to rely on news reports.

However, the Rambam (*Sefer Ha-Mitzvos*, prohibition 11; *Mishneh Torah, Hilkhos Avodah Zarah* 6:6) defines a forbidden monument as one where people gather. In order to fall under the biblical prohibition, it need not be made of a single stone nor be used for sacrifice or any other form of worship. The *Chinukh* (403) explains that since monuments were used for idolatry, we may not use them for anything, even the service of God. While only a minority view, the Rambam's position cannot be easily dismissed. The codes and responsa literature do not offer much guidance on this subject.

II. Gravestones

However, the Rambam himself (*Mishneh Torah, Hilkhos Avel* 4:4) rules that we must erect gravestones for the deceased. Is this not a monument that should be biblically forbidden? The Rambam here follows the Mishnah (*Shekalim* 2:5), and its accompanying Talmud Yerushalmi which states that a Torah scholar does not need a gravestone because his Torah insights serve as a memorial. However, everyone else requires a gravestone, which the Mishnah calls a "*nefesh*," literally, "soul."

At the unveiling of Rav Moshe Sofer's (the *Chasam Sofer*) gravestone, his son and successor, Rav Avraham Shmuel Binyamin Sofer, asked why we erect a monument for Torah scholars against the conclusion of the Yerushalmi and Rambam (*Responsa Kesav Sofer, Yoreh De'ah* 178). He explains that for most people, we write their names on their gravestones so their relatives and friends will pray for them. The gravestone is intended to benefit the deceased's soul (*nefesh*). Righteous people do not need this help. Their gravestones are for the visitors to pray in the merit of the righteous, a service to others and not the deceased.[116]

Rav Yitzchak Ya'akov Weiss (*Minchas Yitzchak* 1:29) explains that a gravestone is not important in and of itself. It is secondary

---

116. See also *Minchas Elazar* 3:37.

to the grave and therefore not comparable to an idolatrous monument. He was asked whether a community could erect a monument for Holocaust victims. He answered that this would be biblically forbidden according to the Rambam unless they include the remains of someone deceased, such as ashes or soap made from humans, which would render the monument a gravestone.

Rav Weiss quotes two halakhic authorities who disagreed with him. Rav Yehudah Leib Tzirilson (*Ma'archei Lev*, no. 42) and Rav David Sperber (oral communication to Rav Weiss) argue that since monuments for the dead are never used for idolatry, they are not subject to the prohibition, even according to the Rambam. Rav Weiss was not convinced by this argument.

III. Gravestone Substitutes

Rav Moshe Feinstein (*Iggeros Moshe, Yoreh De'ah* 4:57) implicitly disagrees with Rav Weiss. He was asked whether someone who does not know where his parents are buried is still obligated to erect a gravestone, perhaps at an empty plot in a cemetery. After discussing and rejecting various prooftexts, Rav Feinstein concludes that there is no basis to obligate a child to erect a gravestone in such a situation. His discussion assumes that erecting a gravestone without a buried body in the grave is permissible, implicitly ruling against the Rambam or interpreting his position differently.

Rav Feinstein proceeds to deciding the most appropriate way to memorialize a deceased relative whose burial site is unknown, making a crucial distinction. A gravestone without a grave gives honor to no one. And if we cannot directly honor the deceased among the dead, we should honor him among the living. Therefore, Rav Feinstein suggests, a child should honor the deceased by erecting a building—or donating partially to a building—that will be used for educational or charity purposes. Let his name be remembered as enhancing religious lives.

IV. Museums and Monuments

We see three methods for memorializing the dead, each appropriate in different circumstances:

1. We place a monument, a gravestone, near the burial place for the sake of the deceased's soul.
2. For the righteous, we place a gravestone at the burial place for the benefit of visitors.
3. Elsewhere, a monument is either forbidden (Rav Weiss) or inappropriate (Rav Feinstein). Instead, we build educational or charitable institutions.

A 9/11 monument, listing the names of the deceased, is appropriate for the site where some remains still rest. It is a burial site, a grave for individuals for whom the nation mourns. Some of the buried may qualify as righteous, whether as victims of a vicious attack or would-be saviors, rushing to assist the injured. The monument commemorates the fallen and allows us to pray for them and for ourselves.

If a graveside monument is impossible, an educational institution—including a museum—is a proper additional commemoration. It should not be a place to merely revisit the tragedy. As an educational institution, this museum must teach the lessons of 9/11. To me, those lessons are about patriotism, bravery, and selflessness. When I think of 9/11, I think of firefighters rushing to the scene to help. I see Abe Zelmanowitz, from my neighborhood, who stayed behind to help his quadriplegic colleague. And I think of the remarkable national unity that followed the tragedy. Teaching those lessons to a future generation would be a fitting commemoration of the martyrs of 9/11.

Vehicular Homicide in Jewish Law

Driving a car is operating a dangerous weapon. An accident can cause significant financial damage and physical harm, even death. But who is responsible for the damage?

An article in the journal *No'am* (no. 10, p. 41, quoted in *Yechavveh Da'as*, vol. 5 no. 16 n. 2) quotes Rav Shmuel Aharon Yudelowitz as saying that generally a driver is not liable for killing someone in an accident. A car goes forward and the driver merely modulates the gas with his foot on the pedal. If a person enters the car's path, a driver is obligated to save that potential victim by stopping or moving the car. Even if the driver intentionally allows the car to hit the victim, he is only guilty of failing to save the person, not of killing him.

Rav Ovadiah Yosef (*Yechavveh Da'as*, ibid.) disagrees with this analysis. He compares driving a car to throwing a stone into public property (*Makos* 8a). If that stone hits and kills someone, you are considered an intentional murderer because you should have been more careful. Ramban (ad loc.) and Tosafos (*Bava Kamma* 32b s.v. *meisivei*) explain that you are considered a near-intentional murderer (*shogeg karov le-meizid*) because of the negligence. Similarly, argues Rav Ovadiah, a speeding driver who kills someone in an accident is negligent because he should have been more careful.

However, it seems to me that we can divide drivers who have had accidents into three categories:

1. Those who drive poorly and disobey traffic laws, for example a speeding driver who hits a pedestrian or another car.
2. Those who drive properly but encounter difficult conditions and make a mistake, for example a driver who panics when his car skids and steers his car into another lane and hits a car.
3. Those who do everything right but get into an accident for other reasons, such as when a pedestrian enters the street without looking to see if a car is coming.

It seems that Rav Ovadiah discusses the first and third cases. About the first case, he quotes the early authorities who considered it near-intentional. Others go so far as to consider a reckless driver a pursuer (*rodef*), at least on some level. Rav Yosef calls the third case entirely unintentional (*annus le-gamrei*). He does not discuss the second case, in which the driver follows the rules. I suspect he would call it accidental (*shogeg*).

A *kohen* who kills someone may not recite *Birkas Kohanim* (*Berakhos* 32b). May a *kohen* who killed someone in a car accident recite these blessings? The *Shulchan Arukh* (*Orach Chaim* 128:35) rules like the Rambam that even if the *kohen* repents, he cannot recite the blessings. The Rema (ad loc.) disagrees and rules like Rashi that a repentant *kohen* may recite the blessings. Rav Shmuel Wosner (*Shevet Ha-Levi* 1:43) rules like the Rema, although his case includes other reasons for leniency. Characteristically, Rav Yosef follows the *Shulchan Arukh*.

However, in the third case above of a completely unintentional accident, Rav Yosef combines the lenient view of the Rema with the *Eliyah Rabbah's* (128:63) view that even those who are strict should be lenient in an unintentional case (even though the *Pri Megadim* 128, *Eishel Avraham* 51 disagrees). With this, Rav Yosef allows a repentant *kohen* who completely unintentionally killed someone in a car accident to recite *Birkas Kohanim*. Rav Eliezer

Melamed (*Peninei Halakhah, Likkutim*, vol. 2 12:5) adds that a third party should confirm that the driver was not at fault.

Rav Ya'akov Ariel (*Halakhah Be-Yameinu*, p. 330) explains that repentance in this context does not constitute merely an internal process. While it is crucial for a person to regret his misdeeds, including his accidents, a murderer must do more. Rav Wosner (ibid.) accepts fasting and charity as practical repentance. Rav Ariel takes a somewhat different path.

In the past, leading rabbis sometimes advised accidental murderers to leave town, mirroring the biblical exile of an accidental murderer (Num. 35). Rav Ariel first suggests that someone who kills another in a car accident should similarly move his home. He then suggests that a more fitting act of repentance is supporting the family that lost a loved one or, if that is not possible, another orphan or injured child. Support in this context means assisting financially and religiously, helping the children grow into healthy religious Jews.

Community Burial

I. Separate Cemeteries

Jews and Gentiles share many aspects of their lives, but in death they must separate. Halakhic authorities over the centuries have consistently ruled that Jewish cemeteries must remain exclusively for Jews. In early nineteenth century, Rav Shlomo Kluger strongly opposed joint cemeteries, and decades later Rav David Tzvi Hoffmann demanded that a Jewish cemetery exclude (halakhically non-Jewish) children of Jewish fathers and Gentile mothers (*Tuv Ta'am Va-Da'as* 3:2:253; *Melamed Le-Ho'il* 2:127). Rav Avraham Kook (*Da'as Kohen* 201), the *Minchas Elazar* (2:41), the *Tzitz Eliezer* (16:36) and Rav Ovadiah Yosef (*Yabia Omer* 7:YD:36) are just some of the recent authorities who have insisted on maintaining this tradition. What is the reason for this practice?

When Rus, the paradigmatic convert, indicates her intention to join the Jewish nation, she tells Naomi: "Your people are my people, and your God is my God. Where you die, I will die, and there I will be buried" (Ruth 1:17-18). The Talmud (*Yevamos* 47b) explains that Rus was saying that Jews bury the righteous and wicked separately (see *Sanhedrin* 47a).

This is quite puzzling because Rus was never wicked. She had been a righteous Gentile and became a righteous Jew. Why was she implying that prior to her conversion she would have been buried separately from Naomi?

II. Separate Burial

Elsewhere, the Talmud (*Gittin* 61a) states that the Jewish community buries Jews and Gentiles. The commentaries—Rashi, Ritva, Ran, Meiri—explain that this means that the Jewish community tends to the needs of the deceased regardless of ancestry. However, it does not mean that we bury everyone together. Rather, Jews are buried in a Jewish cemetery and Gentiles are buried in their cemetery.

The Ran, in his commentary to the Rif (ad loc.), states that we cannot bury Jews and Gentiles together because we do not even bury righteous and wicked Jews together. Later authorities, such as the *Bach* (*Yoreh De'ah* 151), phrase it as a logical deduction. We don't bury righteous and wicked Jews together, so certainly (*kal va-chomer*) we don't bury Jews and Gentiles together. But what is the *kal va-chomer* between a wicked Jew and a righteous Gentile?

III. Separate Communities

I suggest that the separation of cemeteries—which requires at least a deep gate and a space of eight *ammos*—is not a function of righteousness but of community. Burial is not just a sacred religious rite but also a lifecycle ritual. We perform those ceremonies as a community, practicing our religion as only a society can.

Those who are distant from our religious community are excluded from these rituals. While denying access to non-religious Jews is an obviously sensitive subject, those who are executed by a religious court (the subject of the talmudic discussions) are more easily turned away. They have been tried and convicted of irreligiosity and cannot be buried with our community.

Righteous Gentiles share a bond with religious Jews but only as like-minded people within different communities. Therefore, while we take care of their burials needs, we require that they have their own cemeteries. If even wayward Jews are excluded from a Jewish community cemetery, then certainly Gentiles must be as well.

Abortion and Fathers' Notification

Tosafos (*Kesubos* 31a) record a debate about the Torah's case of an attack that leads to miscarriage (Ex. 21:22-25). If a man attacks another man and accidentally hits a pregnant woman, causing her to miscarry, his punishment depends on whether the woman survives. If she dies, then the attacker is executed for murder. If she survives, then he has to pay damages to the husband for the aborted fetus. On the one hand, we see here a differentiation between an adult and a fetus, a living person and a soon-to-be living baby. Murder of the woman is punished with execution while destruction of the fetus is punished financially.

The Talmud generally only allows for one punishment per crime, the harsher punishment (*kim leih bi-de-rabbah mineih*). However, that is in the simple case in which an attacker commits an act on one person—he either pays damages or is flogged or is executed. The question remains open regarding someone whose two punishments are each owed to different people. If someone commits an act that causes financial damage to one person but requires flogging for the offense to another, does he only receive one punishment?

I. Who Gets Restitution?

Tosafos (ibid.) record a disagreement between Rabbenu Tam and Ri. Rabbenu Tam notes that an attacker who murders a pregnant woman deserves execution for the attack on the woman and owes damages to her husband for the fetus. That is a case of monetary punishment to one and execution to another. According to an explicit verse, the attacker is only executed and need not pay damages. Therefore, Rabbenu Tam infers, even when dealing with a capital crime that incurs damages to another, when there are two victims, the court only administers the harsher punishment.

Ri disagrees with his illustrious uncle. After all, he argues, the fetus is part of the mother's body. It is hard to consider this a case of two punishments each owed to different people, because the damage is all done to the mother.

I have not found any analysis in the commentaries of these two opinions. While Ri's point that the fetus is part of the mother's body is certainly true, that does not change the fact that the damages are owed to the father. It seems that Ri and Rabbenu Tam disagree whether the damages are inherently financial or physical. According to Rabbenu Tam, the damage caused is financial and therefore the payment goes directly to the father, who has a financial interest in the fetus. However, according to Ri, the damages emerge from the physical injury and therefore must be considered primarily owed to the mother since her body was harmed. The father's financial responsibility for the child makes him the recipient of the payment, but the damages paid are a function of the mother's physical injury.

In other words, according to Rabbenu Tam, the damages are financial and owed directly to the financial victim. According to Ri, the damages are physical and therefore owed to the physical victim but paid to the responsible financial party.

II. Fathers' Rights

What emerges, particularly but not only from Ri's view, is that even though the fetus is part of the mother's body, the father still has a financial interest in the baby. When an attacker causes a miscarriage, the father is paid damages.

Therefore, I suggest, a father has a say in even a halakhically unjustified abortion. Halakhic views on abortion are complex and the weight of tradition permits abortion in many cases beyond life-threatening danger to the mother.[117] A father has an interest in the fetus and therefore a halakhic right to object to an abortion. Any abortion against the father's will is a violation of his rights. Rape is an extraordinary case—one that demands an exception, not one that determines the rule.

This raises all sorts of practical problems. What if the father is a difficult individual? What if he refuses to sanction an abortion solely to irritate the mother? What if the mother is scared to even contact the father?

No woman should ever be placed in life-threatening danger due to her husband's or partner's financial rights. The general rule is that you may save your life even if it causes someone else a financial loss. If someone is being chased by a terrorist, he may steal a car to escape the danger. However, after the danger passes, he must return the car and/or repay the person whose car was stolen. Danger does not permit theft.

No woman should be forced to bear a baby she did not choose to have. However, that choice begins with intimate relations. Once a man and woman join together to create a fetus, even by accident, they both have rights and responsibilities. A father who refuses to support his child is liable to pay, and a court will force him to do so. It seems from the above that a woman who aborts a fetus without the father's consent is technically liable to pay the father for financial damages, although I cannot imagine any court enforcing this payment. But at the very least, absent extenuating circumstances, the father must consent to an abortion. Paternal

---

117. This is not the place for a discussion of the parameters and debates. See Rav David M. Feldman, *Birth Control in Jewish Law* (New York University Press, 1968).

notification seems a minimum required by this law. If we are going to force the father to pay for the baby, he should have a say in its prenatal development and survival.

PART 11: MISCELLANEOUS

Nail-Biting in Jewish Law

Nail-biting is a habit that many consider improper yet still continues, out of both nervousness and convenience. This practice is hardly new and, despite its lack of sophistication, enjoys halakhic benefits in certain situations. The Gemara (*Mo'ed Katan* 18a) even tells that Rabbi Yochanan bit his nails on at least one occasion.

I. Shabbos

The *Shulchan Arukh* (*Orach Chaim* 340:1) rules that you may not cut your hair or nails on Shabbos. Doing so is biblically forbidden, similar to shearing a lamb's wool. Some might suggest that cutting fingernails is different than shearing wool because the shearing yields useful wool while fingernails are discarded (more on that later). Perhaps cutting fingernails is only rabbinically forbidden. However, Rav Ovadiah Yosef (*Yechavveh Da'as*, vol. 4 p. 279) quotes numerous authorities who hold that cutting fingernails is biblically forbidden.

The *Magen Avraham* (340:intro) differentiates between using a tool (scissors or clippers) to cut your fingernails and doing it manually (peeling with your fingers or biting). Using a tool is biblically forbidden but manual removal is only rabbinically forbidden. This becomes important when a hanging nail causes pain. The *Shulchan Arukh* (*Orach Chaim* 328:31) rules that if your fingernail is mostly disconnected (hanging) and is causing you pain (not just discomfort put pain), then you may remove it manually but not with a tool. Peeling or biting the nail that is mostly removed is a double rabbinic prohibition (*shevus di-shevus*), which is permitted in a case of pain. Using a tool on a nail that is mostly removed is problematic because a single rabbinic prohibition remains in force even when there is pain, unless it reaches the point that one would be classified as ill.

The *Shulchan Arukh* (ibid.) quotes a disagreement between Rashi and Rabbenu Tam about the permission to bite off a hanging fingernail or piece of skin that is causing you pain. According to Rashi, you may only bite that nail off if it is coming off toward the fingertip. According to Rabbenu Tam, it must be in the other direction, toward the palm. The *Shulchan Arukh* rules that we must be strict for both opinions, which effectively means that you may never bite off a nail in that situation. However, many authorities rule that this limitation only applies to skin and not nails. Among them are *Chayei Adam* (21:4), *Kitzur Shulchan Arukh* (80:55), and *Shemiras Shabbos Ke-Hilkhasah* (14:54). *Piskei Teshuvos* (new series, 338:56) says that if you do so, you have authorities on whom to rely. *Peninei Halakhah* (*Shabbos*, *Harchavos* 14:2:1) suggests that you can even be lenient regarding skin, because Rashi and Rabbenu Tam really agree that anytime there is pain, you can be lenient on a double rabbinic prohibition. While his argument regarding skin makes logical sense, his textual support seems very lacking. But regarding nails, he has ample support.

II. Chol Ha-Mo'ed

In order to encourage people to take a haircut and shave before Yom Tov, the Sages forbade doing so on Chol Ha-Mo'ed, the intermediary days of the holiday. Some authorities rule that if you shaved before Yom Tov, you may shave on Chol Ha-Mo'ed. However, the *Shulchan Arukh* (*Orach Chaim* 531:1) rules that regardless of whether you shaved before Yom Tov, you may not shave on Chol Ha-Mo'ed (some say that shaving today is different than it used to be, but that is a separate discussion).

What about cutting your nails? The *Shulchan Arukh* (ibid., 532:1) rules that even though you are supposed to cut your nails before Yom Tov, the Sages' decree does not apply to nail-cutting. Therefore, you may cut your nails on Chol Ha-Mo'ed. However, the Rema (ad loc.) records the Ashkenazic ruling forbidding nail cutting on Chol Ha-Mo'ed. The *Magen Avraham* (ad loc., 1) rules that if you cut your nails before Yom Tov, you may cut them on Chol Ha-Mo'ed as well. His reasoning is as follows: Since many permit shaving on Chol Ha-Mo'ed if you shaved before Yom Tov and many also permit cutting your nails regardless, we can at least permit cutting your nails on Chol Ha-Mo'ed if you cut them before Yom Tov.

However, if you neglected to cut your nails before Yom Tov, then you have to wait until the festival is completely over. There is one other option. The *Mishnah Berurah* (532:3) permits peeling or biting your nails on Chol Ha-Mo'ed. Even though this is forbidden on Shabbos and Yom Tov, on Chol Ha-Mo'ed the rule is more lenient since some permit even cutting. Therefore, even though you should prepare for Yom Tov by cutting your nails, you may still bite your nails on Chol Ha-Mo'ed.

III. Mourners

Many of the rules of Chol Ha-Mo'ed apply to a mourner. Among these prohibitions is that a mourner, both during the week-long *shivah* and the month-long *sheloshim*, may not shave or cut his nails (*Shulchan Arukh, Yoreh De'ah* 390:7). However, the *Shulchan Arukh* (ibid.) records explicit permission for a mourner, even during *shivah*, to peel or bite his nails.

IV. Washing

After cutting your nails, you are required to wash your hands (*Shulchan Arukh, Orach Chaim* 4:19). Do you also have to wash after biting your nails? What if you only bite one nail, do you really have to wash your hands? *Piskei Teshuvos* (4:21 n. 206) quotes the Malbim (*Artzos Ha-Chaim*, ad loc., no. 18), *Kaf Ha-Chaim* (ad loc., no. 28), and *Tzitz Eliezer* (7:2) who say that you have to wash even after cutting only one fingernail. However, he quotes (ibid., n. 208) in the name of the *Chazon Ish* that you do not have to wash after cutting (or biting) part of a single nail. Rav Shlomo Aviner (*Piskei Shlomo*, vol. 1 p. 10), in the context of ruling that you do not have to wash after filing your nails, quotes the same from the *Chazon Ish. Piskei Teshuvos* (ibid., n. 209) also quotes the *Ben Ish Chai* (*Rav Pe'alim* 2:4) that you only have to wash after cutting nails that extend beyond the fingertip. Most nail-biters have shorter nails than that.

V. Order and Disposing

It is a mitzvah to shower and groom oneself before Shabbos (*Shulchan Arukh, Orach Chaim* 260:1). The Rema (ad loc.) quotes a specific order in which you should cut the nails of each finger and hand. I am unsure whether that order also applies to biting your nails. However, the *Taz* (ad loc., 2) quotes the Arizal as saying that there is no need to follow that order. He also quotes the *Tashbetz* as saying that the Maharam of Rothenburg personally did not follow the order. The implication of the *Taz* is that he rules that you do not have to follow the order. The *Magen Avraham* (ad loc., 1) says that the Arizal even mocked the order of cutting fingernails. However, the *Magen Avraham* concludes that you should be strict anyway, which the *Mishnah Berurah* (ad loc., 8) follows. The *Arukh Ha-Shulchan* (ad loc., par. 6) says that some follow the order and some do not ("those who are careful are careful, and those who are not are not"). Personally, I am not too worried about biting my fingernails in the proper order. If you are only biting the nails of one or two fingers, then this does not apply anyway.

The Gemara (ibid.) says that we should be careful how we dispose of fingernails. It says that a *tzaddik* buries his fingernails, a *chasid* burns them, and a *rasha* just tosses them down. The Gemara is concerned that a pregnant woman might step on the discarded fingernail and feel so much pain that she miscarries. Therefore, the Gemara concludes, you can throw fingernails on the ground in a place where women do not normally walk, such as in a *beis midrash* (the Gemara's example) or the men's section of a synagogue. However, you are not allowed to throw your fingernails on the subway (which I see frequently) or anywhere else that women walk. Instead, you must discard them in a sanitary way.

Some authorities say that nowadays it is best to flush the cut fingernails down the toilet or down a sink. *Piskei Teshuvos* (new series, 260:9 n. 91) quotes this from the *Ben Ish Chai* (year 2, *Lekh Lekha*, no. 14), Rav Betzalel Stern (*Responsa Be-Tzel Ha-Chokhmah* 2:35), and Rav Moshe Stern (*Responsa Be'er Moshe* 6:133). Rav Yisrael Belsky also held this way (Rav Moishe Dovid Lebovits, *Piskei Halakhah of Harav Yisroel Belsky on Orach Chaim and Yoreh Deah*, p. 61). While some are still strict and require burning (see *Piskei Teshuvos*, ibid., n. 92), flushing fingernails seems to be a widespread practice. This applies to fingernails bitten off, as well.

VI. Bad Habit

Rav Eliezer Melamed (*Peninei Halakhah, Shabbos*, vol. 1, English translation, p. 278) writes:

> One should make every effort to stop biting his nails entirely; apart from being impolite, a habitual nail biter is likely to bite his nails on Shabbat as well, thus violating Shabbat.

While Rav Melamed does not cite a source for this ruling, *Piskei Teshuvos* (4:22 n. 209) writes similarly and quotes a story that the *Chazon Ish* rebuked a habitual nail biter, saying that he is presumably a Shabbos violator. This sounds to me like strong advice, not a halakhic ruling.

From Ethiopia to *Shulchan Arukh*

Rabbi Dr. Sharon Shalom immigrated from Ethiopia to Israel at the age of eight, eventually studying in Yeshivat Har Etzion and Bar Ilan University and currently serving as a congregational rabbi in Kiryat Gat. *From Sinai to Ethiopia: The Halakhic and Conceptual World of Ethiopian Jewry*,[118] originally published in Hebrew and now translated into English, is part memoir, part communal history and part halakhic treatise. When Rav Shalom began studying in Yeshivat Har Etzion, he confronted one of the *rashei yeshiva*, Rav Yehuda Amital, and asked why Ethiopian students are required to convert. Rav Amital responded wisely and honestly: "If someone comes to me tomorrow and expresses an interest in you for a *shidduch*, I don't want to have to hesitate before recommending you for a match.... We want you to be an inseparable part of the student body." This summarizes the complex process of Ethiopian Jewry's integration into Israeli society. With centuries of history, Ethiopian Jews have their own customs and halakhic practices that sometimes differ greatly from the rest of the Jewish world's. How do they rejoin the community after such a long isolation? Rav Shalom's answer: With great pride, slow compromise, and understanding on both sides.

The bulk of this book consists of *Shulchan Ha-Orit*, a halakhic compendium of laws where Ethiopian practice differs from widely accepted *halakhah*. In a brilliant but controversial move,

---

118. Gefen, 2016

Rav Shalom offers different rulings for the first and subsequent generations of Ethiopian immigrants to Israel. Those who grew up in Ethiopia will have more difficulty changing the practices of their youth. Those who come of age in Israel, surrounded by Israeli culture, will want to join with their friends and may reject Ethiopian tradition altogether if a compromise is unavailable.

For example, Ethiopians celebrate the new year on the first day of *Nisan*, in spring time. Those familiar with talmudic literature will recall the debate over whether the world was created in *Nisan* or *Tishrei*. Rav Shalom recommends that the first generation of Ethiopians continue celebrating Rosh Hashanah in *Nisan* while subsequent generations observe the holiday when everyone else in Israel celebrates it, in *Tishrei*.

This fascinating cultural and halakhic study is accompanied with rabbinic approbations from Rav Nachum Rabinovich; Rav Shabtai Rappaport; Rav Yosef Hadana, the Chief Rabbi of Ethiopian Jews in Israel, and others. However, recently Rav Shlomo Amar—Chief Rabbi of Jerusalem—and former Chief Sephardic Rabbi of Israel, and some Ethiopian elders have expressed strong opposition to the author's approach of compromise.

Jews Attending Church

Rav Haskel Lookstein generated a storm of criticism when he attended the inaugural church services for President Obama and recited a non-denominational prayer. Many pointed out the questionable halakhic basis for such a practice, and Rav Lookstein himself agreed that he would only attend such a service in the exceptional case of a request by a world leader. Many others noted that English Chief Rabbis have historically attended select church services.

I do not know if anyone quoted the following from the former Chief Rabbi of England, Rav Immanuel Jakobovits, upon which I recently stumbled. He discusses the issue twice in his 1995 book, *Dear Chief Rabbi: From the Correspondence of Chief Rabbi Immanuel Jakobovits on Matters of Jewish Law, Ethics and Contemporary Issues, 1980-1990.*

In one letter (p. 46), Rav Jakobovits writes:

After consultation with the [London] Beth Din, my own practice is occasionally to attend Church services on royal and state occasions to represent the Jewish community. But I never actively participate, nor do I wear cap and gown. I find that my Christian hosts usually show understanding and respect for this attitude and its reservations.

Note that he visibly refrained from participating in the prayer services. Also note that he received approval from his *beis din* to attend.

In another letter (p. 49), he writes:

> Naturally I often face the problem of having to respond to invitations to take part in interfaith services, sometimes at the highest level for royal and national events. My attitude invariably is that I cannot take an active part in a religious service of any except my own faith, and this is always understood and respected. But I do on occasions attend such services as a representative of the Jewish community, though without wearing canonicals or "officiating" in any other form.

He continues that a cantor wishing to take part in an interfaith memorial service televised in a church may pre-record an appropriate prayer elsewhere to be played before or after the church service.

I make no claim that Rav Jakobovits' views (and that of his *beis din*) should become normative. I am describing, not prescribing (nor proscribing), them. And even he would agree that the permissive practice only applies to state and royal functions at the highest levels.

Lift-and-Cut Shavers

There is a website dedicated to adjusting Norelco Lift-and-Cut Shavers called Kosher Shaver. I always found this a bit strange because when I was in yeshiva nearly everyone used a Lift-and-Cut, after a senior *rosh yeshiva* declared it permissible (as is this *rosh yeshiva's* policy, he does not want his name mentioned in the media). His reason: He tested it out on his hand and found that the shave was not very close. I used a Lift-and-Cut for a number of years, until I grew my current beard, and found no difference in the shave between that shaver and a screen shaver. I still had the same small stubble that I could feel with my hand after using either kind.

On the Kosher Shaver website, there is a write-up on the subject of electric shavers from the Torah sheet *Halacha Berurah*.[119] The write-up is fairly comprehensive, in that it discusses whether electric shavers are permitted at all—many *posekim* forbid them entirely; others, such as Rav Chaim Ozer Grodzinski, Rav Tzvi Pesach Frank, Rav Yosef Eliyahu Henkin and Rav Moshe Feinstein, permitted their use. I confirmed that Rav Joseph B. Soloveitchik, when he had a goatee, used an electric shaver. Rav Henkin's reason to permit electric shavers is that there is still a remaining stubble. Rav Moshe Feinstein allows them because the cutting is done through both the screen and the blade, thus acting like scissors rather than like a single blade razor.

119. Available online at http://www.koshershaver.org/why.htm

The article then progresses to Lift-and-Cut shavers and claims that according to Rav Moshe Feinstein's position, these shavers would be prohibited because the hair is lifted up by one blade and then cut by another, single blade rather than by the screen and the blade. This is acting like a razor and not like scissors. The article's author writes that he confirmed this understanding with Rav David Feinstein, Rav Reuven Feinstein, and Rav Yisrael Belsky.

Evidently, the *rosh yeshiva* I mentioned at the beginning, who permitted Lift-and-Cut shavers, held a position similar to Rav Henkin's—that the shave must be close in order for it to be prohibited. Despite company marketing, in my experience the shave is not noticeably closer than most other shavers.

Missing from the article is the position of Rav Nachum Rabinovich. In his *Melumedei Milchamah* (no. 128), Rav Rabinovich rules that all electric shavers are categorized as *melaket* and *rahitni* because they cut hairs individually, as opposed to razors that cut a large number of hairs at a time. Therefore, according to him, there is no difference between a screen shaver and a Lift-and-Cut shaver, and the latter is entirely permitted.

Rav Moshe Feinstein's grandson-through-marriage, Rav Shabtai Rappaport, wrote an article on electric shavers. Not surprisingly, he follows his wife's grandfather's position on electric shavers in general. However, when it comes to Lift-and-Cut shavers, he takes this reasoning in a different direction than described above:

Norelco (Phillips in Europe) developed a shaver that they claim (though other manufacturers denied their claim) gives a totally smooth shave. It is made of two interlocking sets of blades, with one of the blades of the first set placed between two of the second. The function of the first blade is to pull out the hair from the skin. Before it has a chance to sink back below the skin, the second blade cuts it off, achieving a very smooth shave.

It seems that this shaver is also not operating as a razor, but as a combination of a tweezers (melaket) and scissors. If one would pull out hair from the skin with a tweezers and then snip it off with scissors, one should also achieve a close shave; but the Torah never prohibited such a process. This similar process, though it achieves a very close shave, is not a razor cut.

The above is not intended to argue in favor of using a Lift-and-Cut. My point is that you should not assume that it is prohibited. As should be obvious, ask your rabbi about it.

The Living Wage and the Working Poor

A living wage is the minimum income necessary for an employee working 40 hours a week to meet the employee's needs on that single income. Some have argued in favor of a legally mandated Living Wage as an anti-poverty measure. Others have argued against it because they believe it will reduce the total number of jobs. Additionally, the obligation of charity should not be placed solely on the employer but on the broader community.

Historically, Judaism is unfamiliar with the concept of a minimum wage. Laws deal with the timely payment of wages but do not set a minimum wage beyond local practice, whatever it may be. However, a scholar from the confusingly named Conservative Jewish movement wrote, in the context of supporting Living Wage legislation:

> The contemporary situation, then, differs from the reality upon which biblical and rabbinic wage laws are based. The rabbis are familiar with workers who live "check to check," but do not consider the possibility that a day's wages might prove insufficient to buy food or other necessities for that day.

While Jewish texts do not advocate a minimum wage, this scholar argues that the situation has changed. In ancient times, workers were always paid sufficiently to survive. Historically, all wages were living wages. This is hard to accept, just as a matter of common sense. Were employers in the past so enlightened that they always paid a sufficient wage? From a textual perspective, I believe Rashi disputes this claim.

There are multiple terms used in the Bible for the poor. In one chapter in Deuteronomy (15), we find "*evyon*" (vv. 4,7,9,11) and "*ani*" (v. 11). The midrash (*Vayikra Rabbah* 34:5) lists eight (some versions have seven) terms that refer to the poor. One of those eight is "*evyon*," which the midrash says derives from the root "*avah*, desire." An *evyon* is someone so poor that he does not have all of his needs and desires more. Rashi (*Bava Metzia* 111b s.v. *evyon*; Deut. 15:4) explains that an *evyon* is poorer than an "*ani*." He cannot acquire all that he needs and therefore, unlike an *ani*, an *evyon* is not embarrassed to ask for charity.

This idea can also be found in *Mekhilta* on Ex. 23:6; *Sifra* on Deut. 15:7; Rashi on those two verses; and *Arukh*, s.v. *evyon*. Radak (*Sefer Ha-Shorashim*, s.v. *a-b-h*) writes: "A very poor person is called *evyon*, because he lacks everything and his desires and wants are for everything." I am not aware of any traditional explanation that differs from the above.

Significantly, Deut. 24:14 states that an employer must pay the wages of both an *ani* and an *evyon* on a timely basis. It seems that an *evyon* is a worker whose wages are insufficient to cover his basic needs. Evidently, the talmudic sages did, in fact, know of a worker whose wages were insufficient. It is therefore incorrect to dismiss the rulings of the sages of the Talmud based on the premise that they were unaware of poor people whose wages could not cover their basic needs.

Afterword

After nearly 400 pages of sometimes esoteric discussions of Jewish law, we do well to close with a concept underlying the entire book. To understand, we have to ask why the biblical Egyptians were punished for enslaving the Jews. After all, they fulfilled God's prophecy to Avraham that his descendants would be enslaved in a foreign land (Gen. 15:13).

Ramban (Gen. 15:14) explains that the Egyptians were not punished for enslaving the Jews but for going beyond the prophecy, for overly oppressing the enslaved nation. Had they merely fulfilled the prophecy, they presumably would have been rewarded. Ramban's approach is surprising but intuitive and consistent. Many commentators ask why people should feel obligated to instantiate a prophecy. Isn't that God's business? The answer to that question explains the Ramban's view here, as well.

Why did Yosef refrain from immediately revealing his identity when his brothers appeared before him in Egypt? Ramban (Gen. 42:9) explains that Yosef wished to fulfill his dreams that his brothers and father would bow down to him. He deceived his brothers so they would bring Binyamin, and eventually their father, to bow down to him in Egypt. Why, many commentators ask, should Yosef feel obligated to ensure the dreams come true (e.g. *Akeidas Yitzchak* 29; *Toras Moshe*, ad loc.)?

The Vilna Gaon (*Aderes Eliyahu*, ad loc.) says simply that Yosef did not want to contradict God's will. His concern was not specifically with serving as the defender of God's words. Rather, he just wanted to be sure that he was on God's side. Fulfilling God's will is not merely praiseworthy; it is a life goal to which all people must strive. Yosef refused to violate God's will by attempting (presumably futilely) to circumvent the prophecies. With this idea, we can understand that the Egyptians should have desired to fulfill God's will, which the Torah tells us included enslaving the Jews. Had they not been overly zealous, their doing so would have been a mitzvah, an accomplishment that moved the divine plan forward.

Everything we have discussed in this book—the biblical and rabbinic commandments, the customs, the ongoing debates—reflects a profound desire to fulfill God's will as revealed in the Torah in its broadest definition. Our continued study of this Torah in all its complexity demonstrates a yearning to understand God's will. I pray that it has succeeded even a little in advancing that desire.

Made in the USA
Columbia, SC
08 September 2022

66465263R00238